EVOLVE OR BE SLAUGHTERED

NEGOTIATION FOR THE 21ST CENTURY

UPDATED 2025 EDITION

DERRICK CHEVALIER

EVOLVE or Be Slaughtered: Negotiation for the 21st Century (UPDATED 2025 EDITION)
Copyright ©2024, 2020, 2015, 2008 by Derrick Chevalier

For more about this author please visit www.linkedin.com/in/derrick-chevalier-6323272

This author is not engaged in rendering legal, medical, or psychological services, and this book is not intended as a guide to diagnose or treat legal, medical or psychological problems. If you require legal medical, psychological, or other expert assistance, please seek the services of a duly qualified, and licensed professional.

All rights reserved. No part of this publication may be reproduced, distributed, or transmitted in any form or by any means, including photocopying, recording, or other electronic or mechanical methods, without the prior written permission of the publisher, except in the case of brief quotations embodied in critical reviews and certain other noncommercial uses permitted by copyright law. Please do not participate in or encourage piracy of copyrighted materials in violation of the author's rights.

No part of this book may be used for the training of artificial systems, including systems based on artificial intelligence (AI), without the copyright owner's prior permission. This prohibition shall be in force even on platforms and systems that claim to have such rights based on an implied contract for hosting the book.

Library of Congress Control Number: 2024918961

Paperback ISBN: 978-1-965092-53-8
Hardcover ISBN: 978-1-965092-54-5

    1. Main category—Business & Money › Management & Leadership › Leadership & Motivation
    2. Other category—Self-Help › Success
    3. Other category—Books › Business & Money › Management & Leadership › Negotiating

Published by: AR PRESS
Roger L. Brooks, Publisher
roger@americanrealpublishing.com
americanrealpublishing.com

BOOKS BY DERRICK CHEVALIER

The Beyond Negotiating Series:

EVOLVE or Be Slaughtered: Negotiation for the 21st Century
(Revised/Updated 2025 Edition)

EVOLVE or Be Slaughtered: Negotiation for the 21st Century
(2020, 2015, 2008)

Influence – Rapport – Results
(2015, 2009)

From Fear to Fearless
(2005, 2003)

Other Books:

ROADMAP to Success, featuring Dr. Steven Covey and Dr. Ken Blanchard

Dedicated to the life and work of Vincent Van Gogh

Table of Contents

EVOLVE or Be Slaughtered: Negotiation for the 21st Century
Foundations and Rudiments ... ix
Chapter 1: Six Foundational Tenets ... 1
   First Tenet: Predict Responses ... 1
   Second Tenet: Test Assumptions,
   Presumptions, and Estimates ... 3
   Third Tenet: Influence Actions ... 3
   Fourth Tenet: Minimize Risks ... 4
   Fifth Tenet: Maximize Results ... 4
   Sixth Tenet: Increase Knowledge and Skills ... 6
Chapter 2: The CNSUF™ Continuum ... 8
Chapter 3: Mode Groups & Modes ... 13
   The Omni Mode Group ... 16
   TYPES OF COMMUNICATORS ... 29
   The Conditional Mode Group ... 44
   The Competitive Mode ... 45
   Range of Conditions ... 53
   Relevant Conditions ... 57
   Seven CNSUF™ Competitive Rules ... 62
      Rule Two ... 71
      Rule Three ... 76
      Rule Four ... 82
      Rule Five ... 100
      Rule Six ... 106
      Rule Seven ... 109

Price Cost Value ... 93
The Co-Operative Mode ... 116
Chapter 4: Competitive Intelligence ... 148
Chapter 5: Overcoming Objections ... 155
Chapter 6: Dynamic Closing Techniques©
An Abbreviated Survey ... 192
Chapter 7: The Calculus of Deadlock ... 227
Conclusion ... 249
Harrison-Chevalier Programs & Services ... 253
Acknowledgments ... 255

Exhibits

Exhibit I: CNSUF™ Continuum ... 8
Exhibit II: CNSUF™ Continuum Cont'd ... 9
Exhibit III: Mods Group & Modes ... 13
Exhibit IV: Omni Modes ... 16
Exhibit V: Triangle of Inter-relationship ... 40
Exhibit VI: Conditional Modes - Competitive ... 44
Exhibit VII: Spectrum of Light - Relevant Conditions ... 57
Exhibit VIII: Competitive Example ... 58
Exhibit IX: Competitive Example Cont'd ... 59
Exhibit X: Degrees of Separation ... 105
Exhibit XI: Co-Operative Mode ... 112
Exhibit XII: Co-Operative Mode Cont'd ... 120
Exhibit XIII: Co-Operative Mode Cont'd ... 122
Exhibit XIV: All Win Mode ... 135
Exhibit XV: Triangle of Conditional Dependence ... 136

EVOLVE or Be Slaughtered: Negotiation for the 21st Century

Foundations and Rudiments

EVOLVE or Be Slaughtered: Negotiation for the 21st Century, newly revised and updated for 2025, is by no means a complete work in itself. By design it is the evolution of work that began with *Beyond Negotiating: From Fear to Fearless*; *Beyond Negotiating: Influence – Rapport – Results*; and "The Power of Influence in Negotiation," which is the chapter included in a collaboration project titled *ROADMAP to Success* that featured chapters by Dr. Stephen Covey and Dr. Kenneth Blanchard, among others. Insights and lessons inspired by those listed in the acknowledgments and many other directly and indirectly related articles and submissions throughout the past two and a half decades have contributed as well.

Much of the content included here has been gleaned and inspired by observations and experiences from more than twenty-five years of continuous traveling across the United States, Canada, and Mexico, flying more than three million miles, sitting in airports, navigating through rainstorms, floods, and blizzards on small back roads and in big cities, as well as doing profit and nonprofit work with clients in the Caribbean, Africa, and Europe. That travel and work has involved a vast range of consulting projects and the customization and facilitation of executive educational events and workshops for individuals, mom-and-pop enterprises, small businesses, non-profits, medium-size companies, the U.S. Military, and large conglomerates from virtually every profession and business sector; asking questions, doing research, interviewing people, watching, observing, testing, reading, and analyzing, along with thousands of hours during fourteen years as an independent contractor under the tutelage and influence of the twentieth century's most influential negotiation authority, Dr. Chester Karrass.

All of these professional experiences and influences have been supplemented by countless lessons from athletics; service in the United States Marine Corps, including a tour in Vietnam; an unconventional upbringing in a single mom, curated multiracial family; plus marriage, business partnerships, friendships, children, divorce, cancer, great joy, abject sadness in the face of loss, recession, financial ineptness, and periods of prosperity and wealth—along with the occasional glimpse of genius and generosity from men and women who possess these qualities.

EVOLVE or Be Slaughtered is intended to serve as the foundational text of the Comprehensive Negotiating Strategies Universal Framework (CNSUF™), and as a supplemental, collateral reference for those who attend live events, executive forums, and other one- and two-day public and in-house customized workshops, and for those who are individual or corporate consulting clients of Harrison-Chevalier. It is in these environments that the content of the book can be stripped down and applied to the specific challenges and questions of participants and clients.

Ultimately it is the tailoring and application of strategies developed from the foundations and rudiments included in *Beyond Negotiating: From Fear to Fearless, Influence – Rapport – Results, The Power of Influence in Negotiation*, and *EVOLVE or Be Slaughtered: Negotiation for the 21st Century*, skillfully crafted and thoughtfully applied to produce unique and powerful results for today and for business and personal challenges in the future. *EVOLVE or Be Slaughtered*, along with the other books in the Beyond Negotiating series, is the backbone of the Comprehensive Negotiating Strategies Universal Framework (CNSUF™). It is intended to evolve as it is reviewed, refined, and used to address challenges in various professional sectors and personal situations by different types of negotiators.

Readers are invited to be critical, but please do not limit your criticism to what you think or how you feel about what is included here. Experiment, test, implement variations, ask questions, learn the rudiments, and allow them to stretch what you already know and the way you now negotiate. Then become part of the evolution of CNSUF™ negotiators by sharing what you learn with me and with other students of the CNSUF™; *EVOLVE or Be Slaughtered: Negotiation for the 21st Century.*

Visit Harrison-Chevalier online at www.h-c.com, and more importantly, join us for one of our EVOLVE LIVE events, or schedule a customized keynote or in-house program for your group, company, or business division. I look forward to meeting you and to growing with you as we EVOLVE and strive, not just to *win* but to achieve the highest and best possible outcomes, given the challenges and circumstances in each negotiation.

Circumstances do not dictate outcomes!

—Derrick Chevalier

Chapter 1:
Six Foundational Tenets

The Comprehensive Negotiating Strategies Universal Framework (CNSUF™) is built on six foundational tenets. Everything in the CNSUF™ links to one or more of these tenets. If you cannot or do not know how to do that, you should rethink your strategy.

First Tenet: Predict Responses

CNSUF™ negotiators are less concerned with ascertaining their own objectives, thoughts, and strategies than with discovering and understanding the objectives, strategies, and peculiarities of their counterparts.

At the outset of any particular negotiation, what I want is far less important than knowing what you want, how badly you want it, and precisely what you are—and are not—willing to do to get it.

If we understand these things about our counterparts—if we comprehend their geographical, socioeconomic, political, organizational, institutional, personal, and behavioral attributes—then we have a much greater chance of predicting how they will respond to the wants, needs, strategy, tactics, and challenges in front of them. If we can predict our counterparts' responses, we can more accurately tailor our approach to encourage, support, or change not only what they think but what they will do and what they will accept.

Preliminary predictions about our counterparts' responses become raw data for crafting comprehensive negotiating strategies. These predictions vary depending on many specific factors, but they begin with a thorough comprehension of the material in *EVOLVE or Be Slaughtered*, as well as a thorough review and understanding of the material in *Beyond Negotiating: From Fear to Fearless* and *Beyond Negotiating: Influence Rapport Results*.

Predicting our counterparts' responses is more like cooking than baking, because a cook can substitute ingredients, lengthen or shorten cooking times, and add a bit more of this and a little less of that. The end product will have similar characteristics, but it will be different every time, depending on the cook (the astute CNSUF™ negotiator), the circumstances, the ingredients, facilities, and our counterpart(s). No two people make macaroni and cheese that taste exactly the same (without a recipe), but every version contains one form of macaroni and cheese or another. Likewise, a comprehensive negotiation strategy may involve similar tactics, techniques, and elements, yet result in vastly different approaches and outcomes.

Conversely, people who bake know they must use the ingredients, in precisely the recommended order, and bake at recommended temperatures for the recommended amount of time. Sure, the baker may tweak a recipe here or there, but stray too far from the essence of a baking recipe and your lemon pound cake comes out more like a chalky brick than a moist and delicious dessert.

The astute CNSUF™ negotiator is a hybrid. Sometimes we precisely follow a recipe, a strategy, a rule, or a tactic; at other times we are CNSUF™ chefs, adding new elements, adjusting ingredients, being creative, taking chances, blazing new trails, and breaking the rules altogether.

The trick, of course, is to develop sufficient skills and insight to determine when to be a baker, when to be a cook, and when to be a hybrid breaking new ground to achieve outcomes beyond our initial expectations.

We learn to predict our counterpart's responses by probing, testing, listening, and observing present and past behavior, enabling us to gather as much intelligence about the individual as possible, especially when we are likely to interact with the same person or group during a prolonged period.

In addition, we pay close attention to the remaining tenets, as they will enhance our ability to predict the responses of those with whom we negotiate.

Second Tenet: Test Assumptions, Presumptions, and Estimates

Assumptions, presumptions, and estimates are three of the most essential elements in the CNSUF™ because they are among the most misunderstood and misjudged elements in negotiation, which lead to devastating mistakes, miscalculations, and unintended consequences for many negotiators. The astute CNSUF™ negotiator develops a keen understanding of the anatomy, function, and potential of each of these elements, while maintaining a respect for their potential danger and elusive attributes.

Third Tenet: Influence Actions

Influence and persuasion are very different. If you work in a military or paramilitary organization and rank higher than someone else, you tell people of a lesser rank what, where, how, and when to do what you want them to do and expect it to be done. Similarly, in a corporate environment, you tell people of lesser status what, where, how, and when to do what you want them to do, and expect for it to be done, both examples represent persuasion by rank or status—direct and to the point, and that is the way things are supposed to work.

But how many executive assistants have changed the course of history because they had access to a general, a CEO, or a president of the United States? How many husbands, wives, partners, or associates have altered the thinking or behavior of a powerful person simply with a glance or glare?

Influence knows few boundaries and is governed by an abstract yet attainable array of components. Many of these components are detailed in the book, *Beyond Negotiating: Influence – Rapport – Results*, and some will be included and reviewed here.

Astute CNSUF™ negotiators understand not only how to influence others, but also how to protect themselves and minimize others' attempts to exact unwarranted/unwanted/negative influence upon themselves.

One can level a playing field or mitigate disadvantage using the power of influence, but to do so, one must master the rudiments of influence and learn to influence deliberately as well as by natural presence and personality. Influence is as much an art as a skill in the CNSUF™.

Fourth Tenet: Minimize Risks

Predicting responses, testing assumptions, and influencing actions successfully all lead to minimizing or strategically eliminating our exposure to undue or unnecessary risks. But that is not to say that the astute CNSUF™ negotiator should not take risks. The CNSUF™ negotiator focuses on assessing/neutralizing/eliminating unnecessary risks so that he or she can take calculated risks that will improve/test/advance movement toward the highest and best possible outcome, given the challenges/limitations/rewards of each negotiation.

Many of the rules, strategies, and tools included in the CNSUF™ are designed to minimize risks, even—and especially—when we are uncertain about what those risks are or may become. Simply put, it is rarely the risks we recognize that take advantage of us; it is the ones that are hidden and unforeseen and seem to come out of nowhere. Upon careful reflection we often find that the red flags of caution were there long before the negotiator was required to pay a price or endure a negative consequence.

In pursuit of our own ends we ignored the red flags until a flag was thrust in front of us at close range. We may not be able to avoid or eliminate every consequence, but the astute CNSUF™ negotiator can surely learn to minimize negative consequences and risk.

Fifth Tenet: Maximize Results

Simply eliminating or neutralizing our risk does not ensure that we will maximize our results.

Chapter 1: Six Foundational Tenets

Maximizing the results of a negotiation has everything to do with the relationship, wants, needs, and objectives of all parties involved, because the only way to determine what the best outcome can be is to move from left to the far right on the CNSUF™ Continuum (see Exhibit I, p. 8). Anything less and we cannot accurately confirm how much better or worse we might have done. In effect, a decision to settle anywhere other than the All-Win position on the CNSUF™ Continuum is a decision to settle without knowing what the potential of a negotiation might have been. This is one of the proprietary cornerstones of the CNSUF™. (We are not kidding ourselves that we achieved the best possible outcome because we *feel* good about it or because we achieved the goals we set prior to the negotiation).

That said, a decision to settle anywhere other than the All-Win position on the CNSUF™ Continuum is also a decision to limit risk by accepting what may or may not be a better potential outcome in favor of minimizing the concurrent risks of pursuing more than we have achieved at a given point in a negotiation.

Unlike other negotiating frameworks, CNSUF™ does not define success or failure by measuring the closing price or the final outcome. Rather, CNSUF™ measures result by assessing how much of the final outcome, whether it is transactional, comprehensive, complex, tangible, and/or intangible, is based on the discovery or confirmation of elements, information, data, and knowledge that were unknown at the beginning of the negotiation.

There is a good deal of empirical evidence to suggest that the closer an outcome is to the negotiator's original assumptions, presumptions, estimates, and objectives, the more likely it is that either a good deal remained on the table or that the negotiator was duped.

Since CNSUF™ negotiators are more concerned with learning about what they *do not* know, rather than reveling in what they know or think they know before a negotiation actually begins, the outcome is best measured by assessing how much of it is based on information, intelligence, data, relationship, and knowledge that were unknown when the negotiation began.

The astute CNSUF™ negotiator does not claim victory or failure at the conclusion of a negotiation, because doing so is frequently premature. Instead, the astute CNSUF™ negotiator measures results and outcomes primarily as historical reference points long after the outcome has occurred.

Sixth Tenet: Increase Knowledge and Skills

In *Beyond Negotiating: Influence – Rapport – Results* (2015, 2009, 2005), I outlined Three Fundamental Reasons People Fail to achieve elevated levels of expertise in negotiation or other areas. If anything, the reasons detailed there are truer in 2025 than in 2005, when *Influence – Rapport – Results* was originally published. Most people are simply too stubborn and/or too lazy to do what it takes to develop high competency in negotiation. It is really that simple, at least on the one hand. On the other hand, people are also afraid to invest the time, energy, and resources to do what they must to increase their competency, for the same reasons they are afraid to invest what is necessary to learn anything new. Acquiring knowledge and skill is painful; learning new things hurts the body, the mind, and the spirit on so many levels. We inevitably put more energy into figuring out how to avoid learning than we do into learning itself.

We do not like feeling dumb; we do not like having to slow down while we develop the mental and physical dexterity to implement what we are supposed to have learned, and we do not like being told that the way we're doing something isn't good enough.

All of this increases as we age. While change is mind-numbing torture for many who have passed the age of fifty, those in younger generations get bored so quickly that they are compelled to stretch every limit placed upon them—new games, new phones, new computers, new social media, new clothes, latest music, new restaurants, new beverages. New is good. New is even a fundamental requirement for their sanity.

There are exceptions to either category, of course. But in the main, older folks are more resistant to change than younger folks. Like it or not, the world is never going backward—change is inevitable. While I

Chapter 1: Six Foundational Tenets

cannot promise that all change will mean progress, I can guarantee unequivocally that change will remain a constant for the young and the not so young the world over as the present Emerging Integrated Global Economy© (EIGE©) matures.

Resist if you will, but continuous learning and the expansion of our personal knowledge and skills are critical for a high quality of life. These Six Foundational Tenets coincide with every element of the CNSUF™, since every tactic, tool, and section of *EVOLVE or Be Slaughtered*, including the framework itself, is designed to assist in the pursuit of one or more of the Six Foundational Tenets. These tenets are the underpinnings of the CNSUF™. They are why the framework was developed. Astute CNSUF™ negotiators become intimately familiar with these tenets. They learn them and they continually study them to improve their ability to use them to coordinate their tools and strategies.

Chapter 2:
The CNSUF™ Continuum

The heart of the CNSUF™ is the CNSUF™ Continuum.

EXHIBIT I

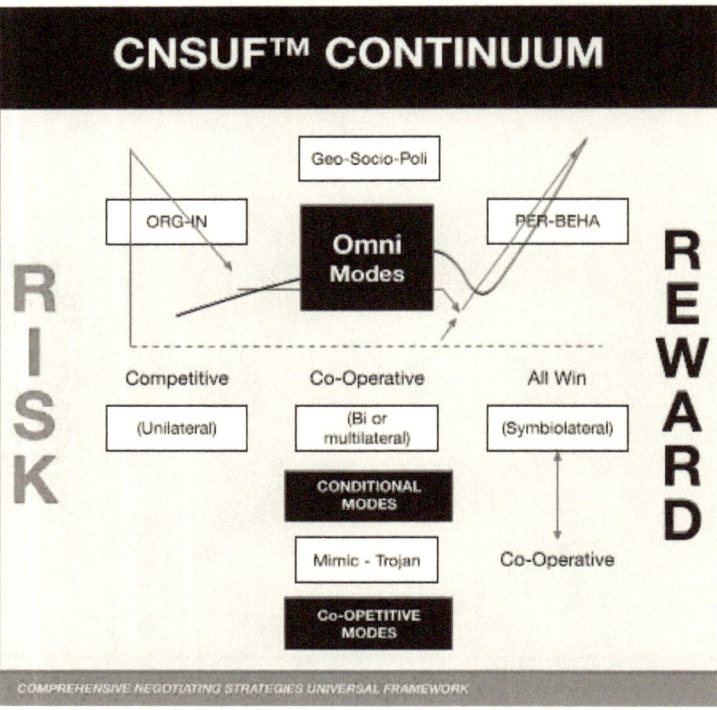

On its face, it is a portrait of squiggly lines and gobbledygook. On closer examination, it becomes a universal schematic that can be adapted to any negotiation, regardless of how simple or how complex.

Chapter 2: The CNSUF™ Continuum

In order to grasp the full essence of CNSUF™, the astute negotiator will memorize every detail of the continuum thoroughly and as quickly as possible, understanding that this will serve as a foundation for pursuing increasingly finer elements of the continuum and of CNSUF™ as a whole, as both the framework and the negotiator evolve.

Short of this, negotiators will familiarize themselves with the continuum, memorize the major components, and refer to the continuum frequently before, during, and after every negotiation.

The development of the CNSU framework is a collaborative endeavor. Every astute CNSUF™ negotiator develops new perspectives that will be added to make the framework stronger and continuously relevant. (See Exhibit II.)

EXHIBIT II

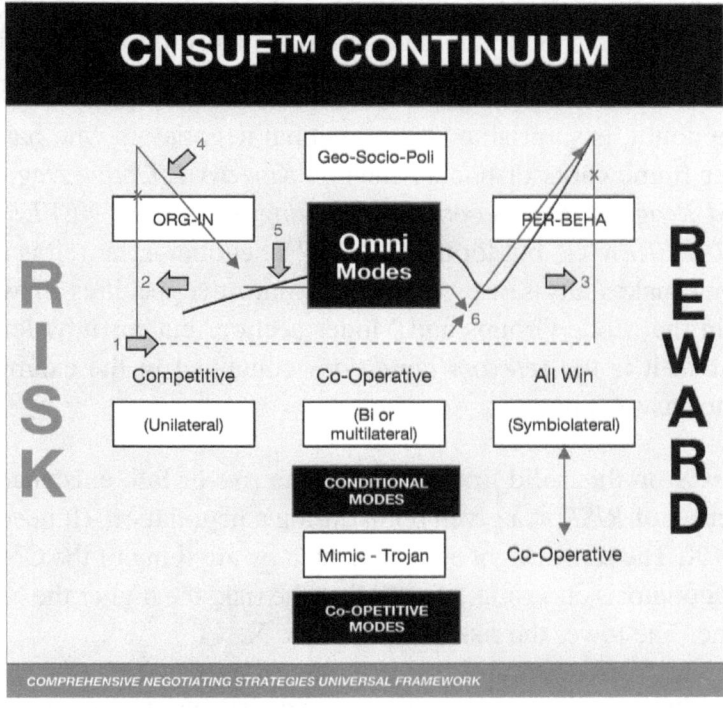

1. This broken line in the center of the Continuum represents its core. It is where we record the status of a negotiation and where we track

the movement of a negotiation from beginning to end. Depending on the negotiators and circumstances, one starts at the far left of the continuum and either remains there or moves to the right throughout the negotiation. This is not to say that the movement occurs in a single direction. We could begin on the far left, see progress, and move to the right toward the middle of the CNSUF™ Continuum, only to digress repeatedly during many days, weeks, months, years, or decades, as with political negotiations in the Middle East and elsewhere.

But let us say you and I have never met—our companies have never done business together—and we want to determine whether we can do business together, such as when a company publishes a Request For Quotes (RFQ) or Request For Proposals (RFP).

If your company writes and distributes the RFP or RFQ, and my company decides to respond, our negotiation is placed on the far left of the continuum.

This, no doubt, is surprising to professional negotiators who have studied other frameworks or books, such as *Karrass Effective Negotiating, Harvard Program On Negotiation, Getting To Yes,* or *NEVER SPLIT THE DIFFERENCE,* but for the CNSUF™ negotiator, far left is the *only* place that makes any sense. We will get into the specifics of why this is true in the Mode Groups and Modes section, but for now let us say simply that it is the *relevant conditions* contained in the example that make the answer finite.

2. An X on this solid line represents the rise or fall, existence or absence, of *RISK* at a given point during a negotiation. (It need not be an X. The same might be represented by anything of the CNSUF™ negotiator's choosing.) The higher the risk, the higher the X on this line. The lower the risk, the lower the X.

We may think we have only a little or no risk because we are not engaged yet and have not put ourselves in jeopardy. But just because we have not decided to become involved doesn't mean others can't or won't

Chapter 2: The CNSUF™ Continuum

take actions that, in essence, force us to engage. We may not want to be involved in a lawsuit, but we cannot stop another party from suing us. And if we decide to do nothing to respond to the lawsuit, we could find we have lost a court battle because we never participated in it.

The less we know, the more that is at stake—and the higher the risk. Risk virtually always exists, whether we perceive it or not. But we know for certain that risk starts, rises, and falls continuously throughout every negotiation, depending on the players, the conditions, the circumstances, and the relevance of the Omni Mode Group.

3. An X that represents a specific action within a specific negotiation on this solid line represents the rise or fall/existence or absence of *reward* at any given point during a negotiation. The higher the reward, the higher the X. The lower the reward, the lower the X.

Unlike risk, reward may or may not be possible on a continuous basis. Sometimes the only reward is to escape becoming a victim of risk.

4. This line indicates that risk fell after some time (as measured by *relevant conditions*). As noted previously, that may not always be the case. Risk does not diminish just because we are negotiating; it falls because there are changes in the *relevant conditions* and as we move from left to right on the continuum.

5. Line five is an example of the *arch* (ebb and flow) of an actual Harrison-Chevalier client negotiation. It indicates that during the course of several weeks, the negotiation was only a small risk to our client. Only minor tangible and intangible consequences for our client were involved at the outset. Over time, those risks and consequences rose and fell until intersecting with line six. Every negotiation will have a distinct arch, depending on many factors. This example merely displays an idea of the arch in a specific negotiation.

6. Line six represents the potential change in the negotiator's risk at the point when he or she decides to move from the center of the broken line (the core) while in the *Co-Operative Mode* toward

the right, where the negotiator believes an All Win© outcome is possible.

For the purpose of simplicity, we will put Exhibit II (p. 9) aside, since lines two through six, as well as other elements of the full continuum, will be unique to each negotiation, depending on the history and specifics of the circumstances, goals, players, risks, and rewards.

Chapter 3: Mode Groups & Modes

EXHIBIT III

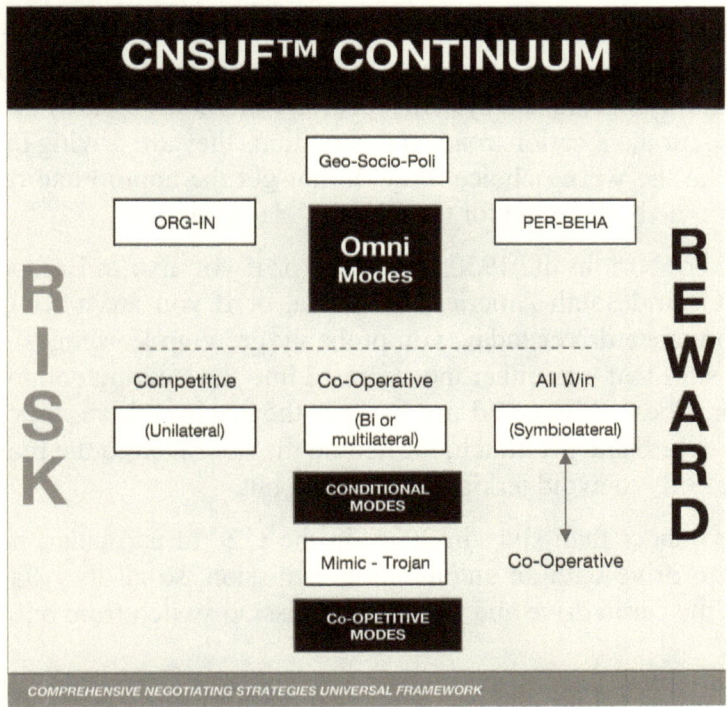

Mode Groups & Modes

Now we are looking at the Core elements of the CNSUF™ Continuum. Exhibit III contains three Mode Groups: the Omni Mode Group, the Conditional Mode Group, and the Co-Opetitive Mode Group, along with the individual Modes within each Mode Group. Because the CNSUF™ negotiator presumes that hidden degrees of risk and reward exist at every stage of a negotiation, our objective is to protect ourselves and our position while discovering precisely what the risks are, and where those risks reside.

Think of each CNSUF™ Mode Group as a collection of gears that interconnect to form a working unit. Each Mode Group and each Mode is independent because each has its own idiosyncrasies. But each Mode Group is also interdependent, because it is an integral part of the CNSU framework as whole.

Each Mode Group and each Mode has a separate function, but each contributes to the overall direction a negotiator chooses to go, and to the momentum generated during the negotiation.

Those who have taken a driver's education course learn to select the combination of gears and systems (accelerator versus brakes) that is appropriate for the location, road, and conditions they are driving in. When they make the wrong choice, they do not get the appropriate response and it is exactly the same for the CNSUF™ negotiator.

If you were born in the 1950s or 1960s, or if you live in Europe, Asia, China, Central/South America, or Africa, or if you are a competitive or performance driver today, you probably grew up learning to drive a manual shift that was either incorporated into the steering column or on the floor. These drivers did not just put the car into drive, they had to learn to coordinate the clutch, located on the floor next to the brake, and shift perfectly to avoid jerking and stalling out.

People younger than sixty in 2025, in the U.S. in particular, probably learned to drive with an automatic transmission, so all they had to do was put the car in drive and let the transmission switch from one gear to another.

Despite my age, I am the last person on earth to suggest that driving a "stick shift," as folks did back in the "good ol' days," is somehow better than learning to drive an automatic. But from time to time, especially while traveling in Europe and elsewhere in the world, I rent a manual shift just to stay familiar with it.

If you are someone who is always talking about how the good ol' days were so much better than today, I am most assuredly not your ally on that point. Sure, I am as likely as the next person of my generation to

Chapter 3: Mode Groups & Modes

wax poetic about the past, but whenever I think yesterday was somehow better than today or tomorrow, I slap myself back into reality by remembering that for everything that was good or better in decades past, there were an equal if not greater number of things that were not so great. Eventually, we will have to deal with the consequences of current sins and behaviors of the past, and things are surely going to change as we move into the future. But the terrible things of the present and future will also include some incredible things as well.

In the CNSU framework, Mode Groups are like the transmissions of many of today's automobiles, and Modes are like the gears. However, at this moment the CNSUF™ transmission and gears have to be manually shifted. The astute CNSUF™ negotiator is encouraged to invest the time and energy to learn how and when to shift gears the old-fashioned way by turning Information into Knowledge, Knowledge to Skill, Skill into Expertise, Expertise into Action, and Action into Results (IKSEAR). (From *Beyond Negotiating: Influence – Rapport – Results, 2015 and 2009, 2005*)

This, of course, will not always be the case, because the future will surely bring automobiles that not only park themselves (there already are models that come with this feature), but that drive and navigate on their own (these are currently being beta tested), as well as applications, artificial intelligence (AI), software, hardware, and various other devices that will automate a good deal if not all of the analyses necessary to develop a coherent CNSUF™ strategy. As with everything else, CNSUF™ is continuously evolving.

The more adept CNSUF™ negotiators are at the fundamentals, the more able they will be to analyze a situation quickly and use their analysis to develop viable intermediate or long-term strategies. Even when technology does most of the analysis and provides competitive intelligence, the actual strategies will need to be implemented by live human beings, at least for the present and intermediate future. A solid foundation of theoretical and practical experience will be the distinguishing factor in the competency levels of negotiators with access to the same tools and technological advances. This is especially true of astute CNSUF™ negotiators, because CNSUF™ is a framework designed to be adaptable to every type of negotiating environment, whether transactional, complex, or comprehensive.

The Omni Mode Group

The first Mode Group is the Omni Mode Group. (See: Exhibit IV.) The word omni is from the Latin word *omnis*, meaning all or everywhere [e.g., omnipresent]. (Reference: *The American Heritage Dictionary of the English Language, Fifth Edition*.) The name of the group indicates that every mode in the group is omnipresent—every mode exists and impacts every negotiation everywhere, all the time without exception! There is never an instance in which the Omni Modes are not affecting the outcome of every negotiation.

Depending on the situation, the degree to which the Omni Modes impact a negotiation rises and falls. The negotiators' focus on one or the other of these modes depends on the specific, *relevant conditions* of each unique negotiation. The critical point here is that the impact and presence of the Omni Modes should not be underestimated.

EXHIBIT IV

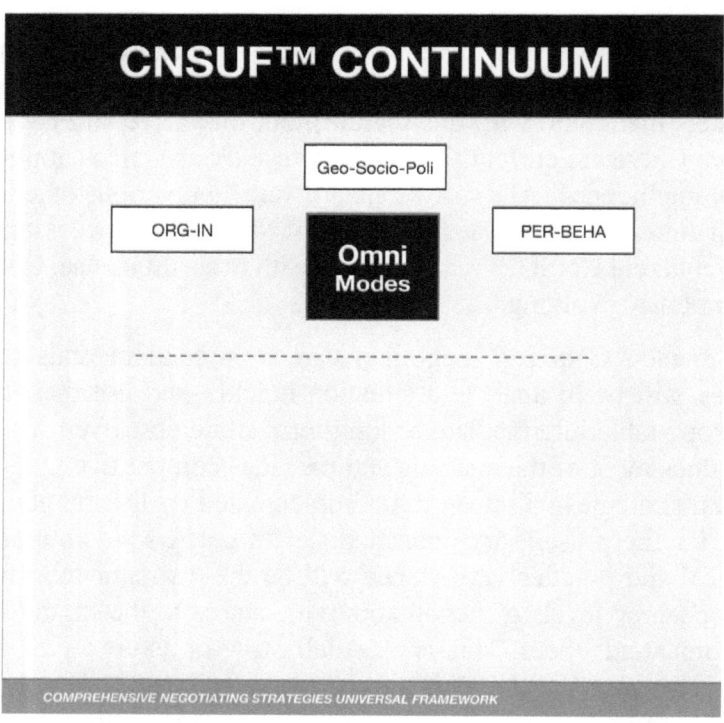

Chapter 3: Mode Groups & Modes

The Omni Mode Group is comprised of three separate modes, beginning with the Geo-Socio-Poli Mode. The term *geo-* is a combining form meaning "the earth," (*geography*); "earth, ground" (*geoponics*); "geography" (*geopolitics*). From the Greek: *geō-,* from *gê* the Earth. (Reference: *Webster's College Dictionary.*)

Geography is hardly the first thing that comes to mind for most negotiators, unless they are calculating shipping/travel costs or deciding what to wear and how much to pack. Yet geography impacts everything from the types of homes that exist in a region to the types of vehicles people buy, the types of IT services that are available, the types of landscapes that prevail, and so on. All of these elements connect to geography.

Under what circumstances should one ignore the role of geography in negotiation? And if we decide to ignore the impact of geography, does that mean the impact is diminished or eliminated? Not by the astute CNSUF™ negotiator.

While the impact and role of geography may not always be obvious, geography impacts every negotiation to some degree. Sometimes geography will be critical in positive ways, such as when farmers get rain, they need to sustain their crops, or when areas dependent on skiers receive an abundant snowpack. At other times, geography can be critical in negative ways, such as when a peasant's subsistence farm is located in the path of government progress and the family is forcibly removed with inadequate compensation; or when the rain that nourishes farmers' crops creates rivers and waterways that spill over or break levees and cause billions of dollars of personal and commercial property damage and destruction.

Other geographical considerations include severe weather incidents, including earthquakes that occur in areas where they don't normally occur, extreme heat and cold, and drought that is rapidly changing every element of life on planet Earth.

Possibly the person you are negotiating with is living next to one of the broken levees. Maybe it is not the person you are negotiating with but someone in the person's family. Either way, geography is a critical part of all negotiation directly and/or indirectly, and the astute CNSUF™

negotiator will seek to identify influencing factors as part of their due diligence preparations and ongoing competitive intelligence.

While many negotiators will miss or choose not to consider the impact of geography, astute CNSUF™ negotiators at the very least will consider the possibilities. This sometimes gives them an advantage because their counterparts never gave geography a second thought. As astute CNSUF™ negotiators, you and I will rarely make that mistake.

The second element of the *Geo-Socio-Poli* Omni Mode Group is *Socio*, a combining form meaning "social," "sociological," "society" (e.g., *socioeconomic; sociometry)*, also a combining form of the Latin *socius*, companion. (Reference: *Webster's College Dictionary*.) More specifically, this includes the socioeconomic factors that have affected those with whom we are negotiating. As related to the CNSU framework, social factors are those elements represented by the culture of a society as well as the economic systems and sub-systems that influence micro-societies within a society.

Note that in the CNSUF™, as related to the Geo-Socio-Poli Mode, when we say *culture,* we are focused on *culture* rather than on race or racial differences. Even some highly intelligent people use the terms *race* and *culture* synonymously, but they most certainly are not synonymous, at least not in the sense that many people think they are.

Few would argue that if two people of purely Caucasian lineage (assuming there are such individuals) traveled to Africa and conceived a child, the child's race would be Caucasian. And if two people of purely Black lineage traveled to Iceland and conceived a child, that child's race would be Black, because the blood in the child's veins is that of Black parents.

It is politics and geographical socialization that have driven the popular misnomer that a person born to a father of purely Black lineage and a mother of purely Caucasian lineage is referred to as *Black,* rather than bi- or multiracial.

Who can say that the race of one child is determined by the blood in their veins and that the race of another is determined by the color of their skin, their socioeconomic status, or the shape of their facial features, and contend that this is a function of culture?

It is a function of geography, socioeconomics, politics, and the fact that "Perception trumps reality" (see *Influence – Rapport – Results,* pp. 83–88). It is not a function of race.

Surely my views on this subject are influenced by the fact that I am of multiracial heritage, so much so that there is at least some chance I may be related to you. Yet the substance of my opinion as related to CNSUF™ is driven by the indisputable distinction between blood (race) and culture.

Culture, in contrast to race, is in part a function of geography, because geography has historically separated people. That separation limits the association of groups and thus leaves people primarily exposed to those around them. It makes sense that our *culture* becomes a reflection of those around us and of where we live on the planet. Beyond that, culture has seven specific components:

a. Food and food preparation.

b. Apparel—body covering, including volume, colors, shapes, and so on of our clothing, jewelry, and bodily ornamentation.

c. Means of exchange—paper, rocks, gold, silver, feathers, dollars, yen, euros, alcoholic beverages, pesos, livestock, seed stock, and so on.

d. Ownership of property—how wealth is defined, and how it is passed down throughout generations.

e. Religious beliefs—what is believed about a higher power, or if it includes ancestor worship or, for some, no such belief at all.

f. Social aspects—marriage, personal and sexual relations, physical closeness, or separation of the genders and/or generations.

g. The Arts—music, musical instruments, rhythms, art, dance, books, and the means of passing along history and customs.

These are the major elements of culture, and they have little or nothing to do with blood. They have everything to do with the historical separation of people by geography, perception, politics, and belief. However, as various means of travel and technological advances have been made, geography has become less and less a cultural barrier, as increased numbers of people worldwide have gained access to the same cultural influences. This is having an enormous impact on the perceptions and beliefs of people across the globe.

As cultures collide, everything comes into question. Those who want one kind of change meet fierce resistance from those who want another and from those who benefit from keeping things the same. This has always been a challenge, despite the indisputable fact that change—evolution—is inevitable. This seems simple enough, yet there are millions of intelligent, educated, moral, loving individuals who reject the argument of race and culture and who, as a result, lump people together based on color, size, and shape.

Why is this discussion about culture and race important as related to CNSUF™? First, because race and culture are components of socio, and socio is part of the Geo-Socio-Poli mode that is part of the Omni Mode Group, which means it is always present. Astute CNSUF™ negotiators are not so much interested in having people agree with their perspective on race/culture; astute CNSUF™ negotiators are interested in determining their counterpart's *beliefs* and *perceptions* on the subjects of race and culture as early as possible.

Agreeing or disagreeing with our counterparts is going to happen, but understanding our counterparts and their perspectives and beliefs is far more important than whether we agree with them initially. Astute CNSUF™ negotiators are not necessarily interested in changing their counterparts' perspectives and beliefs. That comes later. We focus on understanding what those perspectives and beliefs are because that understanding is one of many building blocks that will be used to craft working strategies.

Each element of the Geo-Socio-Poli Mode and the Omni Mode Group contributes to the foundation we need to build on. Each element gives us something that can be contemplated, assessed, confirmed, discarded, or integrated into the bigger picture. Each element is going to tell us something about how a counterpart's perspectives and beliefs shape the actions and choices the counterpart will make, given one opinion or one assumption versus another.

How people or groups are connected to their geography and what they believe about race and culture shape what a person or group believes about the second part of the *Socio* element—economics—in particular the combination of what an individual or group within a society values materially and how those riches are distributed, protected, transferred, and exchanged internally, within a geographic area, group, or groups, and externally, outside a geographic area, group, or groups. I do not believe it is a great leap to suggest that while everything a group or sub-group within a society or culture believes is important, the greatest focus in the larger sense of economics in any geographic area is connected to assets that have the broadest appeal and impact across geographic areas, groups, and sub-groups.

One example involves crude oil. For decades, natural resources such as crude oil have been abundant in geographic areas where many groups and sub-groups did not fully comprehend the enormous value of the resource they had. By the time the realization of the value of oil (internationally) was recognized, billions of barrels had been exported. Further, from the perspective of the economics of those local people, the great question arises as to whether the resources had been acquired by *outsiders* at a *fair* exchange?

Many books, articles, and films are filled with examples of geographic regions where the inhabitants either did not recognize the value of an abundant resource because it held little or no value in their culture, or where they recognized its value but didn't have the means to stop other groups or governments from exploiting and removing it. In many of these cases, the entities that extracted those resources exploited the people with whom they were negotiating by ensuring that the real value of what they were taking was never fully revealed.

Suffice to say that advancements in technology have dramatically changed that calculus in some instances, but in others there remains a long, long way to go. Geographic, racial, and cultural boundaries are still changing in some of those regions, some quite dramatically, and it is likely that this will continue in perpetuity.

From the standpoint of CNSUF™, economics has to do with the possession and distribution of riches, rather than wealth.

Riches, I would argue, have to do with access to and control of an abundance of liquid assets, such as primary currencies (dollars, euros, and so on) in combination with an abundance of other assets, such as gold, silver, commodities, real estate, intellectual property, companies, stocks, bonds, and so forth. People, villages, towns, cities, states, and countries that have control of huge sums of these are *rich*. As it happens, there aren't that many who control an abundance of these assets, as most of them are ironically in the hands of a very, very small minority.

Wealth, by contrast, refers to the control/possession of an abundance of things that riches cannot buy, duplicate, manufacture, market, or sell. Suffice to say there are a great many who are wealthy but lack control of resources or riches.

As an astute CNSUF™ negotiator, it is important to know what you are, who you are, what you believe, and where you stand on the issues of riches and wealth. But it is infinitely more important to understand who your counterparts are, what they believe, and where they stand on those issues. Failure to do this will virtually ensure that you will not achieve the highest and best outcome possible, because socioeconomics and their byproducts, together with the other Omni Modes, are critical elements in every negotiation. They often dictate how an individual or group will respond during the negotiation.

The third element of the Geo-Socio-Poli mode is *poli*, which is the prefix of the word politics. It means *of or pertaining to political* or *concerned with politics*. It can be argued that within the Geo-Socio-Poli mode, poli is the most significant because politics and political elements control the focus of how the geography is going to be used and how the socioeconomic elements are going to be distributed, controlled, and/or governed.

Chapter 3: Mode Groups & Modes

This would include decisions about what will or will not be taken out of or inserted into the geography, and who will or will not benefit from the resources in question. It also involves the size and significance of the military, which is critical because nations have endeavored throughout history to become more powerful by means of acquiring new geography using their military.

Many would point to Russia's 2014 annexation of Crimea, or its invasion of Ukraine in 2022, or to the 2023 Israel-Hamas War as three contemporary examples of this; in the grand scheme of political history, however, I am certain there are at least a thousand other examples involving many other nations that could serve as illustrations.

History is replete with instances where one nation with a superior (though not necessarily larger) military has annexed or subdued the inhabitants of a geographic area, then proceeded to obliterate every element of the socioeconomic and political structure that existed before it arrived, with the intent of replacing whatever existed with its own version of political, socioeconomic, organizational, and institutional governance. The study of almost any historical map suggests that this has been a successful strategy, though not always a long-lasting one.

Although politics dictates how closely the military is connected to the government and political functions, there also are many examples where the military has annexed the government and political system that put it into power. Sometimes this has been done using an apparatus of religion, or of the political system, democracy, socialism, Islam, or communism for instance, that the military once served to accomplish the deed, as occurred in Egypt in 2014, and elsewhere more recently.

Once achieved, the new political structure will decide who will become significant within a geographic area, how they will protect their borders, where those borders ought to be, the size and function of the church, its relationship to the rest of the society, who will control the church (or spiritual life), how the church will support or remain separate from political influence, and what the church owns and how it owns it, if it is permitted to own anything at all. All of this is related to an area of geography, and all the socioeconomic elements are directly and indirectly related to poli in the CNSUF™, Geo-Socio-Poli mode.

The next mode in the Omni Mode Group is the Org-In mode. *Org* refers to organization, meaning a group of persons organized for some purpose. It also can be the administrative personnel or apparatus of a business town, city, nation, and so on.

Without exception, all organizations are products of the geography, socioeconomics, and politics of their origins. Organizations either work to grow and support the dominant religious, socioeconomic, and political elements in the geography where they are created, or they work to change or bring down those organizations and entities.

Simply put, *organizations are groups of persons organized for some work or purpose*. And that group or purpose will be working either to promote or destroy the geography, religion, socioeconomics, and politics that created it.

I have consulting clients who work for Japanese companies with divisions located in the southern United States. I don't think anyone would disagree that Japan is a *long* way from the American South, but ask any of my clients if there is a distinctly Japanese geographical, socioeconomic, and political influence on the way the company operates, even though the division they work for is located in the southern United States, and they will tell you *yes*. They also will tell you that overt actions to change that dynamic will find the proponents of change looking for employment elsewhere.

I have clients located in the Midwest who work for companies that are headquartered in Germany. Ask those clients if there is a distinctly German Geo-Socio-Poli influence on them, even though they work in the Midwest, and they too will tell you *yes, of course*. Clients who work for companies located in other cities throughout the United States, Canada, Mexico, and from around the globe will tell you the same thing—the Geo-Socio-Poli influences that created a company remain a strong influence on the way the organization is run, regardless of where their divisions are located.

Chapter 3: Mode Groups & Modes

That is not to say there are no variations, exceptions, and significant efforts made to allow the geo-socio-poli of the local organization to exist and respond to its local geography and culture as well. But make no mistake—it will be the rare, rare exception when a local geography and culture do not continuously contend with the influences of their parent company. More often than not, local influences and considerations will be subservient to the origins of the organization.

The In portion of the Org-In mode represents: Institution or Institutional, means: of, pertaining to, or established by an institution; for, pertaining to, organized establishments, foundations, societies, or the like, or to the buildings devoted to their work; of the nature of an institution. Characterized by the blandness, drabness, uniformity, and lack of individual attention attributed to large institutions that serve many people. (Ref., Dictionary.com)

Most will agree that institutions are either small and irrelevant or big and impersonal. They are slow to move, difficult to navigate, and difficult to point one's finger at, because it is often difficult to find anyone who takes responsibility for what institutions do and do not do within a geography/society/political system.

What is the institution? Who controls the institution? Who decides what an institution is and what it is not? One will get as many answers to these questions as the number of people one asks, but regardless of what country you are in, it is doubtful that you will find any individual who takes responsibility for the behavior of the institutions that are supposed to serve them. And yet institutions abound in exceedingly small countries and in countries that stretch for thousands of kilometers in every direction.

Suffice to say that institutions represent the collective interests of the geography and the social, economic, and political systems that created them. Institutions define parameters, administer justice, and send people into war as directed by the political dominants of a given time. Their influencers decide what to do when the people they sent to war return home, and what to do when they do not. They administer medical and social welfare and educational systems, and they help to organize, coordinate, and regulate the behavior of the organizations that established them.

The thing is that institutions often outlast political influences—the institution remains long after the political dominants of a given time are long gone. When they do not, or when they become unstable, all the other elements are destabilized. This sometimes leads to social and civil unrest, military intervention or mutiny, economic chaos, genocide, ethnic cleansing, and combinations of these such that the very fabric of a nation can be destroyed. The Org-In mode absolutely impacts Geo-Socio-Poli, but the Geo-Socio-Poli and Org-In have their greatest impact and most notable influence on the final mode of the Omni Mode Group.

The third and final mode of the Omni Mode Group is the Per-Beha mode. Per stands for personal, of, pertaining to, or coming as from a particular person, individual; relating to, directed to, or intended for a particular person. (Ref., Dictionary.com)

As far back as 2003 (and years before) when the first book of the Beyond Negotiating series (*From Fear to Fearless*) was published, I have consistently repeated this simple but critically important axiom: *Circumstances Do Not Dictate Outcomes!* If they did, everyone who was exposed to the same geographic, socioeconomic, political, organizational, or institutional influences would end up exactly the same as anyone else who was a product of those same elements. We would all be clones of the Omni elements and modes in which we were conceived and raised.

The reality is that even identical and conjoined twins have differences. We are all going to act and react to the same stimuli differently, and *thank God*! Can you imagine what the world would be like if this were not true? Talk about boring—that would be boring on steroids! Every human being is unique. Every human being is going to see the same situation through a unique lens, even though they were born and raised at the same time in the same Geo-Socio-Poli and Org-In circumstances as the other people involved in any particular negotiation. And that is *exactly* why using the same negotiation strategy, rules, and actions repeatedly in the same sequence for all of the people involved will work with remarkable success sometimes and fall completely on its face at other times

Chapter 3: Mode Groups & Modes

(exactly as artificial intelligence acts and reacts in its contemporary stage of development).

For the astute CNSUF™ negotiator, every negotiation requires and deserves its own unique strategy, one that is inclusive of tactics, rules, actions, and variations that are specifically chosen for the particular group of people and the specific circumstances of each phase of each negotiation. Astute CNSUF™ negotiators not only analyze each area of the Omni Mode Group in relation to the people involved in the negotiation, but they also take into consideration and analyze the nuances of each of the people, each of the circumstances, and each of the elements of the Omni Mode in every negotiation.

This is precisely why the CNSUF™ is built on the CNSUF™ Continuum. Because minute changes *anywhere* during a negotiation can mean a shift in strategy/timing/choices. CNSUF™ requires that negotiators remain present, active, focused, alive, vibrant, and not glued to six or seven finite rules they learn and then regurgitate for the next twenty years of their careers. CNSUF™ is *personal, of, pertaining to, or coming from a particular person; relating to, directed to, or intended for a particular person;* "evolve or be slaughtered," remember?

The second element of the Per-Beha mode is Beha, which stands for behavioral, the aggregate of all of the responses made by an organism in any situation; a specific response of a certain organism to a specific stimulus or group of stimuli. (Ref., Dictionary.com) "Bam, that is what I'm talkin' 'bout." This is the entire essence of the CNSU framework. The idea today, tomorrow, and in the future is to craft a strategy that responds to and is effective for "…the aggregate of all of the responses made by an organism (or group) of organisms…" at a particular time, given particular parameters, under particular circumstances, dependent on specific goals, limitations, and risk tolerances. In other words, dependent on specific relevant conditions standing in the way of the highest and best outcome.

To achieve that outcome, astute CNSUF™ negotiators use a stacked arsenal of simple and sophisticated hardware, software, psychological, neurophysiological, classic, innovative, and emerging weaponry as though they were a spectrum of colors on a color wheel. We are not looking for the strategy/solution we achieved yesterday or a week ago. We are looking for the tailored combination of elements we need to address the situation we are currently negotiating, while protecting ourselves from negative consequences that might occur in the future.

You want to be aware of what previous strategies or outcomes were, and you want to understand their strengths and disadvantages so you can integrate these into your planning. You should not assume that what happened in the past is not important for you to understand today. It may be important because sometimes you are negotiating today with an individual or group that is totally driven by and is still acting and reacting based on something that may have happened long before you were hired or involved. That thing, whatever it is, may no longer be relevant from your perspective, but it is important *if* it's relevant from your counterpart's perspective, because you aren't going forward at any speed or in any direction unless you identify, neutralize, or eliminate that obstacle or obstacles. (see *Overcoming Objections, Influence – Rapport – Results,* pp. 41–47; see also the section in this book titled "Overcoming Objections, pp. 167-205)

If we do not have what we need to get that done, we use what we do have to create it—we make new weapons or we find somebody who can.

No matter how insignificant or how enormous, every negotiation eventually comes down to those directly and indirectly involved in the negotiating process. It comes down to the personal beliefs and experiences that are influenced by the Geo-Socio-Poli, the Org-In that caused each of those individuals to be who they are and what their Per-Beha attributes are. So, the astute CNSUF™ negotiator seeks to identify and understand as much as possible about each individual and about how each of those individuals acts and reacts, given their similarities and differences.

Many of the tools for doing this are included in the book, *Influence – Rapport – Results*. For example, CNSUF™ negotiators understand the rudiments of Effective Communication. (see *Influence – Rapport – Results*, pp. 73–93) They know the difference between *information* and *communication.* They understand that Carl Jung's insight that "the meeting of two personalities is like the contact of two chemical substances: if there is any reaction, both are transformed" demands that there be not only a reaction (we can't influence anyone or anything if we don't have their attention, change their focus, and cause some kind of chemical reaction), but that we skillfully predict what that reaction will be and, during the course of the negotiation, how we're going to influence it to achieve the best outcome.

Astute CNSUF™ negotiators are not only going to assess the communication styles (see *Influence-Rapport-Results*, pp. 88–93) of each of the individuals with whom they negotiate; they're going to assess their communication type. (Point of clarification: in the book, *Influence – Rapport – Results*, "Types of Communicators" was used to describe what was later changed to "Styles of Communication" during a live workshop and thereafter. Subsequently, four separate Types of Communicators, described under the next heading, have been added to the CNSU framework to further describe the way people communicate.)

TYPES OF COMMUNICATORS

Talkers

It seems simple enough—talkers are the ones who never shut up, aren't they? Well, yes, *they* (okay, *we*) are, so you might think we are not only easy to identify, but easy to tune out, right? Look, there are many variations in styles and types of communicators, but before you dump every talker into one group of people you can ignore and tune out, think again.

The thing about talkers is that because they talk so much, people find it impossible to listen—impossible to actually pay attention—to what is going on, so they simply tune the talker out. But that is like throwing away pots of gold! Many talkers are not actually talking to you; they are talking to themselves—to their self-consciousness—and debating the pros and cons and thoughts or possibilities of an idea.

In some ways talkers are thinkers who process ideas and thoughts aloud. And as they do, they share insights and give information that they would never give if asked for it directly. Talkers might inadvertently tell you exactly what you need to do to change their mind or cause them to shift their own thinking or position.

If you listen to talkers, you will often find that they are actually asking questions, testing limits, and drilling down to the "bottom line," which may not actually come until eons after the talker starts talking. The challenge for many people is that by the time the talker gets to the bottom line, everyone in the room is asleep, ignoring them, or busy checking text messages and e-mail.

But the astute CNSUF™ negotiator understands that there may be gold in the talker's apparent rambling and that, like panning for gold, the words need to be sifted through and washed out a little for their value to be discovered.

Get the talker's attention by being one of the few people to actually pay attention. Ask rhetorical questions and turn the *data* you have been hearing into a succinct *congruence of meaning*. (see *Influence – Rapport – Results,* pp. 87–88)

Doers

Everybody loves the doer; at the very least, everybody knows a doer. If you are a doer, you already know exactly what this section is about, don't you?

The doer is the one person who does as much as the talker talks; he or she never stops doing. The doer is always busy, always moving, always engaged doing something. These folks arrive early and do not stop until it's time to go home.

Among other attributes, the doer is the one person who is absolutely convinced that he or she can *multitask*. You can find doers in their offices on the phone, on the computer, reading a complex report, and making dinner reservations all at the same time—*not*!

It does not matter that it is impossible for human beings to actually *multitask* in the sense of doing several things at the same time. Doers will swear that you are out of your mind for suggesting that they are not doing nine things at once. The fact is that what doers are actually doing is shifting their attention from one thing to another more or less rapidly than someone who does one thing and then does another in succession. (Note that musicians who practice tirelessly over years reading music, and coordinating their left- and right-hand movements, are about as close as most folks get to actual *multitasking*).

The noted inventor and futurist Ray Kurzweil has given a number of technology/entertainment/design (TED) talks related to the expansion of the brain and the expansion rates of brain activity and technology. If my understanding of some of Kurzweil's work and research is accurate, every generation is increasing the useful area of the brain, and simultaneously technology is developing nanobot technology and devices that at some point will be so small that they can be swallowed, interact with the brain, and increase the reservoir of data the brain can access. As this and other things facilitate human evolution, we will likely (at some point) develop the ability to use separate parts of the brain simultaneously, and thus multitask for real. But by then many people, including Plodders, Talkers, and Thinkers, will also have more intellectual capacity and access to nanotechnology. Meanwhile, the doer is a wannabe multitasker who is shifting from one thing to another rapidly enough to make it look like multitasking. We can never forget that *perception trumps reality*—if multitaskers believe they are multitasking, they are multitasking.

What is particularly interesting about doers is that the people around them are sometimes amazed by their energy. Doers often have a reputation for being get-it-done types who never take a break. But look closely and you will find that doers can also be people who, in the words of the great basketball coach John Wooden, "mistake activity for accomplishment."

It does stand to reason that Millennials, who for their entire lives have been working their brains to do many things simultaneously, are better at it than folks who didn't grow up with the plethora of technology that has emerged in the last three decades and that will continue to expand in capability and shrink in cost. No doubt future generations will have full multitasking capability; but for now, it is often people who are consumed with *busy-ness*.

The key to success with doers is to influence and connect them to *specific* actions, targets, deadlines, and consequences.

Depending on what type they are, the doers you deal with will associate consequences as either positive or negative. Some are driven by consequences they see as negative; they need to associate the consequence to something they see as painful or unwanted. This could mean the loss of credibility, a mediocre performance report, the loss of time off, or public embarrassment. For other people, negative consequences will have no impact at all, because not everyone is driven by what they might lose. Some people are driven only by what they will gain and by how they are going to be rewarded. I am speaking here about the doer, but this is applicable to all communication styles and types.

An uncomplicated way to discover the dominant traits of the doer or any other person is to try both at separate times and measure the results; it is empirical for certain, but more often than not you're going to see a pattern. Give someone a negative consequence at one point and a positive consequence at another, and it is highly probable that he or she will produce a more significant response to one type of consequence than another. Try the same experiment on two or three separate occasions and you should develop valuable insight.

Obviously, when given specific tasks and specific time limits, the doer can be exactly the person you want to organize and monitor the progress of a task or project. Doers are often predisposed to get it done, especially if the correct consequences are attached to doing so.

Thinkers

The thinker can be a talker who talks less or a doer who does not act unless he or she considers all of the options and formulates a strategy. Thinkers often want data—something concrete they can sink their brains into before deciding or taking an action. Even when thinkers are provided with that data, though, they will want to take some time, so they will listen or receive the data you have for them and then delay a decision until a later date and time. In part, this may be because thinkers will have other issues on their plate that they have already weighed and thought about, and these are the things they are likely to make a decision about first before deciding about something that has just come to their attention.

There are a good many pluses and minuses to this style of communication that are worth considering. First of all, because they need time to consider the data and weigh the options, thinkers can sometimes be put at a disadvantage when called upon to make a major decision quickly. The kinds of questions the CNSUF™ negotiator asks include: What happens when thinkers encounter pressure—how do they decide then? Who do thinkers depend on for input? Who has their trust when negotiating in the eye of a storm? How do we get that information? These questions are best answered on a situation-by-situation basis, because there are so many variables. But certainly, we can talk to others who have negotiated with thinkers to get their take, unless this is the first time we have dealt with the thinker. There is bound to be someone we know who has had contact with them in the past. We can also look at notes and details from previous negotiations. You do not keep notes and track individual negotiations? Then you are not a fully competent CNSUF™ negotiator. This is part of the Prep & Tracking we do for every significant negotiation, so that as personnel and circumstances change, we change, and we are able to compare what we have done in the past to what we are planning to do today or in the future.

Another important thing to remember is that people are very often creatures of habit and will do the same thing repeatedly when put in the same circumstance. The other important thing is to evaluate the behavior and reactions of the thinker by skillfully using "Minor Concessions."

But even with all this, keep in mind that the thinker may need time to think. These are not people who are likely to make off-the-cuff decisions, so if you have a compelling issue, give them an opportunity to think. There has to be balance, however, between giving them time and giving them too much time. Not enough time and the thinker may just shut down or say, "No." Too much time and the thinker may come to conclusions that are not in our best interest. So, we consider our options: How much risk should we take? Are there others in the organization who can influence the thinker to make a decision in a more favorable time limit? Is there a concession that includes a benefit that disappears if the decision is not made within a specific period of time? Can we use an "assumptive close" combined with minor concessions? Can we change or use a deadline combined with positive and/or negative consequences to encourage movement? These are the types of questions we ask ourselves when dealing with a Thinker, and the choices we make will vary depending on the individual and the specifics of each negotiation.

Plodders

Ah, the plodders, the individuals who are often mistaken for thinkers, because both require time before they decide or act. But there is a world of difference between them. When a thinker finally makes a decision, there is likely a rationale connected to it, and the CNSUF™ negotiator is always going to ask for that rationale. If the rationale is based on technical elements, we will measure those elements to see if they make as much sense (are consistent with all available facts and data) to us as they do to the thinker. If the technical elements check out, we will think about how to handle them. If those elements contain mistakes, we are going to pay attention to and consider how to address those mistakes (and/or nuances as compared to all available data).

If thinkers do not have a solid rationale for their decisions, our antennas go up. They go up either way, but even more so if a thinker's position is not supported by a well-defined rationale. Thinkers rarely act without reason, and when they have a solid case for their position, they share it more often than not, because it strengthens their position, often becoming an inanimate restrictive force. When they do not share their rationale, we want to know why, because that unwillingness may indicate a hidden advantage/disadvantage to us, or a hidden advantage/disadvantage to our counterpart.

When in negotiation with a thinker, pay attention to what happened the last time you interacted with him or her. The only people who are not creatures of habit are well-trained negotiators who recognize the pitfalls of establishing behavioral patterns. So, when someone you are negotiating with has an abrupt change in behavior, especially if he or she is a thinker, there is a high likelihood that what you are hearing has a strategic rationale behind it. You'd better find out what that rationale is, or risk acting without that information and suffer the consequences.

By contrast, the plodder will take a good while to respond and will rarely make immediate decisions or take immediate action. But while the thinker is thinking, the plodder is often just unorganized or incapable of deciding. I find that many plodders are time-challenged—they frequently miss or ignore time deadlines, they are not great about returning calls, or they return a call and say lots of words with very little connection to anything that is relevant. Plodders are masters of the excuse for why something was not possible or why it didn't get done. Thus, they find themselves stretching the truth so much (in order to cover their tracks) that the line between what is true and what is not is often invisible to them.

While there are many passionate people who work for institutions, it is also true that institutions breed plodders whose primary objective is to get through the day and be eight hours closer to retirement. Plodders cost the companies they work for billions every year because they are inefficient and ineffective. In the big picture, there are plodders of every age and description; it is a mindset and a set of behaviors that make plodders what they are—plodders (also called Quiet Quitters).

The plodder is more likely to have more of a reason than a rationale defined by technical analysis, but what makes plodders dangerous is that they are inconsistent, and their plodding brings an inconsistent pattern of behavior that makes them difficult to predict. One week they are a week ahead of schedule, and next week they are two months behind.

The plodder is also someone who mistakes activity (plodding) for accomplishment, but, unlike the doer who is busy doing, the plodder is busy doing little or nothing at all. Plodders can drive some negotiators crazy, and as a result they lash out or take inappropriate action to speed the plodder up. Meanwhile, frustrated negotiators make mistakes, alienate the plodder, and as a result become ineffective themselves.

To negotiate with plodders successfully, you must get their attention and change their focus by establishing appropriate consequences. By understanding the perspective of the plodder, people do what they do partly because they are products of Geo-Socio-Poli and Org-In, but Per-Beha attributes are specific to each individual. What is the payoff for the plodder? Are plodders aware of how they are perceived? Has their experience beaten them down, so they do not feel anything anymore? Are they empowered more by plodding than by any other behavioral choice they could make? Is that their perception? Is it purposeful plodding? Do plodders realize that by plodding, they cause many people to stop asking or go away? Or do people lose their cool and give the plodder a reason to write them off? How does the plodder *feel*, have they been undermined or undervalued?

More often than not, you will find a combination of these and other questions/issues. But it has been my experience that once you discover what is underneath the behavior and establish a meaningful connection, the plodder can become a tremendous asset and a valuable ally.

Of course, there are exceptions, and most people are actually variations of several types and styles of communication. Most of us have a dominant style and a dominant type in each environment. We use a style and type of communication at home, at church, at a party, on a date, and in various social situations that are different from what we use in our professional lives. But when we are in those individual environments, we tend to have the same style and type of communication. Even if we do not want to, those around us expect us to act in the way they know us in that environment.

For example, my dominant type of communication is Talker, so when I am talking, people expect me to talk. The fastest way for me to draw attention to myself is to *stop* talking. When I am talking, people may not listen to a word I say, but if I stop talking you can bet half a dozen people will walk up and ask me, "What's wrong?" Nothing may be wrong with me, but something is "wrong" to those around me; that something is that I am acting outside of the communication type that is expected of me. For that person, something *must* be wrong because the person they know me to be in that environment is a talker, and I am not talking.

Chapter 3: Mode Groups & Modes

If you want to know how people perceive your communication style and type, all you have to do is to communicate in a style and type outside of what is expected in a given environment. Others may not be able to put their finger on it, but they will notice that you are acting differently.

Another way to confirm your communication style and type is to ask people who are close to you. Offer a close friend or relative various choices and ask him or her which of the styles and types most represent you. I can promise two things: the first is that you are going to be surprised by what you learn, and the second is that you are going to be surprised by what you learn about the way people see your communication style and type in various environments.

There are exceptions to this, but they are rare. Think for a moment about stage and film actors and celebrities. If you see someone like George Clooney in a film role, the first person you see is George Clooney. No matter the film, your first impression is that George Clooney is acting out a role—he is playing a character. Brad Pitt is the same; no matter what role he plays, the dominant presence is Brad Pitt. (The recent and notable exception would be his role in the 2014 film, *Fury*.) I am using these two gentlemen as examples because I happen to like and admire them both, and I admire some of the same and some of the distinctive characteristics about each of them. They are not *great* actors, because they mostly act out roles as the characters they play, rather than acting in a role and disappearing into their characters.

When you think of Daniel Day-Lewis, what do you think about? His character. You think about the character he is portraying, because even though we know it's Daniel Day-Lewis, he envelops the roles he portrays so effectively that our first thought becomes that of the character he has embodied. We do not necessarily think Daniel Day-Lewis is acting, because Daniel Day-Lewis is an exception—an actor's actor.

Charlize Theron, in the film *Monster,* won an Oscar because she disappeared into the character. She became the character, she didn't act the role.

Jennifer Aniston is a personality, a celebrity, especially when compared to the likes of Meryl Streep. Streep is an actor, an exception to the exception; she envelops her characters so incredibly well that even when she misses here and there, we forgive her, because she is so incredibly brilliant. Pick any generation of actors and you can find similar comparisons—people who are exceptionally good at what they do and who make lots of money, but whose work is driven by their personality and their celebrity rather than by their exceptional abilities as actors.

Notably one thinks of the Kardashians, who are famous for being famous (and very rich).

The same is true of the way people communicate, of their communication styles and types, and of negotiators in every business sector and profession. Some people are naturally gifted at negotiation or at whatever they do. They personify excellence, and they have never read a single book on negotiation. For example, they have never attended a workshop. They are just gifted, and they are rare. The thing about most gifted people, whether actors or professionals in some other business sector, is that the best of the best usually combine extraordinary talent and potential with an extraordinary work ethic, focus, and, above everything else, an incredible dedication to excellence, or success as *they* define it.

Being a competent CNSUF™ negotiator is a combination of art and skill, knowledge, and execution, and not everyone is going to be a natural. Not everyone is going to have the instincts and intuition that make a truly gifted CNSUF™ negotiator. But anyone who invests the time and effort necessary to learn the CNSU framework and then uses it consistently is going to improve and be a stronger asset for themselves and for the companies they work for; there is no question about it. Those who have modest potential and who dedicate themselves just as people who are great will find unprecedented growth and opportunity as they evolve and as the CNSUF™ framework evolves with them.

That kind of dedication, talent, and intelligence crosses every Geo-Socio-Poli, Org-In, Per-Beha on the planet, but no one truly escapes the impact these Omni Modes have on their lives. We are all products of Omni Modes, whether we want to be or not. I encourage you to focus on becoming the best CNSUF™ negotiator you can be. Do the work and make the investment, and the return on your efforts will multiply many times over.

Yes, we are occasionally going to meet the Daniel Day-Lewises, Meryl Streeps, and Charlize Therons of their profession, and they will be formidable counterparts—difficult to categorize and difficult to predict or detect because we're going to want to believe them. (It must be pointed out that Day-Lewis, Streep, and Theron are not the only actors with these capabilities; there are certainly others who for political and institutional reasons, or policies, are not given the opportunity to demonstrate their full bandwidth.) If you are one of those people, more power to you, but I am more than certain that the vast majority of you reading this book and most of those with whom we are going to negotiate have a dominant communication style and type. Once astute CNSUF™ negotiators understand what that style and type are both for themselves and for those with whom they are negotiating, they are going to more accurately craft negotiation strategies that are effective, given the people and the situations in which they are negotiating.

We start with the Geo-Socio-Poli, and move to the Org-In, but at the end of the day it all comes down to Per-Beha—how have the other modes impacted the personal and behavioral idiosyncrasies of those with whom we are negotiating? The rules, the tactics, the strategies that we create need to be created for each situation, and for each individual. They need to be directed toward the precise Geo-Socio-Poli, Org-In, and the Per-Beha elements of those with whom we are negotiating or interacting.

There you have the primary elements of The Omni Mode Group; while always present, the significance of each will ebb and dissipate like the value of a share of stock from negotiation to negotiation, but the importance of these elements should rarely be ignored or forgotten because all of the modes and mode groups are interconnected to one degree or another.

To help us remember that interconnection, the CNSUF™ Continuum draws a triangle among the Omni Modes that is called the *Triangle of Interrelationship* or the *Axis of Interdependence* (See Exhibit V, p. 40).

EXHIBIT V

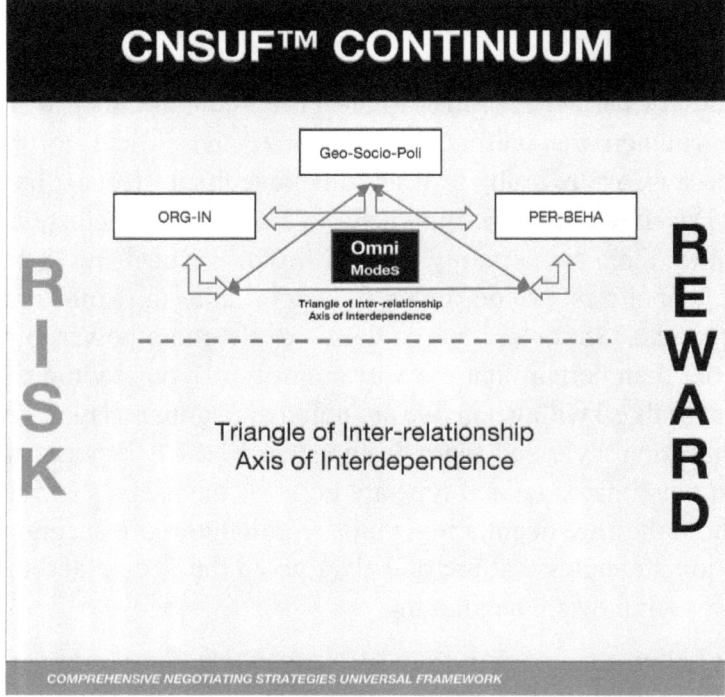

Triangle of Interrelationship or the Axis of Interdependence

The purpose of calling the relationship among the Omni Modes the *Triangle of Interrelationship* or *Axis of Interdependence* is to provide a visual reference for the ever-present and evolving connections between the Omni Modes and each of the elements within each mode.

It reminds us to investigate what the connections might be and what they might mean for a given negotiation. How can we use those connections and interconnections to help us achieve one or more of the six fundamental tenets? Which tenets are most affected by interrelationship(s) during a particular negotiation? We might explore the tangible/intangible risks we are willing to assume versus the potential tangible/intangible rewards that are gained or lost by investing time and resources in answering these and other questions. The product of our analysis will then be used to help determine an overall strategy or to determine the next steps. Sometimes the product of these questions is premature, but we keep it and ensure that it is not lost or forgotten, especially if we are engaged in a long-term relationship or negotiation with our counterpart(s).

Things will change over the course of a relationship, and what is not important today may be monumental tomorrow. Sometimes we miss or miscalculate small bits of information, especially in the beginning stages of a relationship or negotiation. This may be because negotiators are driven by our desire to make the relationship happen, either because we want it or because our organization wants it, and we are charged with making the relationship work. Sometimes we miss the equivalent of a truckload of evidence; we are on a slippery slope and there it is right in front of our faces, but we do not see it, we cannot see it, or we refuse to see it.

This is especially true where our personal relationships are concerned—certainly those outside of our professional lives, but even more so the personal relationships inside the organizations we work for. There we have to navigate protocol. We work with people who are simultaneously our allies and counterparts because of divisional or departmental differences, buyers versus sellers within an organization, engineers versus sales, finance versus procurement, or IT versus administration/management versus the workforce in general. We work for the same company, organization, or government, but often our objectives are not aligned. We have conflicting metrics for success and different definitions of communication and cooperation, yet we are on the same team; this makes a demanding situation even more difficult. What negotiation strategy or tools do you use with the very same people you live and work with or for?

The truth is that we negotiate with people we know all the time. We just do not do it in the same way, and we do not call it *negotiation.* A very good friend of mine calls it *scheming,* which by definition is not at all CNSUF™ negotiation. I have also heard people call it *haggling* or *dickering*, and if these represent the way you think of negotiation, why in the world would you want to do it? You won't want to do it, and you will do everything in your power to avoid doing what is necessary to achieve the best results. Your reward for not learning, for not growing, is that you do not need to learn anything new—you can simply keep doing what you are doing and pretend that it is not possible to do any better.

Negotiation is like chess in some ways and not at all like chess in other ways. Both chess and negotiation involve, among other things, a combination of strategy, mathematics, quantitative analysis, psychology, and intuition. But a chessboard has eight squares down and eight squares across, with every piece having limitations as to where and how it can move, what it can do, and when it can be done.

Negotiation is different because we do not know how many squares there are in a particular organization, and we do not truly know the roles and limitations of each *player* expressly. We can look at a title or at an organization chart, but that is not the same as understanding how individuals operate within those roles—and roles change from family to family, organization to organization, and person to person. Part of the astute CNSUF™ negotiator's responsibility is to determine as precisely as possible how specific individuals function within each organization.

In chess we play the piece first, and then the individual responsible for manipulating the piece because we know that a rook cannot become a queen. By contrast, we have no such assurance in the real world, so CNSUF™ negotiators understand that they are not so much negotiating an issue, a price, or a position. They are negotiating the wants, needs, expectations, and limitations of specific people, organizations, and institutions. The clearer we are about that, the more we understand why having a specific foundation and using it will be better than relying solely on what *we* think or what *we* feel or what *we* did the last time *we* were in a given situation.

There are a hundred reasons why what we see at the beginning of a negotiation/relationship is rarely what we see at the end. Plan on that reality. Use the CNSUF™ to strategize and the CNSUF™ Continuum to track the progress of your negotiations and as a reference point for sharing with others where you are, where you want to go, and the challenges you are facing. Identify and record the actions that both sides have taken in each of the modes that might contribute to one or more of the six foundational tenets and/or to the highest and best outcome.

Before we get to the Conditional Mode Group, I have a question: why the name Omni Mode Group? If you do not know the answer to this question, I strongly encourage you to go back to the beginning of the section on Mode Groups and Modes and review that section until you are absolutely clear about the answer before proceeding.

Chapter 3: Mode Groups & Modes

> The fundamental elements of the CNSU framework are based on principles that can be applied to any form of negotiation, in any business sector or personal situation. That is one of the most valuable aspects of the framework and one of the elements that make CNSUF™ unique. It is also an evolving framework, because there will not come a time when we know everything, when the framework is complete. The world around us is continually changing, layering one bit of insight over another, and resulting in fresh perspectives on the existing body of knowledge in negotiation. When that is no longer true, it will be proof that the world as we know it, has ended.

Keep in mind that many of the words used in CNSUF™ will often be the exact same words you will see in other negotiation frameworks, such as the Karrass Effective Negotiating framework, the Harvard Program On Negotiation framework, and others. It is not the words themselves that make the difference; it is the unique combination of proprietary elements—such as the order of the words and, more importantly, the specific definitions that are associated with words—that makes *all* the difference in the world.

No other negotiation framework arranges the elements of the Omni Mode Group the same way and labels it the Omni Mode Group based on the root definition of the word Omni. That is significant because the word Omni suggests that the elements included in Omni Mode Group are *always* present and *always* relevant in *all* negotiations. When the CNSU framework uses the word Omni, it means that the modes in that group are present everywhere, every day, in every country, in every language, for every person of every size, shape, color, and socioeconomic background. So, in the CNSU framework, definitions truly matter; use them on purpose and treat them with reverence.

The Conditional Mode Group

EXHIBIT VI

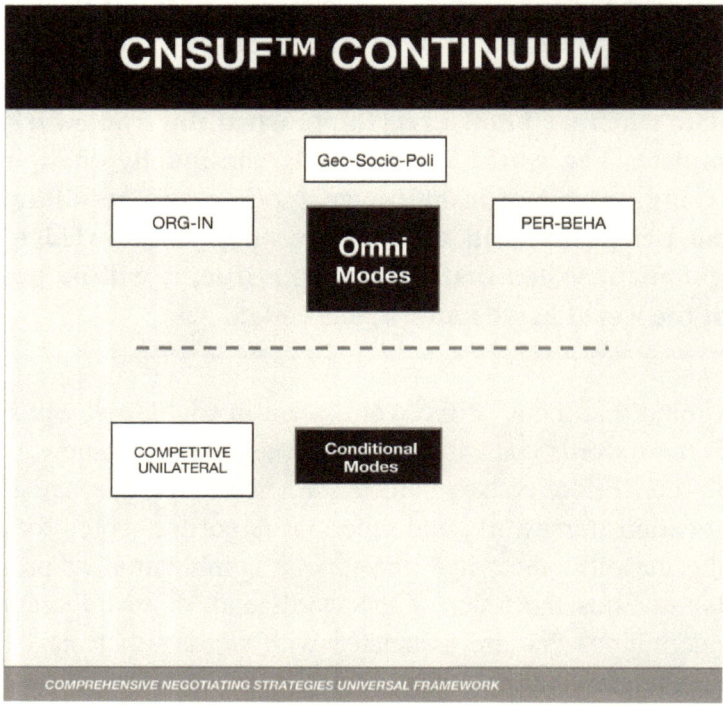

Virtually everything written about negotiation will include something about competitive, cooperative, and some form of the "win-win" or "both-win" mode of negotiation. But what makes CNSUF™ unique is that no other framework puts these modes into a single category or group defined as *conditional*. And no other framework defines these terms precisely the same way. So, while some of the words are the same (and some have been modified to indicate their particular definition within CNSUF™), the definitions, the meaning, and the substance of these words, as used in CNSUF™, are completely different from any other negotiation framework.

The Omni Mode Group is so called because all of the elements are *omni-present* (always there), whereas the Conditional Mode Group is so called because each element's presence is not always there. It is dictated by the existence of one or more specifically defined *relevant conditions*.

The word "condition" refers to a restricting, limiting, or modifying circumstance; it can happen only under certain *conditions*.

The word "conditional" refers to imposing, containing, being subject to, or depending on a condition or conditions; not absolute or allowed on certain terms. Synonyms for the term conditional include *dependent, contingent, relative*. The Conditional Mode Group contains modes that are present only when certain conditions exist.

Furthermore, the CNSUF™ negotiator is looking for a specific kind of condition—*relevant, bearing upon, or connected with the matter in hand, pertinent*.

The CNSUF™ negotiator first analyzes the relevant conditions that exist among the parties involved in a negotiation. Based solely on those relevant conditions, the CNSUF™ negotiator determines the mode of negotiation. This is essential because it means CNSUF™ negotiators are not relying on their emotions, feelings, or objectives to determine what mode of negotiation they are in. They rely on an assessment of the *relevant conditions* in the same way meteorologists rely on relevant atmospheric conditions to predict the weather.

The Conditional Mode Group contains three modes: the Competitive Mode, the Co-Operative Mode, and the All-Win Mode. The presence or absence of each of these modes is dependent upon specific *relevant conditions*.

The Competitive Mode

The competitive mode is beyond a doubt the mode that is most familiar to everyone. I daresay I have never encountered a human being past the age of five who isn't on some level familiar with the word "competitive."

Depending on who you ask, the word competitive conjures up responses ranging from deadly to bullheaded, domineering, spoiled, angry, exclusive, excluding, mean, self-centered, the attitude of "my way or the highway," and more.

According to Webster's Online dictionary, the word competitive means: *of or relating to a situation in which people or groups are trying to win a contest or be more successful than others.* But what does the word competitive mean to *you*? If someone walked up to you at work and asked you to define competitive, what would you say? No matter what that is, the first thing that comes to your mind will be exactly how you define competition for yourself.

More often than not people, even very smart people, find it difficult to define the word competitive succinctly. In thirty years of asking thousands of people from many professions, I have never had anyone give me a precise definition, and I have certainly *never* had anyone, other than clients and those who have attended CNSUF™ Live or its predecessor, give me the CNSUF™ definition. Rather, people tend to respond, then stop, ramble, squirm, and then start to see pictures in their head that describe their definition of competition. And the pictures they see and the definition they give will be tied to their unique Geo-Socio-Poli, Org-In and Per-Beha idiosyncrasies.

I encourage you to do a simple experiment: Ask the next ten people you talk to, "How do you define the word competition?" and see for yourself the range of their responses. Odds are your results will be remarkably similar to the responses I have received. (Depending on when you are reading this book, you may have a few people answer the question succinctly, and if they do, the first thing you should ask is whether they have read this book or attended a live CNSUF™ workshop or event). One thing is certain: if someone answers that question succinctly, you may well be dealing with an experienced, well-trained negotiator. Another thing to remember, if you conduct this experiment and everyone you ask gives you the CNSUF™ definition, it will mean that CNSUF™ has become mainstream and it will mean that you either need to step up your CNSUF™ IQ or find another negotiation framework ASAP, preferably yesterday!

In the CNSU framework, the definition of the word competitive is a fundamental and proprietary element with universal application; there are no exceptions to its essence. Whether or not people understand the concept, the word competitive always comes down to a single synonym:

Chapter 3: Mode Groups & Modes

unilateral. What is universally accurate about the term competitive is that it refers to the interests of one entity as they differ from the interests of another entity.

When we use the word competitive in the CNSU framework, we are saying that our interests, loyalty, objectives, focus, allegiance, commitment, thoughts, and actions are centered around, dedicated, and inextricably tied to our team, employer, country, brand, process, objectives, and self-preservation. If these *relevant* conditions do not exist, then we are not in the competitive mode.

If, for example, you say the Pledge of Allegiance and commit your allegiance to America, yet simultaneously pledge your allegiance to some other country, where is your allegiance? Your allegiance to America is by definition in competition with your allegiance to whatever other country you pledge your allegiance to, isn't it? Is it possible to give total allegiance to two countries or two teams or two of the same anything simultaneously? No, because when we *decide* to give allegiance to one thing, we simultaneously cut off allegiance to anything else. In fact, the word *"decide"* actually means: *"to cut away"* (from the Latin word *dēcīdere*), as I shared in *Beyond Negotiating: Influence – Rapport – Results*.

When I joined the Marine Corps at seventeen years old, I swore allegiance to the Marine Corps and to the United States of America, despite all my doubts, opinions, questions, protests, and the like. Many years later I am still a proud American and a Marine at heart. But the Marine Corps is a branch of the military, and America is a country. The point is that I could not have been committed to the Marine Corps and the Army and the Navy and the Air Force and the Coast Guard at the same time. A contract to serve in one branch during one period precludes the ability to sign a contract to serve in another branch at the same time. For clarification, my allegiance to the Marine Corps does not preclude my admiration for the people who serve and who have served in the other branches of the Armed Forces. I admire all those who have served our country and recognize that we all, regardless of our branch of service, serve the same great country.

Remember Webster's definition of competition? It is of or relating to a situation in which people or groups are trying to win a contest or be more successful than others; relating or involving competition, relating to, characterized by, or based on competition, inclined, desiring, or suited to compete.

An important question is this: when we are in a competition, whose interests are we bound to represent—the team we play for or the other team? Where does our allegiance reside—with our employer or with the employer who hired the people on the other side of the table? The simple answer is that we are duty-bound to represent the interests of the team we are on, whether it is in sports or in business. In fact, doing anything less can be unfair, unethical, immoral, or downright illegal. If you are professional in the financial sector and you are managing a client's resources, don't you have a fiduciary responsibility to do everything in your power to grow that client's portfolio and to provide truthful (to the best of your knowledge) recommendations that assist the client in achieving his or her financial goals? What if you are a lawyer? Don't you have a responsibility to represent the best interests of your client?

This does not mean that everyone who is supposed to represent the interests of one party instead of another always does what he or she is supposed to do. It means that in a perfect world, it is what people are *supposed* to do, understanding that there will be many who will fall short of their obligation to do so. History will forever be filled with examples of how and where those who were supposed to do something did not do it or violated the principles and commitments they had made to uphold a particular set of standards or ethics.

I am certain that what we know is only a small drop in the bucket compared to what we will never know about the competitive nature of human beings and their allegiances.

Have your allegiances ever been in competition with one another? No? Are you sure about that?

Have you ever had to decide between what was best for you or for your family versus what was in the best interest of your employer? Have you ever made a decision that involved a good friend versus a family member? Have you always made the right choice, or have you ever found that you chose to do what was best for you or for your family ahead of what might have been best for the company you worked for? Have you ever looked back and realized that you sided with a relative instead of a good friend because you concluded that blood is thicker than friendship?

If you are more than ten minutes old, you have been in competition with something or someone every day of your life, whether you believe it or not.

From the beginning of time, human beings have competed, just like the birds of the air and creatures of the field. Everything from atoms to microbes competes, and those who do not are doomed.

Beyond all of this, there is one indisputable fact about competition that dictates how it is viewed and defined by the astute CNSUF™ negotiator. No matter what you or I believe about the definition of competition, we will be hard-pressed to find ten random people in a thousand who share our exact definition and viewpoint. Please do not just believe me on this; simply ask the next ten people you talk to at random what their definition of the word competition is, and listen to their answers.

The ironic thing is that many readers will be so competitive that rather than simply asking ten people, "Hey, what is your definition of the word competition?" they will ask leading questions like, "Don't you think that competition should be defined as—" and they will fill in the blank with whatever they believe. These are the same people who will swear that they are not competitive.

Rather than doing a variation of this, I am asking you to simply ask the next ten people you speak to this question: "What is your definition of the word competition?" Pay close attention to the looks they give you, and then simply repeat the question.

After asking this ten times at random, you will most assuredly learn that everyone defines competition differently. You will also learn that most of the answers are connected to the Geo-Socio-Poli, Org-In, and Per-Beha of each individual. And you may find it surprising to learn that even people who come out of the same family or out of the exact same Geo-Socio-Poli and Org-In have vastly different ideas about the concept of competition.

Of course, you are going to find similarities, too, because many of the answers you will hear will contain fragments of the same answers. You will even find that some people have the same definition exactly, but this will be an aberration if you are asking people at random. You will no doubt find that, generally speaking, women are more likely to connect competition to seeking the best outcome and that, generally speaking, men will connect competition to winning. (see *The Fundamental Purpose of Competition, Influence – Rapport – Results,* pp. 29–39)

Once you have completed this experiment you should be much better able to compare the way you define competition with the way all those you asked do. You will find that your definition has changed by virtue of what you have heard from others, because their opinions will have influenced your own perspective. You will find that every definition you hear will have one thing that is consistent. Every definition will come down to the fact that all competition involves the interests of two or more unilateral entities. There must be two or more entities with separate interests, loyalties, focus, or objectives without which you cannot have competition. If the interests of two or more entities are the same, then it is not competition but some variation of cooperation.

And here there are no exceptions.

In fact, the very root of the word competition, *competere,* means to come together. If we are meeting within our own brain or coming together with another individual or group, competition requires more than one party, or entity, with contrasting functions, interests, goals, access, and intentions.

For the astute CNSUF™ negotiator, the competitive mode comes down to one word: *unilateral*—unilateral interests, objectives, functions, wants, and needs. From a military or corporate perspective, when two unilateral parties with different goals come together, they engage in "warfare" to determine whose goals will prevail. The *means* of negotiation are a combination of distinct types of "battles" and diplomatic interactions that often occur simultaneously, and these activities will go on until one party dominates the other on the "battlefield," or at the negotiating table, a combination of these, or when the parties come to an agreement. But how is that different from spouses coming together to decide whether the toilet tissue in the bathroom will go under or over the top? How is that different from a person selling his or her house and asking a half million dollars for it and a buyer who comes along and offers four-hundred and fifty thousand? Or when lawyers present their arguments before a judge or jury?

It does not matter who the players are or what the issue is, a negotiation is competitive whenever two or more entities with different interests come together. Of course, the real difference in the examples is *consequence*—people die in war or suffer horrific physical and mental injury, husbands and wives separate or divorce over issues as seemingly insignificant as which direction the tissue in their bathroom should go. And decisions as to who wins or loses in a courtroom are decided by either a judge or jury.

This shift in perspective regarding the nature of competition represents a quantum leap in negotiation theory, because it fundamentally changes how negotiators look at competition. It does not change the definition of competition; it changes the way the definition is comprehended. It changes what we do, what we think, and how we react to competition. It changes where we place our focus and where we invest our resources. Seeing the competitive mode as the *coming together of two or more unilateral entities* turns attention away from assumptions, presumptions, and emotions toward gathering the resources, information, and insights we need to craft a viable negotiation strategy.

In other words, when the CNSUF™ negotiator is in the competitive mode, we are focused on three questions: How are we going to find out what we do not know? How are we going to find out what our counterparts know (or think they know) about us? How are we going to protect ourselves and our interests while we are figuring things out and seeking answers?

The cornerstones of our approach are built on top of the Six CNSUF™ Foundational Tenets, and on the *Relevant Conditions* that exist between the parties. Remember: *relevant conditions* dictate the mode, the mode dictates the position the negotiation takes on the CNSUF™ Continuum, and the position and mode(s) together dictate the tactics and tools that will be used to build and implement strategy.

You may be thinking, "What if my objectives are the same as my counterpart's? For one thing, the answer depends on what you mean when you say that your goals are the same. How do you know that? If you know it because you have had access to the same resources and knowledge as your counterpart, that is one thing. But if you *know* your goals and your counterpart's are the same because you believe it, because you feel it, because you think it, or because they said it, then that is quite another thing indeed.

A couple of things come into play here. First, if you know your goals are the same, and you and your counterpart agree they are the same, then you are no longer at the extreme edges of the competitive mode on the CNSUF™ Continuum, because you are no longer two or more unilateral parties coming together in a negotiation. You begin to move from the competitive mode toward the co-operative mode, because the relevant conditions have changed.

But even though we may find during the negotiation that both parties have objectives in common, we rarely *know* that at the beginning. If you answered Yes, how do you know? Is it because they tell you that their interests are the same as yours?

That reminds me of a teenager telling their girlfriend, boyfriend, or significant other, "Trust me," in the back seat of their first car! If you were the parent of the teen hearing that message, would you tell them to "trust" everything their admirer said to them? No, you would not. But you are willing to believe your counterpart, who works for a different company, is located in a different country, has a different Geo-Socio-Poli, Org-In, Per-Beha than your own or that of your colleagues, when they tell you "trust us, our interests, and objectives are the same as yours," even before the negotiation begins? Perhaps you believe them because your counterpart has published a Request for Proposals (RFP) or Request for Quotes (RFQ). Certainly, any legitimate RFP or RFQ will

Chapter 3: Mode Groups & Modes

contain some accurate information and detail, but virtually no RFP or RFQ is all-encompassing. For every detail included in an RFP, RFQ, contract, agreement, or proposal, there are a dozen relevant details that are omitted by default or by happenstance. RFPs, RFQs, initial contracts, agreements, and proposals are only a small part of the total picture or process, and therefore they raise as many questions and issues as they answer.

Still many successful and intelligent people are willing to trust what their counterparts tell them or include in an initial RFP, RFQ, treaty, contract, or agreement. When I asked them "why?" they tell me, "He's/she's a really nice person," or "Oh, they seem really honest," or "We feel really good about them," or "We've done business or have negotiated before." That is it? That is your strategy? You *feel* like they are "really nice people"? Reading it on paper makes this approach look a lot dumber than it feels when people do it in real life, especially to those who have made the mistake of trusting their counterparts simply because they *seemed* like nice people. The fact is, we do not truly know what our counterparts' objectives, wants, or needs are until we have confirmed tangible evidence or until after the negotiation has concluded. Even then we should test and re-test what we believe and move in Appropriate Degrees of Separation (ADOS/MADS).

Range of Conditions

The questions raised above are sufficient to support the conclusion that we do not know exactly what our counterpart's intentions are. We do not have access to the same information they do. We did not attend their meetings. We were not on their conference calls. We did not receive the same memos. Though we may know one or two of the people who will be participating in the negotiation process, we do not know that they will be the only people involved as the negotiation progresses.

These are things we know. We do not have to guess, and we do not have to conjecture—we *know* we were not included in the internal strategy sessions conducted by our counterparts. Therefore, we could not possibly know that the intentions and goals of our counterpart are exactly what they have shared with us. Bottom line, should this knowledge be taken into consideration and factored into our strategy and behavior? Of course it should. Yet how many times have we walked away from the negotiating table and thought, "We got a good deal" or "They seem to want a win-win outcome"? By contrast, how many times have people walked away from the negotiating table, and as soon as the door closed behind them, their counterpart thought while beaming, "Wow, if they had waited another ten seconds before they accepted our offer, we would have given them twice what they got"?

Because we never really knew our counterpart's objectives, how could we conclude that we achieved the highest and best outcome? Consider this scenario: Your counterpart was not there when you set X as your goal. What you did not know was that if you had set X higher or structured it differently and focused on finding out what you did not know, rather than negotiating based on what your counterpart told you, the outcome might have been much different. Getting the highest and best outcome is what astute CNSUF™ negotiators are working to achieve, not feeling good based on a negotiation they had with themselves.

I have facilitated a thousand live negotiation workshops throughout the United States, Canada, Mexico, and elsewhere around the world for businesses and organizations from every conceivable business sector on a wide range of issues. I have witnessed the overwhelming majority of people and organizations measure their success in negotiation by labeling the process as "Competitive, Cooperative, Win-Win, or Win-Lose," based either on how they feel or on goals that left them negotiating with or against themselves. Frankly, that just is not good enough now, and it certainly is not going to be adequate as the emerging integrated global economy continues to evolve—because negotiators do not know whether they have achieved the highest and best outcome most of the time, and because they certainly aren't able to accurately declare success or failure based on the empirical evidence they have at the moment most negotiations conclude.

That is why CNSUF™ redefines the terms competitive, cooperative, and win-win. This redefining includes a critical but often missed mode of negotiation in the Co-Opetitive Mode, rather than repeating the historically prolific standard of assuming that everyone understands these terms the same way, as is the case with other significant negotiation frameworks.

This redefining of important negotiating terminology, combined with the concept of relevant conditions, together with the CNSUF™ Continuum, moves away from the idea that outcomes in negotiation are finite or certain and moves toward the idea that outcomes in negotiation are primarily tentative and evolutionary. It moves toward the idea that a range of relevant conditions leads to a range of possible competitive or co-operative outcomes. In the CNSU framework, outcomes are relative (based on a range of specific conditions), rather than finite. Some competitive behavior is different from total competitive behavior. Some co-operative behavior is different from total co-operative behavior, since the outcome is measured by a range of conditions.

Rather than seeing a negotiation as solely competitive or cooperative, the CNSUF™ negotiator uses the CNSUF™ Continuum to note that there are degrees of both competition and cooperation, not the fixed positions that so many are accustomed to recognizing. The rationale is simple: the vast majority of negotiations do not conclude with a clearly discernible winner or loser. Even in sports, where there are scores to reflect who won and who lost, any avid sports fan will tell you that the scoreboard often does not reflect the total details of what happened. Isn't it obvious today that the industrialization of America throughout the nineteenth and twentieth centuries contributed to the current worldwide environmental, Geo-Socio-Poli, Org-In, Per-Beha issues of today? So, who has won and who has lost? Clearly it depends on who you are, your age, your race, your experience—all the considerations of the Omni Modes. Outcomes occur on a continuum and then devolve and evolve over time.

Negotiations are primarily completed in shades of gray rather than black and white. That has always been true, it is true today, and it will continue to be true as AI and other software and technology lead us into the future. This is another reason astute CNSUF™ negotiators must evolve or be slaughtered. The CNSUF™ Continuum characterizes base competition (the fundamental purpose of competition) as darkness, the complete absence of light. It is a unilateral perspective that is satisfied *only* by the annihilation of anything outside of its own goals. In the CNSU framework, the Competitive Mode starts there and moves only as relevant conditions evolve, expand, and/or contract.

Remember, *The Fundamental Purpose of Competition* (see *Influence – Rapport – Results*, pp. 29–39) argues that despite all thought to the contrary, the fundamental purpose of competition is to "obliterate" the competition. Who can argue that the history of the world is not replete with examples of how those who built the world did so by dominating the people and core industries of countries without regard for establishing monopolies or who was crushed in the process? Who can argue that in order to build industries across America, millions of Native Americans were forced from their land, or that over sixty-million buffalo, the bedrock of the plains tribes, were purposely obliterated in order to do it?

While there are people who will argue anything for the sake of argument, the facts indicate that history has defined the fundamental purpose of competition as the obliteration of everything in its path just short of extinction, because those who are dominated are then put to work building the victors' monuments and infrastructure. Once the monuments and infrastructure are completed, crumbs of benevolence emerge to support the perception of refined culture and humanity as defined by the victor.

At its core, competition wants to obliterate or, at the very least, dominate its counterpart. But for many reasons (Geo-Socio-Poli) it does not, and thus compromise is accepted as an interim point of resolution. There are certainly exceptions, but from a macro point of view nobody compromises unless they have to, unless they perceive it as convenient or advantageous to do so. Why would individuals, an organization, or a country cooperate if competitive domination with acceptable consequences is possible? Compromise and cooperation happen only because there is something in it for the entities that tolerate or promote it.

The challenge is getting your counterparts to see what you want them to see from your perspective or position so thoroughly that they are persuaded, influenced, or compelled to accept your highest and best outcome. Therefore, rather than seeing the outcome of a negotiation as finite, the astute CNSUF™ negotiator recognizes that the outcome of the vast majority of negotiations more often than not is relative, reflecting a range of relevant conditions, a range and combination of competition(s), and cooperation.

So, visually the Competitive Mode on the CNSUF™ Continuum, as represented by a spectrum of light (see Exhibit VII), starts on the far left, where the absence of light represents the fundamental purpose of competition. It gradually moves right to its antithesis, the total absence of darkness, to the CNSUF™ All-Win Mode (not to be confused with Both-Win or Win-Win).

EXHIBIT VII

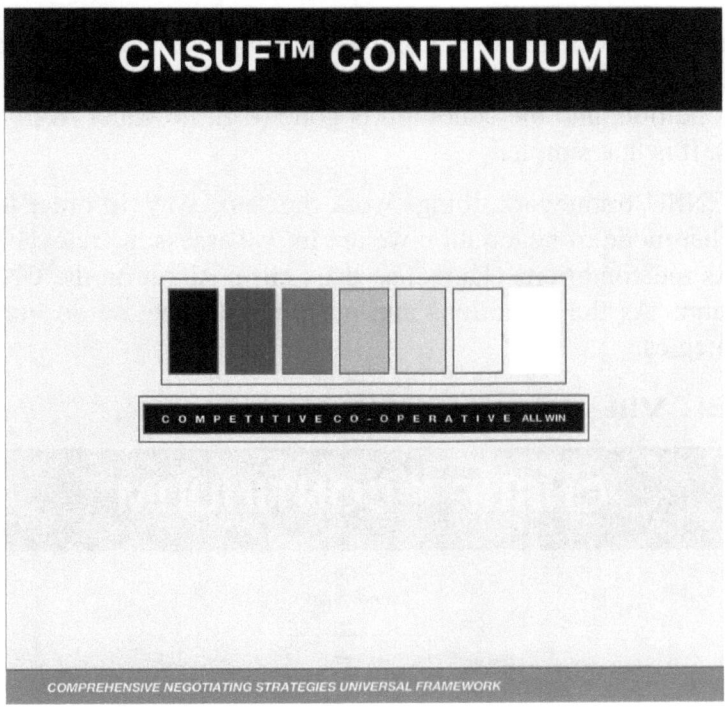

Relevant Conditions

If you are outside as you read this, take a few moments and look around you. What do you see? Are there clouds? What color is the sky? What is the air quality? What is the temperature? Is it hot? Is it cold? Is there any wind? In what direction is the wind blowing? If you are inside as you read, take a look around you. What color are the walls? What kind of light is filling the room? Is it fluorescent? Is it ambient? Is it incandescent? What is the temperature? Is it warm? Is it cold? Is there carpeting on the floor, or is it wood or ceramic tile?

Now, how do you *know* that the *conditions* you observe or experience *are* the conditions you are observing or experiencing? Yes, this is like the question: if a tree falls in the forest and nobody hears it, did it make a sound? I am simply asking, for example, if it is raining or not, how do you know? Hopefully, we can agree that the answer would be the same whether you are inside or outside. You know it is raining because there are raindrops falling. (Granted, someone could be using a rain machine or water hose to make it seem like it was raining.)

The way we answer any one of those questions is to take a look around, assess the relevant conditions, and respond accordingly. Remove the relevant condition, and the condition is gone (e.g., no water from the sky, no rain). It is that simple.

In the CNSU framework, things work the same way. In order to determine what mode of negotiation we are in; we assess the relevant conditions. As the conditions change, so does our position on the CNSUF™ Continuum. As the conditions and positions change, so do our tactics and strategies.

EXHIBIT VIII

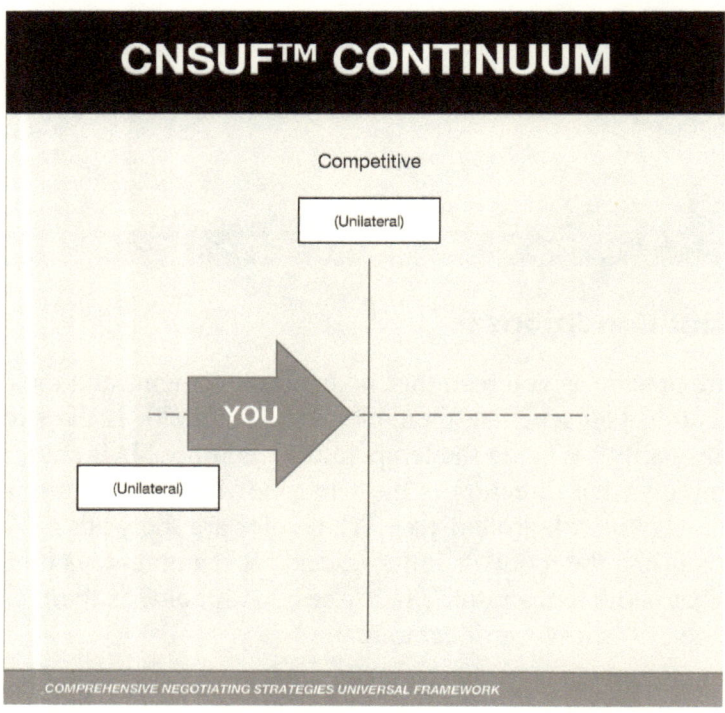

Chapter 3: Mode Groups & Modes

Exhibit VIII shows the Competitive/Unilateral Mode. The arrow represents you—your interests, the interests of your company and internal counterparts. The horizontal line in the center of the exhibit represents any obstacle between you and your internal/external counterparts. Because you have limited access beyond the horizontal line at the beginning of a negotiation, you are in a competitive/unilateral mode.

The primary relevant conditions here are the limited, unverified, and/or unknown elements of access to your internal/external counterpart's resources and knowledge.

Exhibit IX introduces your internal/external counterparts who are separated by the horizontal line that indicates the limited, unverified, or lack of access they have to the same data, resources, and knowledge you have. Limited access is one of the relevant conditions that create the competitive/unilateral mode.

EXHIBIT IX

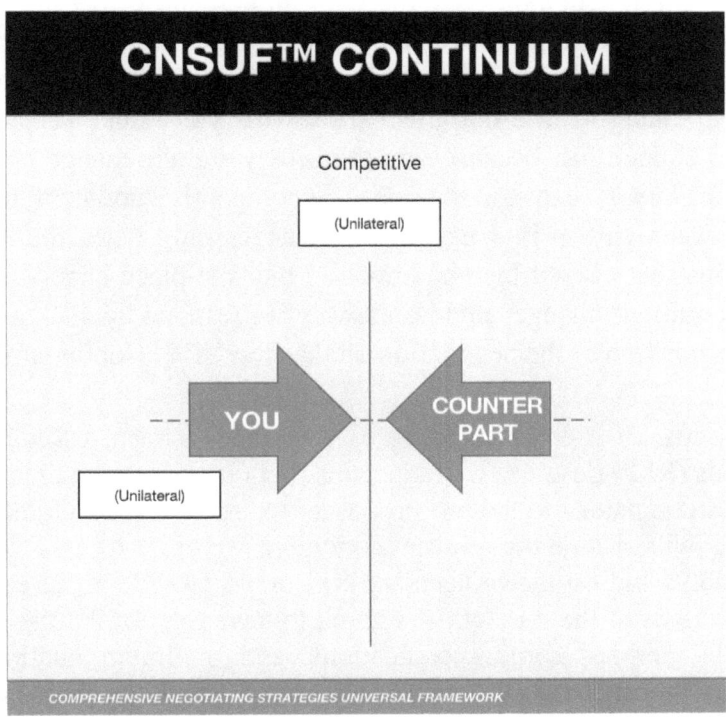

EVOLVE or Be Slaughtered

At the beginning of a negotiation, you may or may not know your objectives. You may not know the extent of your authority, or who will intervene during the negotiation. But you do know what information you have, what has occurred in the meetings you have attended, who has said what on the conference and video calls you have participated in, and the contents of memos you have read. And no matter how small or insignificant, all of these things add up and give you a great deal more insight than your counterpart, who may have had no access to the data and communications you have had.

The exact opposite is true of your counterparts. They know what they have been exposed to, they know about the meetings they have attended, what has occurred during the conference calls they have heard, and what was in the memos they have read. There is a great deal they may not know, but they have far greater insight into what has occurred in their own company than you do. These are *relevant conditions*. Like raindrops that tell us it is raining, the lack of access to data and knowledge between the parties in a negotiation are the relevant conditions that bring about the competitive or unilateral nature of the relationship. These relevant conditions have nothing to do with how you feel about your counterpart. Relevant conditions are not affected by what you think. They are not going to change just because you think they should change any more than your *thinking* can stop the rain. The competitive/unilateral relationship between parties in a negotiation changes only when the relevant conditions that caused the conditions in the first-place change. As relevant conditions change, so does the way we respond to change, and so does the position of the negotiation on the CNSUF™ Continuum.

For example, if a company were to write and publish a Request For Proposals (RFP) describing a large construction project and then invited qualified companies to submit proposals for review, the publication of that RFP will change the relevant conditions. In order to have prospective vendors bid on the project, the RFP must provide some access to the objectives of the project. It is going to have to describe the project, timetable, perhaps some specifications, and minimum qualifications necessary to bid. Relevant conditions change simultaneously for those submitting proposals as well, because they must provide a good deal of information about their company, their management team, previous projects, their capabilities, financials, and whatever else the RFP is requesting, in order to compete for the work.

If a company does not follow the instructions and requirements, or if it does not meet the minimum qualifications or submit a proposal by the deadline, then that company may not have an opportunity to have the project awarded to it. Without a proposal, the prospective client cannot evaluate it against other proposals, theoretically speaking.

Once a company decides to respond to an RFP for a significant project, it has to commit tangible resources in the form of employee hours for meetings, strategy sessions, conferences, and/or video calls from every department that must take part in the development, and deliverables required by the RFP. There are actual costs involved in the development of mockups and models, blueprints, photos and whatever else is necessary to comply with the requirements of the RFP. And then there are the intangible costs. What happens to a company's reputation if it repeatedly publishes RFPs for projects that are never awarded? It suffers, doesn't it? (Many governments and institutions notwithstanding.)

The reality is that there will always be some combination of tangible and intangible costs associated with the development and submission of an RFP of any kind, and these costs can limit or negatively impact the ability of some companies to submit proposals, and thus they cannot or do not win the project.

The point here is that the moment your counterpart writes and publishes an RFP, the moment you decide to respond with a proposal and all that entails, relevant conditions begin to change. The negotiation begins moving from completely unilateral to less and less unilateral as you share information, gain insight, go through the process of evaluation, and develop more knowledge.

All of this brings us to a summary of the specific relevant conditions and the introduction of the competitive rules that help us achieve the Six Foundational Tenets of CNSUF™ as we move through the Competitive Mode.

Relevant Conditions: Competitive Mode

1. Limited or no access to the same resources (Geo-Socio-Poli, Org-In, and/or Per-Beha). The less access, the higher the risks, the more entities involved, the farther left on the CNSUF™ Continuum.

2. Limited or no verifiable information (Geo-Socio-Poli, Org-In, and/or Per-Beha). The less access, the less verifiable, the farther left on the CNSUF™ Continuum. When these two relevant conditions exist, we are in a unilateral position. We have access to resources and information from our company, but we lack that same degree of access to information from our counterpart's company; therefore, we are in the Competitive Mode as defined in the CNSU framework. In order to assess, change, determine our strategy and protect ourselves, astute CNSUF™ negotiators will consider and employ:

Seven CNSUF™ Competitive Rules

Rule One. Ask IWWWWWH (Pronounced "IOWA") questions. (IWWWWWH is the acronym for *If, Who, What, Why, When, Where, and How*) The two most important skills the astute CNSUF™ negotiator must acquire and continuously refine are:

- Learning to ask the right questions at the right time, for the right reasons, and in the appropriate manner.
- Learning to listen twice as much as one speaks but, more importantly, learning to distinguish the difference between what is being said and what is being *communicated*.

These skills are always critical, but they are particularly important during the initial stages of a negotiation. Without these skills, the value of everything else the negotiator does will be severely diminished if not rendered entirely impotent.

Understanding the rudiments of effective communication and of the power of influence (as I detailed in *Beyond Negotiating: Influence – Rapport – Results*) includes the ability to identify the five styles of com-

Chapter 3: Mode Groups & Modes

munication and their corresponding attributes, matching them to the four major types of communicators (Talkers, Doers, Thinkers, Plodders), and using that knowledge to guide the choices one makes while interacting with different individuals. It is also imperative that the astute CNSUF™ negotiator becomes familiar with the basic components of influence to assist in selecting appropriately tailored components for a negotiation strategy.

Asking the right questions at the right time, for the right reasons, and in the right manner begins by understanding that questions that can be answered with a simple yes or no generally make those with whom we are communicating get the feeling that they are involved in an interrogation or interview, rather than a conversation. Because of this, yes-or-no questions inadvertently create a competitive feel. This is especially true if the questions are being asked over the telephone or in a text or e-mail, and there is not an established relationship with the other person in the conversation. It should also be said that yes-or-no questions give away a negotiator's power by giving the counterpart the option of answering "No.

I have said that "feelings are not facts," and that is absolutely true. Feelings and facts are often vastly different, but the fact is that how someone feels during a conversation will affect the substance and quality of a conversation, because, factual or not, "perception trumps reality."

Keep in mind: a good deal of communication is not verbal, it is subliminal. If people feel they are being interrogated, they function as though they are being interrogated. If they are being interrogated, they usually do not have the warm and fuzzy neurophysiology that generates spontaneity and fluid conversation. It has been made clear throughout the past few years that one cannot always rely on what people say when they are being interrogated/interviewed, because they are most likely going to tell you whatever they think will look best in print or whatever they think you want to hear. The astute CNSUF™ negotiator will avoid more than the occasional question where yes or no is the likely response.

CNSUF™ negotiators think IWWWWWH questions when they are crafting questions or strategy. *If, Who, What, Why, When, Where, and*

How? questions should be treated like the friends and family that you love and enjoy spending time with.

They should be entertained frequently; they should be nurtured, engaged, and appreciated. Sure, IWWWWWH questions can also intimidate and shut down a conversation, but when they are used appropriately, they are the cornerstones of every conversation or interaction.

"Appropriately" refers to the way a question is asked, the tone of voice, and the speed of the question—all of the elements described in Chapter 8 of *Beyond Negotiating: Influence – Rapport – Results.*

I once heard James Gunn, director of the Marvel film *Guardians of the Galaxy*, explain in a radio interview that the character played by the actor Vin Diesel was called upon to say the line "I am Groot" repeatedly throughout the film. Each time he said it, there was either a single line or an entire page of back story explaining the underlying meaning of the line in each instance that it was used. Mr. Gunn explained that only he and Mr. Diesel had the back story, but that Mr. Diesel had spent so much time thinking about, developing, and perfecting his delivery of the line that other actors in the film seemed to understand the intended meaning, even though they did not have the backstory, and even though the words were exactly the same every time.

James Gunn went on to explain that Vin Diesel recorded the line dozens of times for each instance it was used in the film, perfecting the tone, rhythm, inflection, pitch, and other components in order to communicate exactly the underlying meaning for each particular instance in the film. Mr. Gunn went on to say that it was Mr. Diesel's performance that had received the most mention from those who had contacted him. Having seen the film, I understand and agree with Mr. Gunn's assessment.

There are many other examples, including Rob Reiner's film *When Sally Met Harry.* Recall the restaurant scene when Sally fakes an orgasm and a woman (Mr. Reiner's mother in real life, by the way) sitting nearby says, "*I'll have what she's having.*" All she hears is the sound of Sally's demonstration. Nobody has to tell her what is being demonstrated. She knows *exactly* from what she hears. How about this example: how does a new mother or father know the precise difference between the crying

Chapter 3: Mode Groups & Modes

of their child when they need to be changed and when they are hungry? It's not like the kid sits up and says, "Hey, don't you get it? I need to be changed!" Good parents know instinctively how to interpret the pitch, tone, and timing of their infant's demands.

Turn away from comic-book-inspired superhero theatrical productions and iconic films and all one has to do is listen to any news program or read any credible news publication to see where asking yes-or-no questions and getting yes-or-no answers drives major influencers, financial institutions, and governments to do things that literally cost people their livelihoods, threaten the health of everyone and everything on the planet, and in too many instances cost people their lives. *"Do they have weapons of mass destruction (WMDs)?"* "Should we go to war?" "Is that nuclear facility safe?" No doubt there are times when a simple yes-or-no answer is warranted, even exactly what is needed, but where the answer to any question carries grave consequences, the astute CNSUF™ negotiator is well advised to err on the side of IWWWWWH questions.

It isn't just the words that do the actual communicating. It is the way the questions are phrased, the timing of the questions, and other factors matched to the individual (Per-Beha) who is asking and being asked the questions, and the situation (Geo-Socio-Poli, Org-In) and individuals involved in the conversation. Each of these factors plays an important role in the use of IWWWWWH questions, and the better we are at developing a range of ways to ask each of these questions, the better we are going to be at using IWWWWWH questions. They will help build the knowledge we need to understand our counterpart's assumptions, their major and minor objections, concessions, wants, needs, and timing. All of these help to shape our strategy, minimize our risks, and achieve the best outcome possible.

Ask IWWWWWH (Note that "If" questions should usually be used in combination with WWWWWH) open-ended questions. Ask them thoughtfully, frequently, and repeatedly. It is equally important to ask IWWWWWH questions in a timely manner and with a range of inflection, tone, meter, and pitch appropriate to the situation and to the style and type of communicator(s) involved in the negotiation process.

The second and more important element of asking IWWWWWH questions is the skill and habit of listening carefully. While you and I work to develop our ability to ask IWWWWWH questions and pay attention to the properties of effective communication, we have to focus on the fact that the entire purpose of doing all these things is lost if we do not listen effectively. Listen to what is being said, both verbally and non-verbally. Listen to understand how Geo-Socio-Poli, Org-In and Per-Beha are affecting what is being said, and listen to move the conversation from talking and listening to *effective communication*.

Many times, negotiators are so busy pursuing their own agenda that actual communication is impossible, and they end up engaging in what have been called "conversations of the deaf." These are conversations where people who appear to be engaged in a conversation are just watching each other's lips move and figuratively covering their ears while they contemplate their next rebuttal.

If you want to see experts in this type of communication, spend a couple of hours watching a Senate or congressional hearing, or turn on FOX, CNN, CNBC, CBS, financial or political commentary. More often than not, speakers are interested only in advancing their own point of view. Guests of many programs are actually booked only because they are going to advance a specific point of view, and rarely is either side genuinely interested in hearing what the other side has to say or understanding what the other side wants to *communicate*.

Have you ever interrupted someone while he or she was still speaking? Unless you cannot grasp or do not know the difference between a comma and a period, how could you possibly be listening to other people and interrupting while they are still speaking? This behavior is either a purposeful tactic or lacks sincere commitment to listening.

Be clear that for the CNSUF™ negotiator, communication is not the exchange of information. As written previously in *Beyond Negotiating: Influence – Rapport – Results:* "Communication…occurs when the meaning associated to information or data is congruent and consistent with the meaning that was intended by the party providing the information or data." For the CNSUF™ negotiator, listening is effective only when the product is *effective communication*—when the listener clearly and fully comprehends the meaning (not just the words themselves) that is intended by the person(s) who is speaking.

The astute CNSUF™ negotiator will pay attention to words but will seek to understand the meaning of what is and is not being said, especially in the competitive mode, for many reasons. Consider the tool or weapon (depending on its use) of reframing. Reframing is the skill of restating as close to verbatim as possible what has been said by the other party, and then continuing to repeat and restate what is said as the speaker clarifies, until the speaker acknowledges that the listener has a clear comprehension of his or her words. When used as a tool to achieve clarification, reframing can lead to clear communication. But when used as a weapon, it can shield the underlying intent of the party using it to gain an advantage.

An example: If negotiators from neighboring countries were negotiating a ceasefire during a conflict, the negotiator from one side might say, "We propose a ceasefire for the period of twenty-four hours so that humanitarian supplies can be brought in for our civilian population."

The other party might reframe that statement to say, "As we understand it, you are proposing a ceasefire for a period of twenty-four hours so that humanitarian supplies can be transported in for your civilian population. Is that right?"

"Yes, that is what we are proposing."

Now, in your view, have the two parties communicated?

On the face of it, many would assume that the parties certainly have communicated. But what exactly has happened between them? From the CNSUF™ perspective, all that has occurred is the acknowledgment that one side is proposing a ceasefire for a period of twenty-four hours so that humanitarian supplies can be brought in for the civilian population, and the other side has acknowledged what its counterpart has said. In reality, there has been only an exchange of information and a reframe, not true communication.

One of the powerful aspects of the reframe, when used in competitive negotiation, is that once the party making the proposal sees that their counterpart has taken the time to reframe the proposal, rather than rejecting the proposal or making a counterproposal, the party making the proposal will often interpret the reframe as an indication of agreement. The simple fact of reframing, rather than responding any other way, is immensely powerful.

If such a negotiation were to end at this point, it would soon become evident that no communication had occurred if the party that proposed the ceasefire, having left further details unaddressed, found that their counterparts permitted the delivery of humanitarian supplies only to resume destroying infrastructure in areas away from roads and lines being used for that purpose. When accused of breaking the ceasefire, the party who had used the reframe could argue that their agreement did not, in their view, preclude the destruction of targets that did not interfere with the delivery of the supplies in question. And they would be correct.

In such an instance, the reframe would have been used as a weapon rather than a tool for the negotiation of a fully bilateral and sustainable ceasefire, yet both sides could argue publicly to the international community and to their own constituents that it was the other party who broke the ceasefire.

In order for true communication to have occurred, the parties would have had to spend a good deal of time breaking down the words that had been exchanged to clarify the full meaning of "ceasefire." Examples include the questions; When does it start? What does it exclude? Where are the boundaries? Who will determine what can and cannot occur during the period of the ceasefire? But in the competitive mode, why would the party with the superior military capability want to do that?

Effective communication, as defined in the CNSU framework, could eliminate a military advantage and the opportunity to achieve an unwanted unilateral strategic objective. Reframe, then, can be used to promote the exchange of information, which would yield a unilateral advantage, or to enhance the exchange of effective communication which might well take the option of destroying a perceived enemy asset off the table, while at the same time allowing for the delivery of needed humanitarian supplies and assistance.

While this is a hypothetical example (with substantial historical evidence behind it), I can assure you that even as you are reading these words, no matter when that might be, there is a chance that variations of this example are occurring in locations the world over at this moment. Pick up a newspaper, visit a prominent online current events news outlet, turn on your radio, or, for many, simply look out your window to see specifics that support this illustration. Be clear: this is only one example of the power and flexibility of the reframe. It can be tailored for use in virtually any personal or professional situation where two parties are engaged in a negotiation. Have you ever needed to influence someone who held a superior position to your own? Ever wanted to get someone to alter their instructions or requirements of you but have not had the power or ability to refuse or reject their leadership? Reframing is the perfect tool.

In the first place, most of us rarely say what we mean with the first words that come to mind, especially when we are under pressure or when we are negotiating or giving instructions or guidance to someone else. All you have to do to see this is repeat what someone says when you ask him or her IWWWWW questions.

For example: "Who should we send to Dallas to address the issues we are having there, and what do you want them to say to reduce the tension we are having with ABC company, an important client?

Now, you think Ann should go, but you don't have the power to recommend that. If you do recommend it, your experience is that your VP, a woman of conviction and a bit of an autocrat, will certainly send John. She says, "Send John, he's got the most experience."

"To be clear," you respond, "you're saying to send John because he's got the most experience; what about the fact that he's completely tied up with the Hamilton situation?"

"No, that is not what I mean. We'd better send Ann. She's probably a better fit anyway."

"So, Ann is a better fit, and we are sending her?"

"Absolutely. Get Ann down there as soon as possible."

"And what should Ann say to reduce the tension?"

"Tell her to give them a reduction in our terms."

"Tell Ann to give them a reduction in our terms, what if she sees a better option?"

"No, that is not what I said. Tell Ann to do whatever she thinks is best and to keep me posted on what happens."

"So, you want me to tell Ann to get down to Dallas as soon as possible, do what she thinks is best, and to keep you posted?"

"That's what I said, yes."

Which one of the communicators in that example controlled the conversation? Which one has the title, and which one used the power of *modified reframing* (not repeating every word, while influencing the direction and substance of the conversation) and suggestion to influence the outcome?

Following a consultation with my client, a director of operations, this is pretty much the way we rehearsed the conversation prior to its occurrence. We had previously discussed the type of communicator and style of communication the VP typically used to dominate conversations, bark out instructions, and flex her authority. I assure you that to this day, she is under the impression that it was her decision to send Ann down to Dallas. The power of reframing and influence by using IWWWWWH questions is enormous.

At the end of the day, the only situations that will be effective for you will be those that impact your own personal and professional life. So do not just sit here and read this book. Put the tools and knowledge to the test and tailor them for as many of your personal/professional situations as possible. Practice, reflect, and then get into action. If you get stuck, pick up the phone and schedule a consultation with me or with one of our negotiation consultants. Go out and work on achieving one or all of the six foundational CNSUF™ tenets by asking open-ended IWWWWWH questions and using reframing. Listen to what is and isn't

Chapter 3: Mode Groups & Modes

said, and continuously work to improve your skill and knowledge of effective communication, influence, and IWWWWWH questions.

Rule Two. Test all assumptions, presumptions, and estimates. This is one more area where laymen and professional negotiators alike are certain they know the answer. But when asked simply and directly, "What is an assumption?" many gulp and hesitate to answer. Don't look down at the definition. I'm asking a simple question: what does the word assumption mean to you? If I walked up to you on the street and asked you to define "assumption" or "estimate," what would you tell me? How would you answer? Since the rule here is to test all assumptions, presumptions, and estimates, it seems appropriate to ensure that we are on the same page about the definitions of these words, as associated with the CNSU framework. According to virtually any dictionary, the word assumption is defined as: *something taken for granted or a supposition* (e.g., a correct assumption).

Okay, that may be the definition, but it is likely that *"something taken for granted"* isn't the first definition that popped into your head when I asked the question. And what does that mean anyway? In the CNSU framework, we break down the meaning of "assume" to a single word, "Belief." When we assume something, we are saying that we believe it is correct. Thus, *all assumptions are beliefs.* Unlike facts that do not care what you or I believe, beliefs often do not care about facts. The fact is that you and I, and most people on the planet, have all kinds of beliefs that are not factual—they may, in fact, be absolutely *wrong*. Still, we believe these things for any number of reasons: our parents told us these things were true when we were children; we read them in a book; we saw them on television or in a movie.

Case in point: When I was nineteen years old, I came home after serving a year in Vietnam. I was so physically changed that when I knocked on the door to our home, my mother asked, "May I help you?"

Shocked, I looked down at the name tag on my shirt then my eyes darted back up at my mother. Simultaneously, she looked more closely at me, thinking she knew she had a son in the Marine Corps, but "This couldn't be my boy." Then she asked in a doubtful tone, "Derrick? Derrick, is that you?"

We both figured out quickly that I was me and that I was in the right place. And so began my reintroduction to what Marines serving in Vietnam called "The World."

A few weeks later, I awoke early at my mom's house—it was Easter Morning—and, as I had done since the time I was four or five years old, I began looking all over the house for my Easter Basket. When I didn't find one, I wrote a note that my mother has kept ever since. Scribbled on a piece of paper, I wrote: "Looked all over, couldn't find my Easter Basket!"

It turned out that she had no idea a nineteen-year-old Vietnam vet could still believe in the Easter Bunny and want an Easter Basket. Truthfully, I wanted the jellybeans, but, yes, even a nineteen-year-old Vietnam vet still believed enough in the Easter Bunny to expect a basket, with maybe some extra jellybeans, considering I did not get a basket the previous two years.

As I have said, beliefs do not care about the facts. This is one more reason that "perception trumps reality," which remains true in the twenty-first century, just as it has been true at any time in the history of the world. It will continue to be true as technology and AI continue to blur the lines between now and the future.

It is a personal and maybe even a silly example, but it does speak to the fact that assumptions are beliefs, and in the CNSU framework All Assumptions Are Beliefs! It makes complete sense, then, to follow this simple rule: Test All Assumptions.

Another critical term in negotiation is the term presumption, what is a presumption? Again, do not keep reading. Ask yourself that question and answer it in your head before you look down at the definition. What is a presumption?

Presumption/Presume is a verb (used with object), meaning 1) to take for granted, assume, or suppose: I presume you are tired after your drive, and 2) Law to assume as true in the absence of proof to the contrary.

Chapter 3: Mode Groups & Modes

Surprise, surprise! It looks like the number one definition of presumption is to assume. Again, according to this first definition, a presumption is also a belief. However, in the CNSU framework we prefer to use the second definition of the word presumption: the legal definition—*"to assume as true in the absence of proof to the contrary."* Mind you, the legal definition is not necessarily any better at telling fact from fiction. It just admits that it is willing to be wrong until proof to the contrary shows up.

This could not be more evident than in the fact that a growing number of people exist who were convicted of crimes by judges and juries because there was not enough evidence to prove their innocence until the use of DNA testing. I would say the many people rotting in prison based on a lack of evidence to prove their innocence makes *presumption* worth paying considerable attention to, wouldn't you?

Somewhere along the line it has occurred to me that the real difference between an assumption and a presumption is *action*. Consider that when an investor assumes that a stock will increase in value, he or she thinks about buying the stock. Case in point: believing or assuming that a stock will rise in value and thinking about buying it is quite different from *presuming* that a stock is going to go up in value and actually buying it.

So, in the CNSUF™ we recognize that an assumption is a belief, and we espouse that nobody can argue that another human being does or does not believe something. We do not argue with anyone's beliefs for that reason. But astute CNSUF™ negotiators see presumption as a belief that they or someone else is willing to *act* on. This can be likened to the time I presumed that I needed to serve my country during the Vietnam era. I quit high school on a Monday, joined the Marine Corps, and left for boot camp that Friday. I based this on a presumption—my belief that led to action (otherwise it would have been just another assumption).

But beware: just because we take an action does not prove that our belief is factual or correct—it is just that we have taken an action.

Another consideration regarding presumptions is this: Why would people waste their time assuming or presuming something if they *knew* for certain that what they assume or presume is factual? If investors presume a stock is going to go up, they buy a certain number of shares, depending on the risk they are willing to take. But if an investor *knows* that a stock is going to go up, why wouldn't he or she put every penny they have on the trade?

Knowing something with certainty eliminates risk; eliminating risk turns a presumption into a fact. If I *know* that a stock is going to rise in value, I can put every dime I have into the stock and reap the benefits when the stock goes up. If I *presume* a stock is going to go up, buy it, and then find that my presumption was wrong, I am dead broke. When investors presume and put every penny they have on a trade, it's more like gambling than investing. When investors *know* a stock is going to go up and put every penny they have into a trade, it is likely going to be insider trading. That is why most successful investors use a combination of investment tools, preparation, knowledge, experience, and intuition to balance risk and reward. They understand that aside from illegal insider trading, an investor never really *knows* (with certainty) whether a stock is going to go up or down on a specific date or at a specific time.

If I know that two plus two equals four, why would I assume or presume that two plus two equals anything more or anything less? We do not, do we? We do not presume two plus two is four; we make a statement that two plus two is four. If our calculation turns out to be mathematically incorrect, we say that we were flat-out wrong. No one presumes that we are wrong when we speak of fact—we are either correct or we are not. We either presume we know something and act, or we assume we know something and merely believe we are correct.

Because the CNSUF™ negotiator recognizes that presumptions are "*assumed to be true in the absence of proof to the contrary,*" and because we know that just because we act on something doesn't mean that it is factual, CNSUF™ negotiators remain as cautious about presumptions as we are about assumptions until we know the facts. And remember, facts do not care how you feel or what you think. They are facts precisely because they are not moved or altered by what someone says or what they believe or what they do—unless what they do has proven that the presumption in question is based on fact, in which case we have no need for presumption at all. Remember: ***Test All Presumptions***!

Chapter 3: Mode Groups & Modes

Beyond assumptions and presumptions there are estimates. For years I have asked professionals and folks in casual situations alike if they have ever seen or been aware of an accurate estimate. Overwhelmingly people respond "yes," they have.

Think about that. Engineers, politicians, political staffers, consultants, administrators, procurement professionals in every sector imaginable, sales professionals, non-profit executives, teachers, doctors, and lawyers young and old alike believe they have seen an accurate estimate, and all are dumbfounded to learn that, by definition, there neither is, nor can there ever be, an accurate estimate—because it is impossible for an estimate to be accurate:

> Estimate(s) Verb (used with object), to form an approximate judgment or opinion regarding the worth, amount, size, weight, etc., of; calculate approximately, 2) to form an opinion of; judge.

The definition of the word "estimate" tells us that the phrase "accurate estimate" is an oxymoron. If an estimate is accurate, it is, by definition, not an estimate at all. How is it possible that millions have made it all the way through prestigious business schools and accomplished amazing things all under the assumption or presumption that estimates can be accurate? My thought is that this point is so simple and so obvious that very smart people may have just missed it.

The more important thing about the fact that no estimate can be accurate is that it teaches us that *all estimates are wrong*! The question the astute CNSUF™ negotiator asks is this: "How wrong is the estimate?" If an estimate is only slightly wrong and fits within a prescribed margin of error or standard deviation, it may be of little concern. On the other hand, if the estimate is very wrong and falls outside of a prescribed margin of error, it may matter a great deal. In fact, an estimate that is significantly incorrect can mean the difference between life and death, success, and abject failure on any number of levels. Whenever I see an estimate, I ask two simple questions: "How wrong is it?" and "What do we need to do to find out how wrong it is?" Those two questions lead to other questions and often to specific actions that help to lower my clients' risk and maximize their results. All estimates are wrong!

Rule Three. Establish/Test Timeframes. In addition to our negotiation consulting, mediation, and executive education programs, Harrison-Chevalier has offered business skills workshops and consulting for a number of years. One of our most successful programs is Dynamic Time Management (DTM). And one of the most important questions we ask participants during those workshops is whether they have ever known anyone or heard of anyone who has said, "I don't have enough time in the day." Inevitably, people raise their hands to indicate that they *know* someone or have heard someone say they do not have enough time.

Now, both the participants and the facilitator know that the "someone" who has talked about not having enough time in the day is the same person sitting in the workshop. We have all said or felt at some point that we just do not have enough time in the day, haven't we?

Yet the fact is that none of us is so important that we do not get exactly as much time as every other human being on the planet. We all get the exact same amount of time each day. It just is not true that everyone else you know gets twenty-five hours and you get only twenty-four.

What is different about each of our days is not how much time we get, it's what we do with that time. How do we invest our time? How do we value it? How do we use it to gain influence and to mitigate challenges in negotiation and life?

Because time is finite, it is one of the most valuable tools CNSUF™ negotiators have if they understand how to use it and how it is often used to impact our thoughts and behavior. Giving time or taking time away, even giving or taking the perception of time away, is one of the most universal ways to create and to alleviate pressure in a negotiation.

Let us start with the issue of power as related to time in negotiation. Generally speaking, who has the most power in a negotiation? Is it the person who sets the deadline, or is it the person who has a deadline put on him or her? The person with the real power, generally speaking, is the person or organization that establishes the deadline. For them it isn't

Chapter 3: Mode Groups & Modes

really a deadline at all, since they can change or eliminate the deadline altogether. I say *generally speaking*, because it isn't something negotiators always realize. Most people see deadlines as finite, when often they aren't finite at all for the people who set them or for the people who know how to challenge and test them.

For example, the federal government of the United States requires that all taxes be filed by April 15. But if April 15 falls on a Saturday or Sunday, the government changes the deadline to the end of the next business day. Beyond that, all one needs to do to avoid significant penalties is to file an extension. You are not going to avoid paying interest on the tax you will owe, but you aren't going to be charged the penalties and the interest on the penalties that would be due if you don't file a return or an extension by April 15.

However, even if you fail to file a return, fail to file an extension, and pay no taxes at all for a prolonged period, you may still be able to reduce or eliminate a significant portion of your accrued taxes and penalties by working with the tax collection arm of the IRS. You must provide an explanation and supporting data and request the abatement of some or (in some cases) most of the taxes and penalties you owe.

Sure, the systems are vastly different in other countries, but the point is that in many of the situations where deadlines are set, there are exceptions and ways to negotiate those time limits. Whether you live in the United States or elsewhere, there is a great deal we can learn from the example described above.

In the first place, we can take note of the fact that even in critical situations where deadlines appear to be non-negotiable, there may be more room or alternatives than we think. Look for that room, seek out alternatives, and remember that no matter what the deadline, we should *always* test the parameters and possibilities. (For specific steps and strategies for testing time limits and deadlines, see *The Calculus of Deadlock, p.227-248)*.

Another vitally important realization for the astute CNSUF™ negotiator is to recognize that deadlines should virtually *always* be measured against tangible and intangible consequences. If there aren't any tangible or intangible consequences involved in missing or ignoring a deadline, then there is no deadline, is there? The same is true when we recognize that the tangible and intangible consequences of missing or ignoring a deadline are palatable or can be withstood or neutralized with little or no significant impact consequences.

In fact, when we realize that the tangible and intangible consequences can be absorbed with little or no significant impact or cost, we may have a perfect opportunity to reverse or shift the balance of power away from the person or organization that set the deadline in the first place. One strong example would be to ignore the deadline and, by doing so, cause our counterpart to be left wrestling with why we missed it. Did we have alternatives our counterparts were unaware of? Are the terms of their proposal or contract unacceptable? Is their price too high? Are we terminating the relationship? All these questions and more may be going through the minds of our counterparts, especially (as is often the case) if some of the negotiators on their side were actually opposed to setting a deadline in the first place. They now rise to express that their reservations about setting the time limit should have been taken more seriously, which can produce an advantage for us by dividing their resolve and/or their cohesiveness. Of course, we don't have to tell our counterpart that we missed or ignored the deadline on purpose. That is a mistake that often takes the negotiation to a very personal level for the person who was in favor of setting the time limit while others on their side were against it. We should share our rationale for missing a deadline only if it creates an opportunity to recalibrate, assess, or diminish/raise the value of the relationship in question.

And no, we don't have to lie about why we missed the deadline. What we need is a *reason,* and the more truthful, sincere, and detailed the better. You will not believe what you are going to get in return for missing a deadline for strategic purposes. It can range from an entirely new time limit to changes in scope, reduction in costs, increases in quality, expansion of services, and even the possibility of a more cooperative relationship and/or a shift in the balance of power or perceived power. This approach is particularly relevant where diplomacy, politics, military, and corporate issues are involved.

Chapter 3: Mode Groups & Modes

Results are not guaranteed, but this is an example where actual results have been obtained by Harrison-Chevalier consulting clients when we've worked with them to implement a multifaceted strategy to shift the balance of power or nullify the impact of a deadline. Even when we don't achieve the exact result we want, many Harrison-Chevalier consulting clients have determined that the consequences of using this tactic as part of a comprehensive strategy more often than not make it worth serious consideration. If all we do is level or recalibrate the playing field, we have gained an advantage.

If we miscalculate the consequences and our counterpart responds with a "nuclear" retort, then yes, we may suffer some damage. It may hurt, but we also learn a great deal that we did not know before. And that consequence will be analyzed and calculated before we make the decision to take that risk. Remember we see and move in shades of gray, how close we come to the line, what we risk, and when we risk it, is considered on a case-by-case basis.

When we think about it, why are deadlines so effective in negotiation? There is not a single answer to this complex question, in large part because of the Omni Modes that are always going to impact the thoughts and beliefs of our counterparts, as well as what we think and what we do. The question of why deadlines are so effective in negotiation will highly likely include the issue of pressure. Deadlines often create pressure, or at least the perception of pressure. What is the primary strategic purpose of establishing a deadline? Beyond internal and external logistics, what is an important byproduct of establishing a deadline—particularly when the entity setting the limitation or deadline knows it can be changed?

An important byproduct of a deadline is that it creates pressure or the perception of pressure, especially as the deadline comes closer. The advantage for the entity that sets a deadline is that as the limitation approaches, they are not worried about it at all. What about the party who has a deadline, especially if he or she has not measured the tangible and intangible consequences? What are they doing and what are they thinking as they scramble to meet the deadline? They may be running around like chickens with their heads cut off, scrambling to get something done that often did not have to be done at all within the given timeframe.

How many times in your life have you scrambled, bolted, given up weekends, worked late, come in early, sacrificed time with your loved ones, and broken promises to your kids and significant others to meet a time limitation, only to find out that no action was taken on the work or project that you sacrificed and rushed to get completed? How many times have you discovered that had you simply asked for an extension or asked what the consequences might be if you did not get the project completed on time, that extra time would have been granted?

If you have ever served in the military—any branch of the military—I know you are familiar with the phrase "Hurry up and wait!" If you have not served in the military, I am still pretty confident that you have fallen victim at one time or another to a deadline that lacked significant consequences or teeth. You might have wondered why you had to work so hard to meet the deadline.

What do you feel as a deadline approaches and you aren't quite ready? Your heart rate increases. Your palms start to sweat. You may speak choice words to yourself or aloud that really aren't appropriate for the workplace environment, but you do it anyway. You want to drink an entire bottle of wine, or something stronger. You want to smoke an entire pack of cigarettes, and you stopped smoking years ago. All of these and more are part of the response as time limitations and deadlines loom in front of us and come to a head. Every bit of it is connected to the fact that we feel pressure.

The great irony is that pressure truly has nothing to do with deadlines, because pressure is really just another face of fear. We "feel" pressure because we focus on consequences that we often don't even know and haven't asked about. We "feel" pressure because we associate time limitations to something bad happening or to something bad that happened at some point in the past. We feel pressure, but we don't all feel pressure the same way, do we? While some of us have hearts that are pounding out of our chests, look around and you'll see that other people with the same consequences, in the same room, at the same time, don't feel the way we do, partly because they remain in the present and address the issue, while we focus on the future and allow our feelings to dominate our common sense.

Chapter 3: Mode Groups & Modes

If I give you a deadline, I can be a thousand miles away, yet I can look at a clock and calculate when you are going to feel the most pressure to respond to it. You are going to feel it and react to it most as the limitation or deadline approaches.

For example, I had a client explain to me that he "had" to grant a 6 percent increase in the price of a commodity he was purchasing from a vendor because he was told that it was "take it or leave it." Accept and price the increase or they stop shipment.

"Why didn't you call me?" I asked him.

"We did not have enough time to call you. What difference would it have made? What could we have done?"

"That is exactly the question we should have explored *before* you agreed to the increase," I replied.

You and I both know that the vendor in this instance did not send an email at two in the afternoon and tell this client, "Take it by sundown or we stop shipping." The client had time but was so focused on the consequence of the possible stop-shipment that he didn't make prudent decisions about how to handle the situation. Score one for the vendor. Well, not exactly. After further discussion and renegotiation, we eventually used a *reverse escalation* to recoup a considerable portion of the promised 6 percent.

By the way, this particular client is an excellent negotiator. But even with education and skill, a deadline can pose a significant challenge to many. The truth is that this particular situation is exactly the reason my clients are consulting clients. No matter how many classes someone takes, it's difficult to remember it all. But working with someone who focuses on strategy and negotiation every day and collaborating with colleagues using a qualified Harrison-Chevalier negotiation consultant are of critical advantage when running into a challenge. We can help craft solutions for difficult issues. On a scale of difficulty, this particular example rates at best a one or a two on a five-point scale, but it reflects a common challenge for many professionals who negotiate

The point is that deadlines create the perception of pressure, proving once again that "perception trumps reality." That is why they work so well. The bottom line is that deadlines should be analyzed and connected to consequences, and we react to and treat the time limitation or deadline accordingly.

Finally, for those who have this question rolling around in their head, "What if we don't know or aren't able to calculate the consequences?" The answer will depend on factors unique to each negotiation and to the idiosyncrasies of the negotiators. Generally speaking, you should already know the answer to that question:

STOP.

Move backward on the CNSUF™ Continuum toward a more competitive position.

Follow CNSUF™ Competitive Rules one through seven.

How can we use time to create pressure on the counterpart?

What reasons exist for the counterparts not to act, even if they are able to do so?

How can we heighten the counterpart's perception of our strength/options?

Reevaluate, revisit, and reinvigorate our Competitive Intelligence.

Rule Four. Identify/Test Major and Minor Concessions. By now it should be clear that the CNSU framework is firmly focused on asking IWWWWWH questions and on finding out what we don't know before we determine the best course of action, rather than providing quick-fix, one-size-fits-all answers to challenges that require strategies based on specific circumstances, Omni Mode particulars, and goals. Competitive mode rule number four is no exception. It starts with some basic but critical IWWWWWH questions: What is a major concession for you? What is a major concession for your counterpart? What is a major concession for your organization? What is a major concession for your counterpart's organization?

Chapter 3: Mode Groups & Modes

One thing is certain—the answers to these questions will change not only during the course of each negotiation you are involved in, but they are likely to change several times during the same negotiation. So, it is important to have a solid understanding of concessions in order to drive toward the best possible outcome.

Concessions are like gold, but this *gold* can be tangible or intangible, gargantuan, or imperceptible—important to one but not important at all to someone else. Everything we have covered related to assumptions and estimates is especially important and germane when it comes to accepting or giving a concession. For one negotiator, a pound of gold is worth selling his or her soul. For another, that same pound of gold may as well be a gallon of raw sewage. Come to think of it, for some negotiators, a gallon of raw sewage can be more valuable than a pound of gold.

What matters is not so much what I think about a concession but that I understand how the other party perceives a concession, because their perception will influence their actions, and their actions will influence what I do, along with many other factors. While I can change what I do and what I think about a concession, it is often more difficult for negotiators to change the way their counterpart sees a concession, because "Perception Trumps Reality." That is not to say that we shouldn't seek to influence the way our counterpart sees a concession. Often, we can influence our counterpart to see and do things that are in our best interest, but in order to influence effectively, we first need to have a clear understanding of our counterpart's point of view and perception of a concession.

Just for reference and to put concessions into context, we will consider an example. Just before I sat down to work on this section of the book, I was discussing an issue of concession with a client who is a physician. After months of negotiation, he decided to give up a medical directorship at a hospital when the administration decided to cut the compensation for medical directors in half. My client is enormously hardworking and excellent in his field of medicine. He works many hours, including weekends, nights, and early mornings. He does whatever is necessary to achieve outstanding results; excellence is part of his DNA.

I suggested that he give up the medical directorship because I presumed he would work just as hard for half the compensation, and I had a strong sense of what would happen: every time he thought about doing so much work for half the compensation, a part of him would be diminished, and the damage to his self-esteem, combined with the tax on his time with a young family, would cost him many times more than the monetary compensation. This client is necessarily focused on dollars and cents—but dollars and cents are a tangible representation of the hospital's regard for his time, skill, and administrative contributions.

In this example, the doctor gave up the tangible concession of compensation and the intangible status of the title of director. He gained the tangible concession of time and the value of additional interaction with his family. He also gained time to conduct research and writing, things he had not been able to do as director.

By contrast, the administration of the hospital gained unpaid compensation but lost the far greater skills and services of an extraordinary physician. The physician is a skilled businessperson who can grow programs and teach and increase the reputation and market share of the hospital. This rare combination of excellence as a physician and as a businessperson will cost the hospital many, many times more than it will gain.

Looking at it this way, giving up the directorship seemed an easy decision to me, but it took a while for my client to see it the way he does now. Ironically, had the hospital increased his compensation for the directorship by 20 or 25 percent (after six years at the same level) when his contract came up for renegotiation, it is likely that my client would have accepted the position and worked even harder to bring more revenue and accolades to the hospital. Over time, which might be many, many times more valuable than the few dollars the hospital saved by losing my client's contribution in the role of director. Once more, if the hospital came back to my client now to offer the return of the compensation they took away, I am certain he would turn them down. This was an example of "penny wise and pound foolish" on the hospital's part.

At this point, what is a major concession for you in your business or employment? What is an example of a minor concession?

Chapter 3: Mode Groups & Modes

In the CNSU framework, a major concession is any concession that has an excessive cost/value to you or to your organization. What is a high value? During live workshops, I explained many times to a participant that I did not have any cash to buy a soda or bottled water, and I asked him or her for a dollar. The only time a participant refused to give me a dollar was when he or she did not have a dollar in cash. And even on the very few occasions when this happened, many of those participants returned from a scheduled break in the program with either a soda, a dollar, or a soda and a dollar. Once it was a soda and a five-dollar bill, insisting that there was no need for me to return the soda or the money.

Sure, there are lots of reasons that people have been willing to give me a dollar for soda. I am facilitating the program, but most of the time it has nothing to do with that. It has to do with the fact that I am asking for something that has extraordinarily little value to the person I am asking. People are willing to part with a dollar pretty quickly, not just to me but to strangers on the street (I've done that as well). On the other hand, when I have asked participants for a hundred dollars in cash, there are many more people who don't have it. Even if they did, there have been very few people willing to give me a hundred dollars just because I asked for it. Why? Again, there are lots of reasons, but one big reason is that most people are likely to place more value on a hundred dollars than they do on a dollar.

Because people place more value on a hundred dollars, they are far more reluctant to give it away without conditions—without knowing when and if they are going to get it back, or without expecting some kind of interest. So, on the simplest level, I am suggesting that people are less likely to part with something they perceive as having a high cost or value.

But let's say that a couple of people give me a hundred dollars and feel it's a significant gesture. Does that make their gesture a major concession? In their mind it might, because they think a hundred dollars is a lot of money to give to someone you've just met. But what if they think it's a major concession, and I think that, given how much money they have, they should have given me a thousand dollars. Is it still a major concession? No, it is not—not unless I perceive it as a major concession. This means that a major concession has a unilateral definition in the CNSU framework. It means that if a major issue is a concession that has a high cost or value to the person receiving it, it doesn't necessarily matter how the person giving the concession feels about it.

If I like calf brains and scrambled eggs for breakfast, and you give me a plate of delicious calf brains and scrambled eggs, then your gesture may be a major concession for me. You, on the other hand, might think that calf brains and scrambled eggs are disgusting. The point is that the way you perceive the value of calf brains and scrambled eggs has absolutely nothing to do with the way I perceive the value. If I see it as a major concession, it is a major concession to me, no matter how you see it (assuming of course that you do not insult me by telling me you feel the dish is revolting).

For the record, I have never eaten calf brains and scrambled eggs, so I can't comment on the culinary elements of the dish one way or the other. I am simply pointing out that if something has a major value or importance to you but has little or no value to the person you are giving the concession to, then it is not a major concession, and he or she isn't going to respond with heart-pounding gratitude.

This explains why you may have given someone a gift that cost you a lot of money or that in some way meant a lot to you, but the person's subdued reaction told you it did not have the same meaning to him or her. If you have had an experience like that, then you know exactly what I am talking about.

It is the same thing in personal negotiation or the most comprehensive, multilateral professional or diplomatic situation. Major concessions have to be major concessions to the person or group receiving them.

In a military conflict involving Iran, Israel, or Ukraine, for example, there is a high probability that a ceasefire would be rejected if the European nations and the United States put together a negotiation and presented it to one of them. No matter how much a country might want it, accepting the ceasefire would signal weakness on their part. This would be true even if the other nations offered major concessions to demonstrate their desire for and commitment to peaceful resolution.

Chapter 3: Mode Groups & Modes

That said, in the CNSU framework, concessions are major only if those receiving the concessions value them as major. If they do not, it is often possible for an astute CNSUF™ negotiator to find ways to enhance their perceived value and craft a proposal that meets or exceeds their expectations. This might include giving them a major concession in exchange for something that achieves *Equity of Risk,* where the tangible and intangible perceived or actual cost or value associated with an asset, idea, position, or concession in a contract, partnership, or association is the same for each involved party. (see pp. 38-39, *Influence – Rapport – Results, 2009 and Equality of Transparence*) The transparency of information and access provided by each side is relatively equal in substance, value, and significance to the respective parties.

On the other hand, what is a minor concession? Think about what you do, whether it is international diplomacy, non-profit administration, corporate leadership or governance, politics, teaching, engineering, law, medicine, buying, selling, or housekeeping/child rearing, whatever. What is a minor concession for you in your personal/professional roles?

In the CNSU framework, minor concessions are pretty simple, yet they are extremely important. They can be complex, depending on the circumstances, issues, and players involved in a negotiation. Unlike major concessions that are unilateral by definition, minor concessions in the CNSU framework have a bilateral definition, which often makes them infinitely more important and more complex than major concessions. Minor concessions have a low perceived value to the person giving the concession and a high perceived value to the person receiving the concession. This means that a minor concession is bilateral in nature, because it involves the participation of at least two entities, each meeting the defined criteria. Obviously, this is the polar opposite of the major concession, where the opinion or position of only one of the involved parties is pertinent.

For example, if I give you something that cost me a penny, put a price tag of a hundred dollars on it, and offer it to you as a concession, and you not only want what I am giving you but see it as something worth a hundred dollars, is that a major or a minor concession? Low cost to me, high value to you equals minor concession in the CNSU framework.

From my perspective, the ability to trade minor concessions for major concessions is one of the most valuable skills the astute CNSUF™ negotiator can develop. This can increase our ability to influence the equity of risk, the balance of power, and the outcome of the negotiation/relationship without giving up anything that is important or of significant value to us.

Far beyond dollars and cents, minor concessions can be tangible or intangible and can range from pennies and dimes to billions of dollars to every sort of condition involved in mergers and acquisitions, real estate, hostage negotiations, and everything in between. In addition, concessions often affect the perception of mode in negotiation. If I give you a minor concession, is that a competitive or a cooperative act? Are we negotiating in the competitive or the cooperative mode? Remember, you believe you have received something of value and that it was of high value to me. More often than not, this will be seen as a cooperative gesture.

The conundrum, however, is that a cooperative act in itself does not mean that we are in the cooperative mode. We simply do not know. What we do next is evaluate the relevant conditions and act based on those conditions, not on the basis of a single cooperative act.

What happens if the minor concessions I am offering you are also minor to you? Since the definition of minor concession in the CNSU framework is "a concession that has a low cost/value to the giving party and a high cost/value to the receiving party," if both parties perceive the cost/value of a concession as low, then by definition it is not a viable minor concession. It is inconsequential. However, if both parties perceive the value of what they are getting as high, but what I get from you gives me more knowledge about you, your strategy, resources, and timing than what you are getting from the minor concessions I am giving you, then eventually I'm going to be in a better position to influence/dominate the negotiation.

CNSUF™ negotiators who understand the power of the minor concession understand a great deal about the way their counterparts determine what is or is not a minor concession. Not everywhere in the world, but

Chapter 3: Mode Groups & Modes

surely in the vast majority of the world, the *ease* of access determines the perceived value of a concession. In most cultures, the value of something can be measured by how difficult it is to obtain. Things people give away easily are often either abundant or not perceived as valuable to the enhancement or continuation of life, so they have less value to basic sustenance or the enhancement of life (Geo-Socio-Poli). The same principle is true in many businesses, organizations, and institutions (Org-In). Where things are abundant and easily obtained, they have less value than things that are not abundant and are difficult to obtain.

Because "perception trumps reality," the value of a concession can therefore be enhanced by withholding it, restricting access to it, or attaching costs or consequences to the concession that make it appear more valuable than it is. When you do this, your counterpart will often associate the consequences that you have attached to a concession as evidence of its importance to you, and thus will enhance the concessions he or she is willing to make in order to remove the consequences.

From a transactional standpoint, these principles are found everywhere. The airlines, for example, eliminated services and added fees for baggage, food, seating, boarding, and so on. By doing that, they eliminated costs and increased their bottom line. By adding fees and so on, they increased the value of these amenities to their passengers that, in turn, allowed them to offer "free" or reduced-priced baggage, boarding preference, and so on if you obtain their credit card or fly their airline rather than the competition. How much did you want to pay to check your baggage before most airlines started charging for it as a separate fee? Nothing.

The same principle gives airlines the incentive to do things that make the passenger experience just a little less than miserable. Some examples include putting seats so close together that passengers cannot open a laptop computer or sit without having their knees pressed into the back of the seat in front of them. These changes make passengers miserable, and they are enough to make many of us feel good about paying a premium for a seat the next time we travel.

Have you ever boarded a plane with your carry-on luggage, only to find that you boarded so late that there isn't any overhead space available? The same airline that charged you a fee to check a bag before you arrived at the gate is now willing to check it for *free*, which will cost you time and inconvenience. Is that a benefit? The first thing the flight attendant is likely to ask you, as he or she gives you a bag tag, is whether you have the airline's credit card or know about preferential boarding, as if to say it is your fault you were too cheap to pay the additional fee to board early. You may get mad, but you also may get the airline's credit card to get preferential boarding before you fly again; or you may fly another airline.

However, airlines are not the only ones who do these things with concessions, not by a long shot. Many businesses and many business sectors and governments do similar things, including banks, car rental agencies, colleges and universities, city, state, and local governments, hotels, and many others.

Let us say that you are a supplier of mine and you frequently fail to deliver products on time, or you don't deliver the exact volume of product, or the composition of the product is slightly different from what we agreed upon. Let us also say that every time you make one of these errors I simply say, "no problem."

How do you think my concession of simply accepting these errors as business as usual is perceived? Do you, as the supplier, see my acceptance as a minor or major concession? It is likely that you will see little or no value in it. There was probably some appreciation in the beginning, but it has become a regular part of the relationship.

There are many ways to manage this, but let's say I tell you that any further late deliveries will result in a 10 percent late delivery reduction to our pricing. I then explain that other issues will result in an additional 10 percent penalty. Now, how will you value the concessions you were receiving? Much higher, because now there is a negative consequence.

But what if you, as my supplier, continue to make late deliveries and have no problem with the 10 percent penalty? How would I, as your client, feel now? I would probably feel pretty dumb for not charging

Chapter 3: Mode Groups & Modes

the penalty the entire time. While I thought I was giving you a major concession or intangible courtesy, you did not think anything of it one way or the other. At this point, do you think I should continue to allow you to make late deliveries at no charge, or should I consider raising the penalty?

From a complex or comprehensive perspective, take for example a country that has been isolated from the international community for decades, refuses to allow its citizens to interact with relatives a short distance away, and refuses to talk about its nuclear program or intentions. How does it get international kudos and raise hope for a diplomatic solution to these and other issues? Well, it is not by participating in talks every week or by negotiating with counterparts.

First, they agree to talk or negotiate, then they change their minds, then they sit down to negotiate, break their commitments, or leave the negotiating table, then they make threats about what they will and will not do, restrict travel and communication, and vow to use "any means necessary" to protect their way of life (even though the "way of life" of which they speak has millions of their people starving and being held hostage). After a prolonged period of silence and maybe a salvo or two at their neighbors, they announce that they have agreed to sit down and negotiate, and *voila*! the act of agreeing to negotiate becomes a minor concession (low cost to the country initially, high perceived value to the international community and to the citizens and relatives who see it as the possibility of resolution initially).

Keep in mind that one concession sets up the next concession, because the minor concession here could eventually morph into a major concession for the country if its leaders agree to changes they previously rejected in exchange for goods and services they desperately need.

Another example would be that of a world power set on the annexation of desired real estate whose leaders move troops to the border of that real estate, tell the international community that they didn't know the troops were there, say they are going to order the troops to leave, provide support for separatists who would like to see them be successful in the annexation, and then deny any knowledge or involvement when a commercial plane is blown out of the sky using weaponry they manufactured and provided.

There is no doubt that the tragedy of the commercial aircraft will be followed by minor concessions that will be given to dissipate the ire of the international community. While denying involvement or knowledge, the resolute aggressor will in time suggest that the "tragedy" would never have taken place had it been provided/allowed the access it was seeking that would have prevented such an incident and that will prevent another such incident from ever occurring again. Not that the loss of hundreds of human beings is a minor issue in itself, but compared to what is at stake from a Geo-Socio-Poli point of view, the loss—the tragedy—will, from the perspective of the aggressor, be credited as unavoidable collateral damage (low cost to the aggressor, very high cost to those who lost their lives and to their families).

There are hundreds of examples from the pages of history and current events that illustrate various aspects of minor concessions. Perhaps there will be an opportunity someday to explore a number of examples from various vantage points and sectors using the CNSU framework, but this is not the time or the book to do it. The application of the concession theory must be specific to the circumstances, objectives, stakes, and players involved in each situation. The important thing here is to understand the concepts and the definitions, so that they can be successfully applied to your negotiations. That is where the true value of the CNSU framework can best be measured.

Knowing the power and value of minor concessions, the astute CNSUF™ negotiator will assess a concession by using a variety of tailored tactics to determine whether it has value and whether that value is perceived as major or minor. These include, for example, taking a concession away or introducing a new consequence or cost to the concession that was not previously there, or that is currently being given at no perceived cost, or that has been given freely or easily in the past, to see what the response is.

Major and minor concessions play an enormous role in all modes of the CNSU framework, but in none more than the competitive and co-opetitive modes. They are powerful and, at times, lethal tools that can change the balance of power, open doors, close doors, increase access, limit risk, or bring down an entire superpower. While major concessions are often perceived as big and significant, minor concessions are frequently perceived to be trivial things. Yet they can have huge consequences for those who use them skillfully. So, take the time to understand major and especially minor concessions pertinent to your role, industry, business sector, or profession and those important to the people (concessions tend to be idiosyncratic) with whom you negotiate. Then develop strategies for identifying, testing, offering, and withdrawing concessions to achieve the highest and best outcome in each specific situation.

Price Cost Value

Having just read about major and minor concessions in the CNSU framework, you have encountered the terms price, cost, and value many times. As you read those words, how were you defining them as related to the topic of concessions? And, in general, how do you define these terms for yourself?

Price

How do you define the word price? What does the word *price* mean to you? Do not try to over-think the question, just focus on your initial thoughts about the word.

Price is:

- How much something costs
- What you pay for something
- How much someone is asking for something
- Cost plus profit
- Retail price
- Wholesale cost
- What you have to give up to get something
- What something is worth

Anything else come to mind? Let's face it, whatever comes to mind will certainly depend on who is answering the question and on that individual's Geo-Socio-Poli and Per-Beha preferences and experience. The accountant and the CFO will certainly see this word differently than the sales professional, non-profit executive, or food service worker, but at the end of the day one or more of the phrases listed above will be part of the equation. Each of these phrases will be correct not only from the standpoint that it represents someone's belief or presumption about the word, but also possibly from a factual perspective as well.

None of these phrases will be correct all the time. For that reason, the CNSU framework breaks down the definition of *price* to three simple words or symbols that are correct in virtually every situation:

$ Dollars

. Decimals

% Percentages

Virtually every conversation that includes the word price eventually comes down to some combination of these three words or symbols. When someone is talking about price, even when the issue involves something intangible like the loss of a life due to combat, an automobile accident, a fire, or natural disaster, at some point the conversation is going to involve dollars, decimals, or percentages. The instances where this is not true are so rare as to make it nearly impossible to determine when such an instance might occur. What will occur more often than not is the involvement of the words or symbols for dollars, decimals, and percentages.

This is a small point with huge ramifications, because if we eliminate all the emotion from the definition of the word price, we eliminate the fear and anxiety that comes along with it and can focus on what really matters—cost and the value. In all three instances, the perceived price, cost, and value are most important. Ultimately, the perceived definition of these words and symbols is where the CNSUF™ negotiator will focus his or her attention, rather than simply acting or reacting based on price

Chapter 3: Mode Groups & Modes

as "what something cost," "what something is worth," or "what someone is asking for something."

Cost

How do you define the word "cost," given your unique education and background? On paper, list the terms that come to mind quickly. What terms/phrases do you immediately think of? Do any of the following terms, phrases, or words come to mind?

- Wholesale cost
- How much something cost
- What something cost
- What something is worth
- What someone pays for something
- What someone is willing to give up to get something

What other words or phrases come to mind? It is likely that one or more of the phrases listed above are similar to what came to mind when the question was asked. Each of these responses is correct if it represents your belief or presumption about the meaning of the word *cost*.

Here is another question: does everyone you negotiate or interact with define the word cost the same way you do? Does every company, corporation, country, or individual believe, see, and define cost the same way you do? Which people/entities with whom you negotiate see the definition the same way you do, and which of them do not? We both know the answer: We simply do not know. And even if the individual or company in question does define cost the same, there is no guarantee that their definition will not change at some point without our being aware of it.

For these and other inherent reasons, the CNSU framework breaks down the definition of the word cost to another more accurate and universal word: *liability*. Whether tangible or intangible, individual, company, corporation, male, female, white, black, brown, or yellow, in every country on planet Earth when someone speaks about cost, he or she is speaking about some form of perceived tangible or intangible *liability, subtraction, culpability, risk, consequence,* or the like. When is that not the case?

This is not to say that a cost is not worth the liability. It is simply to point out that rather than defining cost with terms and phrases that are only sometimes applicable, the CNSUF™ negotiator has a greater opportunity to reduce risk and to maximize results by defining cost as perceived tangible or intangible liability. Understanding this, is it incumbent on you as a CNSUF™ negotiator to persuade your counterpart that you define the term cost as a tangible or intangible liability? Absolutely not. What is incumbent on you, as a CNSUF™ negotiator, is to find out how your counterpart defines this and other terms relevant to each situation. You know how you define the term, but how does your counterpart define it? As you gain more insight into that, you gain more access and data to apply to your understanding and knowledge about cost, and you use that insight to influence the behavior and perceptions of our counterpart(s).

Value

Surely the definition of value is clear, concise, and consistent across the spectrum of those with whom you negotiate, correct? Of course not! There are going to be a range of beliefs and perspectives wherever there is more than one person interacting with the same thing. This is a fundamental outgrowth of the Omni Modes. As noted previously, even people who occupy the same body have different perspectives on any number of issues. People who grow up in the same home with the same parents have different recollections about the circumstances and events of their upbringing (or is that only in my family?). The word value is no different, and throughout the years participants at live workshops have told me that value is:

- Cost minus profit
- Low price
- Retail versus sales price
- What you pay for something

Chapter 3: Mode Groups & Modes

- What something is worth
- High discount
- Good deal
- Less than budget
- Price

Add your own terms and what do you come up with? Once again, whatever you produce is going to be accurate for you, because it came out of your brain and because you believe it. But you already know that whatever you believe yourself is not likely to be what everyone else you negotiate with believes. Many of the people with whom you interact do not define the term value the same way you do. If you ignore that fact, you are certain to find yourself in the midst of miscommunication, assumption, and presumption a great deal of the time. That is not where you want to be when so much is at stake in so many of your personal and professional negotiations.

Remember, the CNSU framework applies universal definitions, examples, and anecdotes to critical terms where few if any exceptions exist. From a strategic standpoint, the more universal the definitions and knowledge, the more applicable in an Emerging Integrated Global Economy (EIGE); the more applicable, the higher the chances for gaining insight about those things we do not know. The more we know, the more we can add to what we learn and use the combined data to craft strategy and influence negotiations in directions consistent with our objectives. To that end, the framework defines the word value as *benefits*—tangible and intangible perceived benefits.

Based on these definitions, the CNSUF™ negotiator sees price only as a word or symbol that has absolutely *nothing* to do with cost or value. We see cost only as tangible or intangible liability, and we see value only as tangible, or intangible perceived benefit. Therefore:

Price = $. % (tangible or intangible, quantifiable perceived).

Cost = Liability (tangible or intangible, quantifiable, or perceived).

Value = Benefit (tangible or intangible, quantifiable perceived)

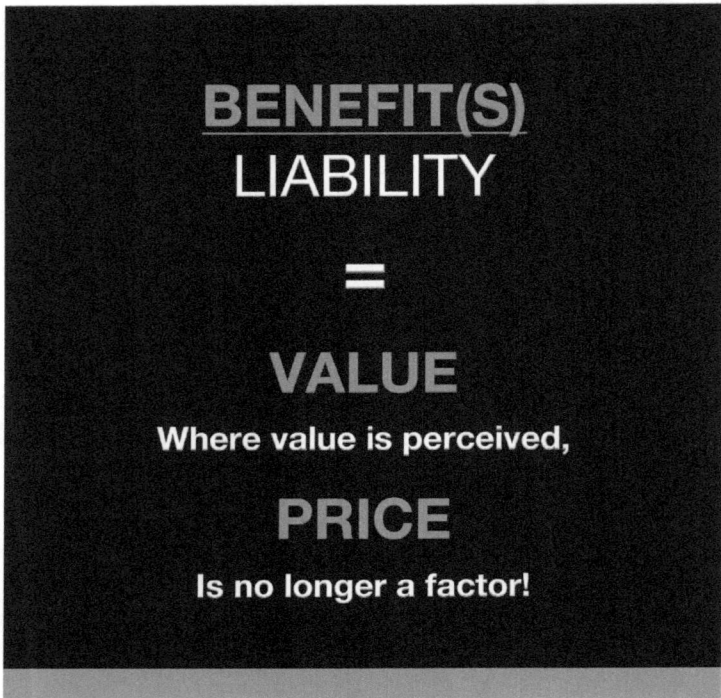

Perceived benefit(s) over perceived liability equal perceived value. Where perceived value is established and codified (tactical denial notwithstanding), price is no longer a consideration, except in the most competitive or co-opetitive modes. Your counterparts may perceive value, but they will not disclose it, because they believe they may be able to do even better or because they believe that some concession will be lost or removed if you know they believe they have an acceptable outcome. It is more accurate than to say that where value has been quantified, price is not a factor. This is not to say that acceptance is guaranteed. There may be other key factors in play beyond price. Everything comes together here: Geo-Socio-Poli + Org-In + Per-Beha + access and capability. Why do some people pay $200,000 for a car they can't get out of second gear in the city where they live? Is it because of comfort, reliability, or the ability to get somewhere faster? Of course, there is no single answer. One thing is for certain: there are plenty of people who would *never* buy a $200,000 car, no matter how much money they had. For them, there could never be enough benefits to justify the dollars, or the liabilities.

Chapter 3: Mode Groups & Modes

How many people who own $200,000 cars own them because they want to demonstrate to others that they can buy one while others cannot? How many people buy a $200,000 car because it makes them feel successful? No matter the reason, the person who pays $200,000 for a car eventually comes to a point where the benefits of owning the car are greater than the perceived price, cost, or liability.

This is no different from the person who will not pay $1.50 for bottled water or soda in a supermarket, but who will pay $10.00 for a small bottle of designer water or for a small soda at a movie theater or sporting event. Why not bring a bottle of water or a can of soda in your shirt, purse, or pocket? In the first place, doing this can be unethical if not straight-out illegal. However, at some point the benefits of bringing in your own soda are bigger than the liability of getting caught doing something unethical or illegal or of paying $10.00 for a bottle of water or small soda.

While some people will take their own soda into a movie theater or to a ballgame if they are with their peers, many of those same people would never do so if they were taking a spouse or date to that same event. Why? There are many reasons, but at some point, the benefits of taking in your own soda or popcorn are perceived as less than the liabilities of having your date find out you are a cheapskate.

The same is true in contract negotiation, procurement, mergers, acquisitions, sales, product development, medicine, engineering, law—you name the sector or the circumstance. At the end of the day, people find ways to do things they would never do ordinarily once they perceive that the benefits or the liabilities are sufficient to warrant the action or choice. Remember: it is the responsibility of the CNSUF™ negotiator to *communicate* concession benefits or liabilities to counterparts in a way that enhances their acceptance, quantification, or perception.

Communication in the CNSU framework involves *congruence of meaning*. You quantify for your counterparts, or your counterparts perceive the benefits or liabilities of a concession, in a manner that persuades or influences them to take actions that are consistent with your objectives. Depending on those objectives, you are seeking to illuminate benefits or liabilities. Where price is concerned, you are illuminating benefits until price is no longer a factor. But if you are on the other side, you are illuminating liabilities until the price is lowered to a point where you are willing to accept it. That means there are not going to be cookie-cutter or rubber-stamped "three easy steps" for achieving the effective communication objective where concessions are concerned. Every negotiation, every concession, every set of circumstances, every Geo-Socio-Poli + Org-In + Per-Beha will require a strategy comprised of unique elements and approaches, closes, and trial-and-error actions until benefits exceed liabilities to create value, or until liabilities exceed benefits to reduce or eliminate value, depending on which side of the equation the CNSUF™ negotiator is on.

In the competitive mode people are not openly exposing where those points are. If they are, they tread lightly. And they will not expose those points unless they make a mistake, are influenced to do so, move toward the co-operative mode, or perceive that there are no better options available to them. Our job as CNSUF™ negotiators in the competitive mode is to create the perceived benefits and/or liabilities necessary to move our counterparts to make choices consistent with our objectives. Remember: people do not compromise unless they perceive that they have to compromise or cooperate. Otherwise, why do it? You have to give something up to cooperate. You may have to increase your risks. Why compromise or cooperate if you can take or demand what you want and get it, unless the certain (operative word, *certain*) benefits of doing so (not perceived but quantifiable benefits) outweigh the liabilities of remaining competitive?

Now, with these definitions for price, cost, and value firmly in your mind, go back and re-read the previous section on major and minor concessions, replacing your original definitions for the terms with the definitions from this section. You are likely to discover that you have developed an entirely new and deeper level of understanding and appreciation for the power and possibilities of major and minor concessions.

Rule Five. Move in appropriate degrees of separation (ADOS/MADS). Where concessions are concerned, questions are going to arise regarding how far and how fast to move from one concession or from one point in a negotiation to another, as well as how much risk to take. These are all extremely important questions.

A survey of numerous articles, books, and negotiation frameworks suggests overwhelmingly that one should start with a high target and then give concessions slowly until some point of resolution is reached. From time to time this may be an acceptable standard, particularly for simple transactional negotiations. However, the astute CNSUF™ negotiator would be well advised to take another path, one that will reduce risk, maximize results, and accommodate both the simplest and the most complex negotiations.

Why not keep it simple and follow the time-tested and oft-recommended "move slowly" approach? To begin with, let us ask a few IWWWWWH questions about the usual approach; it makes little sense to reject something if it remains effective.

The first question that comes to mind is: who determines what a "high" target is and what it isn't? If my objective is to achieve the highest and best outcome, and I set the "high target," I am actually negotiating against myself—against a target that I set using criteria I choose. What if my counterpart uses different criteria and sees a value that is greater or lesser than the high target I set? I would likely leave concessions on the table and essentially cheat myself out of the highest and best outcome. I might get everything I asked for using a predetermined high target, but negotiators often end up with outcomes that are less than the highest and best outcome by doing so.

I am reminded of a couple of examples involving professional sports franchises. The first example is the sale of the iconic and hugely popular Los Angeles Dodgers. In 2004, News Corp sold the Dodgers, Dodger Stadium, and some surrounding real estate for a total of $371 million to Frank McCourt. Eight years later, with the Dodgers losing players and games, with attendance waning, with mounting debt, and with Mr. McCourt engaged in a highly publicized divorce with his wife, Jamie, a number of bidders began scrambling to purchase the team and possibly the real estate.

By all accounts, speculation was enormous that the team would sell for a billion dollars. Yes, a billion dollars. At the time, the most ever paid for a franchise was $1.4 billion, but the Dodgers were a mess. Surely every group that put in a bid assumed that they were close, but they also knew that they were competing against other groups that were going to submit offers, so they had to consider what they might be thinking of as a "high" target. Of course, the most important concession that Mr. McCourt negotiated was that he, not Major League Baseball, would decide on the winning offer; that was brilliant.

At the end of the day, the Dodgers were sold for a packaged deal totaling $2.15 billion—a deal that stunned everyone except Frank McCourt. He was wise enough not to set the value of the team based on his debt load or his divorce or his predetermined "high" target. One has to wonder how News Corp felt about the $371 million they had sold the team for just eight years earlier. I suppose they might have asked for more had they known the team would fetch $2.15 billion in so short a time.

Two years later, in 2014, after making what many considered numbskull remarks about race and trusting his younger companion who taped their conversation, the owner of the NBA Clippers, Donald Sterling, was caught up in a firestorm of public outrage and was forced to sell the team to former Microsoft CEO Steve Ballmer, who, in another surprise move, offered $2 billion dollars. According to reports in the *Los Angeles Times* and other publications, bids started at $1.2 billion. That is a hell of a range. You have to think that the group that bid $1.2 billion did not do so because they knew they were going to be blown away by an offer that was 80 percent higher than their "high" target. Or was it that they just had some time on their hands and wanted to go down in history as the also-ran who were blasted out of the park trying to pay $1.2 billion for a team Donald Sterling bought for $12.5 million in 1981? It is likely that they would never have made the $1.2 billion offer had they anticipated Mr. Ballmer's offer of $2 billion for the same asset.

These are extraordinary examples, but since 2014 there have been many notable others in sports and other sectors, including Elon Musk's purchase of Twitter in 2022 and the collapse of FTX that same year. Going forward, these may be the benchmarks for the sale of professional franchises or the valuation of other business enterprises, but the pitfalls and absurdity of setting "high" targets based on outdated and ill-advised negotiation theory will continue as long as individuals and institutions insist on clinging to old habits and outdated rules.

By contrast, astute CNSUF™ negotiators ask, "How high should my target be?" "What is the highest and best outcome possible?" And "How do I remove any limitation in the way of finding out what that outcome or target can or should be?"

The other concept, encouraged by many negotiation articles and supported by several prominent negotiation frameworks, is the concept of moving slowly once a target has been established. The astute CNSUF™ negotiator is encouraged to follow this approach with great caution. Considering the Omni Modes, it is clear that moving slowly while negotiating some concessions in some Geo-Socio-Poli, Org-In, Per-Beha environments is the correct and prudent approach. But surely there are far more situations where following that old prescription can be a figurative or literal death sentence to negotiating the best outcome.

Sometimes the consequences, liabilities, or benefits of a situation preclude any possibility of moving slowly and achieving the highest and best outcome. I am reminded of clients who work in medicine, law, construction, engineering, IT, and the financial sectors. For many of them, moving slowly is sometimes tantamount to a death sentence for life and for opportunity.

As a result, the astute CNSUF™ negotiator in every situation will move in appropriate degrees of separation (ADOS/MADS) from point of origin or previous point of rest. (ADOS and MADS are synonymous, according to which you will remember more easily.) The starting position of every negotiation will be determined by a thorough analysis of mode, the product of each of the seven competitive rules, aggregate competitive intelligence, the CNSUF™ foundational tenets combined with a harmony of practical experience, and prudent professionalism. From the point of origin or from the last position of rest (the position at which an ongoing negotiation was started or stopped), the CNSUF™ negotiator will either maintain a position or move back and forth along the

CNSUF™ Continuum as appropriate in variable, uneven, erratic degrees of separation, or sometimes not move at all.

The ultimate, underlying drawback to setting a self-proclaimed high target and then moving slowly toward or away from that target consistently creates a pattern of behavior. Once your counterpart has determined/discovered that pattern, you are like a sitting duck. You are vulnerable and weakened by rules and behavior that you imposed on yourself, to the advantage of your counterpart and to your own determent.

All of the points made regarding moving slowly versus adhering to CNSUF™ Rule 5 are magnified enormously when considering the advice of the 2016 best-selling book by Chris Voss, entitled: *NEVER SPLIT THE DIFFERENCE*. In either case, both moving slowly and never splitting the difference inadvertently create the same *Fatal Flaw*, by advising negotiators to create habits that become the equivalent of a *Tell* in poker.

If you are negotiating repeatedly or over a long period of time with an individual, group, or company that consistently moves slowly or never splits the difference, an astute CNSUF™ negotiator will take note of these traits, the way a professional poker player will take note of an opponent's peculiar movement or idiosyncrasy before they make a particular bet or play.

That insight, or *intel*, will be used by an astute CNSUF™ negotiator to confirm and test other elements of their counterpart's ORG-IN and PER-BEHA training, strategy, and behavior to enhance their *mapping*, predictions, and understanding of their counterpart's influences. Over time, astute CNSUF™ negotiators can become so adept at reading our counterparts that we essentially know what they are going to do before they do. (Nonetheless, we do not simply trust our assumptions, presumptions, or previous experience blindly. We test.)

The key here is that the CNSUF™ negotiator must perpetually avoid being lulled into a sense of complacency or self-confidence by repeatedly assessing, reassessing, and applying the CNSUF™ Seven Competitive Rules with vigor and evolving commitment.

Chapter 3: Mode Groups & Modes

Bottom line, move in appropriate degrees of separation, ADOS/MADS. As the renowned martial artist and actor Bruce Lee said, "Be like water.... You put water in a cup, it becomes the cup." An astute CNSUF™ negotiator possesses the knowledge and skill to adapt, morph, and dissolve into any situation "like water," so their counterpart is essentially facing a new, smarter, and better prepared opponent every time they negotiate.

EXHIBIT X

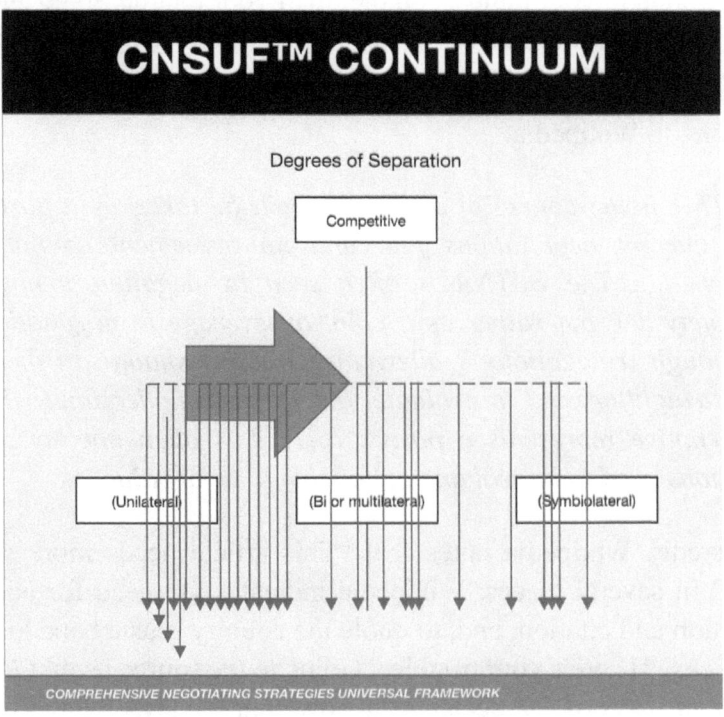

Exhibit X provides a visual representation of ADOS/MADS appropriate variable and uneven, erratic degrees of separation. Depending on an analysis of many factors (detailed above), the astute CNSUF™ negotiator will suggest major and minor concessions designed to influence actions that move the negotiation in the desired direction, limit risks, and maximize results. Exhibit X is an example only, as each negotiation will require a unique set of concessions and ADOS/MADS, depending upon the circumstances and challenges of each situation.

Rule Six. CEATNA© TO BATNA. It is difficult to recall a more iconic or misused concept than that of BATNA. (See *Getting to Yes,* Fisher & Ury, 1981*).* Chances are that even if you've never attended Harvard University's renowned program, the Harvard Program On Negotiation, or any other negotiation workshop or seminar, you are at least somewhat familiar with the acronym BATNA. If you are even remotely connected to the study or practice of negotiation theory or literature, it is virtually certain that you are familiar with this term. If so, the words are already rolling around in your mind or on the tip of your tongue, so go ahead say it: BATNA, *Best Alternative to a Negotiated Agreement.* Now, what does that mean?

According to Wikipedia:

> *BATNA is the course of action that will be taken by a party if the current negotiations fail, and an agreement cannot be reached.... The BATNA is often seen by negotiators not as a safety net, but rather as a point of leverage in negotiations. Although a negotiator's alternative options should, in theory, be straightforward to evaluate, the effort to understand which alternative represents a party's BATNA is often not invested. Options need to be real and actionable to be of value.*

To its credit, Wikipedia notes that "This article needs more verification...." In several places, Wikipedia indicates the need for additional verification and citation, and, to quote the country music band known as The Chicks, "There's your trouble." Going to the source itself, *Getting to Yes, 2nd ed. 1991*, p. 99, declares, "Know your BATNA." Page 100 goes on to clarify that BATNA is "the standard against which any proposed agreement can protect you both from accepting terms that are too unfavorable and from rejecting terms it would be in your interest to accept."

This is insightful and thought-provoking stuff, and I recommend picking up a copy of *Getting to Yes* and refreshing your recollections about the full content on the BATNA. This book contains many substantive insights and remains an important weapon and reference in the negotiator's repertoire. Throughout the years I have come to understand that

Chapter 3: Mode Groups & Modes

while many people can quote the acronym, not many go beyond that point, and thus they have BATNAs that are identified either too late or more often too early in the negotiation process. Either can be a dangerous or limiting mistake, especially in the world's Emerging Integrated Global Economy (EIGE).

The simple truth is, when BATNAs are identified too late, options may no longer be present that were available earlier. But far more often, BATNAs are identified too early and eliminate options or cause opportunities and options to be squandered or missed.

The key to achieving the highest and best outcome is to focus on timing and on the constant testing and reevaluation of BATNA. The astute CNSUF™ negotiator will take a Careful Evolutionary Approach To Negotiating Alternatives, or CEATNA©, to BATNA. Essentially, CEATNA© represents a summary of the CNSUF™ competitive rules with some additions and variations.

When BATNAs are established at the beginning of the negotiating process, as is often the case, including the example used by Fisher and Ury to introduce the concept (*Getting To Yes*, 2nd *ed.*, p. 99), negotiators end up establishing alternatives that are based on their own Geo-Socio-Poli, Org-In, and Per-Beha and are inherently the product of their assumptions, estimates, and presumptions. They end up negotiating with and against themselves by becoming so psychologically and emotionally attached to their own unilateral viewpoints (BATNA) that they miss or eliminate many options and opportunities. For many negotiators, BATNA has unknowingly become more a limitation than an asset.

That said, if your purpose is to influence your company or collaborators toward an outcome they don't initially comprehend or support, the fact that so many are willing and trained to set BATNA early in the negotiating process means you can put aside your resistance to alternatives the group favors. Once the limitations of the alternatives are exposed, and after encouraging CEATNA©, you can introduce your own refined alternatives with more confidence that they will be valuable assets. Remember: you must be willing to accept the risk that goes along with this strategy, but if you have insight, you are going to have to take risks in order to establish and solidify your added value to the group or company at some point anyway.

To avoid the mistakes made by many negotiators who do not follow the CNSUF™ and to maximize the potential for achieving the highest and best possible outcome or BATNA, use CEATNA©:

Careful

Develop IWWWWWH Questions

Identify Your Counterpart's Assumptions, Presumptions, and Estimates (APEs)

Identify Yours also.

Evolutionary

Test APEs

Establish/Test Timeframe(s)

Identify and Test Major & Minor Concessions

Modify BATNA(s) Accordingly

Approach

Move in Appropriate Degrees of Separation (ADOS/MADS)

Negotiate in VARIABLE Speeds

Revise BATNA(s) Accordingly

When in Doubt, Slow Down

The Mine Field (*Influence – Rapport – Results*, pp. 36-38)

Seek Third-party "Devil's Advocate(s)"

Run Modified War Games (MWG©)

Identify and Weigh:

P.A.R.T.S. (Brandenburger & Nalebuff, 1996)

Players

Added Value

Rules

Tactics

Scope

Close Six to Ten Times

Repeat Process – Refine Alternatives

Trial Close

Use Most Powerful Close(s) With Subtle and/or Blatant Variations

Repeatedly Repeat CEATNA

BATNA

Revise & Refine

Implement

Rule Seven. Only Death Is Certain. Who was it who said, "But in this world, nothing can be said to be certain except death and taxes"? If you are thinking Benjamin Franklin or Mark Twain, think again, because according to Fred Shapiro, author of *The Yale Dictionary of Quotations*, the original quote was "'Tis impossible to be certain of anything except death and taxes," said by Christopher Bullock, "The Cobbler of Preston," in 1716, more than seven decades before it was slightly altered and attributed to Mr. Franklin.

More importantly, neither Mr. Bullock nor Mr. Franklin would find either statement remotely true in the twenty-first century. Many of the richest corporations and wealthiest individuals in the world today pay little or no taxes, and millions upon millions of the poorest people can hardly eat, let alone meet or satisfy any tax obligation at all. In the Emerging Integrated Global Economy (EIGE) the only thing that is truly certain is death. Regardless of Geo-Socio-Poli, Org-In, Per-Beha, age, race, wealth or poverty death treats each of us with the same finality, albeit without equal timing, grace, or dignity.

In negotiation there is another certainty—whenever negotiators come to believe that their conclusions, strategy, or intelligence is 100 percent accurate, there is an extremely high probability that they are unequivocally wrong. When they are not wrong, they are just plain lucky, with rare exception. Because of the enormous number of variables in even the most elementary transactional negotiation, certainty is a rare commodity, and its presence should be highly *"suspect."* In some ways, certainty is the mother of *The Fatal Flaw, that point when negotiators believe they have covered every base and planned for every contingency, and they move from caution and co-operation toward an All-Win outcome, only to encounter devastating new truths and sometimes devastating consequences.*

Negotiation is a skill, an art, and a combination of many sciences. Like chess, physics, psychology, medicine, mathematics, and other subjects of substance, negotiation—especially CNSUF™ negotiation—is best approached with reverence and great expectation, but rarely with reckless abandon or utter certainty.

In order to achieve the highest and best possible outcome, the astute CNSUF™ negotiator's objective is not always to be certain, but to be as certain as possible given the risks, goals, time limitations, and challenges of each negotiation.

As a negotiation consultant, I believe that if I could provide my clients with complete certainty, I would be underpaid at any price, and they would be fools not to hire H-C, Inc. Luckily, that is not an issue for our clients or me, and I trust it will not be an issue for you. Remember: *only death* is certain.

Instead of certainty (as related to strategy and the underlying rationale for any strategy), I think of *cautious consideration.* I like to focus as much if not more on what our strategy might be missing and what we haven't considered yet. I do this even after we have run through CEATNA to BATNA and after we've taken a full range of other steps. We remember that the astute CNSUF™ negotiator should measure outcomes or assess the value of an outcome from a negotiation only in hindsight, well after the strategy has been executed and long after the consequences have been weighed and measured. If I do not see where we might have improved, where we might have read or interpreted a piece of data sooner or more accurately, or where we missed an opportunity or left something unnecessarily on the table, then I am certain we did not do our best.

Harrison-Chevalier wants our clients to be rewarded for doing business with us by achieving a measurable ROI that is as far as possible above the tangible and intangible cost of our services. To do that, and to grow our business and retain our clients, we have to be more accurate and more "right," for lack of a better term, most of the time. But that doesn't mean we are afraid to seek out and identify ways we might have done even better for our clients, no matter the outcome.

In order to do that, we have to be self-critical and willing to explore where we can improve at every turn in every negotiation. If we do not do that, we are resting on our laurels in an EIGE. Resting for too long on accomplishments of the past can be the kiss of death for excellence and continued success. My hope is that you will rise to or exceed this standard and expectation of your skills and knowledge of the CNSUF™, and that you will help to improve and refine the framework by sharing your ideas on how to use and improve the system.

Rule Seven reminds us that no matter how things *feel,* how they *seem,* and how bleak or difficult a challenge or negotiation might be, if we are not dead, then we are not done.

If we cannot find a solution today, then we keep working to be better prepared for tomorrow, or for the challenge that follows.

Where long-lasting, hugely consequential, complex issues are concerned, we even think beyond death. We think in decades, we think in quarter centuries, we think in centuries, because many geopolitical battles, for example, aren't going to find static long-term resolutions, and what we do or do not do today will have an impact on our ability to prevail in the future.

If an issue is *really* important, if it matters to you, you do not give up until the *fat lady* is laid to rest entirely, or until the issue is no longer *really* important.

Just because we do not see the solution, just because *we* cannot find or craft the right strategy, that does not mean a solution or strategy is not possible. It means we go back, we check our work, we retrace our steps, we dig deeper into the data, and, where necessary, we get help.

Because where some complex, comprehensive, or substantive issues are concerned, not even death is certain, so DO NOT QUIT!

EXHIBIT XI

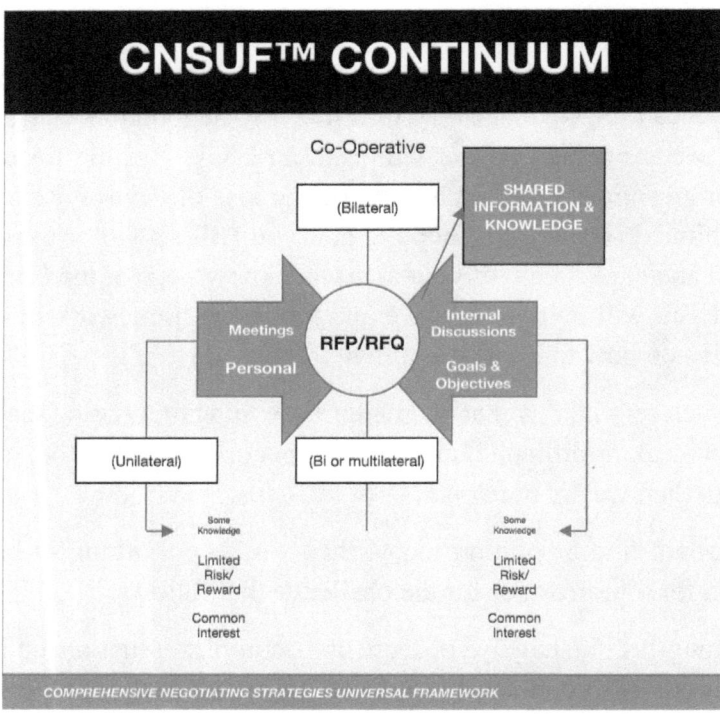

The Seven CNSUF™ Competitive Mode rules are rudiments that should be read, reviewed, and memorized until you can quote them as easily as the multiplication tables. Being familiar with these rules is not enough to become an astute CNSUF™ negotiator, because you won't be able to use them to tailor specific creative/effective strategies or to react on the spot, unless you make them a part of your negotiation DNA. Given that others will have access to the material presented here, its effectiveness will ultimately be based on the knowledge, skill, and execution of each astute CNSUF™ negotiator. The negotiator who reads *and* memorizes these rules and the other rudiments of CNSUF™ will prevail repeatedly against those who simply look at the words or read the book and never pick it up again. The reasons for this are clearly detailed in the section, "Three Fundamental Reasons Negotiators Fail" in *Influence – Rapport – Results*.

Exhibit XI shows a negotiation moving from the far left side of the CNSUF™ Continuum in the Competitive Mode toward a less competitive relationship as each side begins to provide more access to knowledge and shares more information. The example here is *transactional* (involving the buying and selling of goods and/or services) and contains complex elements, because at some point those directly and indirectly involved at the beginning of the negotiation can be replaced and/or joined by negotiators from other departments or organizational entities as the negotiation moves through the process toward final resolution or deadlock, where a leader in, say, the automotive, manufacturing, services, financial, or other sector writes a Request For Proposals (RFP) or Request For Quotes (RFQ) indicating their interest in receiving proposals from qualified suppliers or vendors of specified products and/or services. The RFP/RFQ may then be posted on a company website, emailed, sent to prequalified vendors or existing vendors, posted on a public or private network or third-party website, or any combination of these. The RFP/RFQ will likely specify minimum requirements, including dates and parameters for the format and instructions about what to include. It sometimes will even spell out how the submitted proposals will be evaluated and the process for how and when the business will be awarded. The RFP/RFQ might also include details about whether the company is seeking an all-inclusive price, a price range, a best and final bid, the lowest price, or—depending on the company, the business sector, or the industry—some combination of these.

Once a company's management determines that the RFP/RFQ is something it wants to pursue, it usually will begin the process of reviewing the RFP/RFQ and of writing a proposal, doing its best to anticipate how to make the top two or three finalists among those submitting proposals, and how it can go from there to winning the contract. Then the company will do its due diligence and write and submit a proposal.

Thinking back to the CNSUF™ Continuum (Exhibit I, p. 8), before the buyer has published the RFP/RFQ and before the seller or vendor has submitted a proposal, the two are truly in unilateral competitive positions, because the buyer has not written the RFP/RFQ, and the seller hasn't submitted a proposal. (Obviously, if the parties are in an existing relationship, there may already be a contract in place. This example is for illustration and is provided on the basis that the two companies do not have an existing relationship.)

But once buyers write an RFP/RFQ and the sellers submit their proposal, the relationship changes from one where neither party has insight to one where the sellers know what is contained in the RFP/RFQ and the buyer knows what is contained in the sellers' written proposal. At that point, the buyer has placed the RFP/RFQ and the seller has placed its proposal into a *circle of shared information/knowledge.*

Where would you place the relationship on the CNSUF™ Continuum? Is the relationship still competitive, or has it now entered the co-operative mode? You are correct if you think the relationship is still in the competitive mode. Even though the two parties have placed something into a circle of shared information, they have taken only the very first steps toward reaching a place of co-operation in the CNSUF™ framework. Since all the parties have done is make additional information available, neither has actually had an opportunity to evaluate or scrutinize the validity of what the other side has requested or submitted. This means that far more remains unknown than known. Therefore, the parties would move only slightly from left to right on the CNSUF™ Continuum in ADOS/MADS, dependent on specific Geo-Socio-Poli, Org-In, Per-Beha, circumstances, benefits, and liabilities for each side's short, intermediate, and/or long-term objectives.

As you see in Exhibit XI (p. 112), each side has *some* knowledge, *some* common interests, *some* risk, and the potential for *some* reward. These

Chapter 3: Mode Groups & Modes

elements are limited because neither side has actually put much into the circle. If the two parties were to part ways at this point, neither could calculate what there was to lose or gain beyond the cost and liability they have invested in the negotiation to that point. Maybe there is a great opportunity, but maybe there isn't. How could either party tell, based on an RFP/RFQ where the parties have no previous relationship? For that matter, how much could they tell even if they had a prior relationship? Is there enough to determine that the relationship of the past will automatically lead to the highest and best outcome today? Perhaps one could trust such an assumption in the economies of the seventeenth, eighteenth, nineteenth, or twentieth centuries, although volumes of historical evidence suggest otherwise. In the current EIGE, the astute CNSUF™ negotiator is well advised to test that assumption rigorously.

Whether you are a professional buyer, seller, engineer, attorney, primary, secondary, or collegiate educator, military officer, corporate or non-profit executive, real estate broker, a professional in the financial services realm, or whatever, I would encourage you not to get bogged down by any particular example. If you are having difficulty translating a principle or concept into one that is commensurate with your own profession or experience, ask IWWWWWH questions. These can include: Where does this concept fit into my profession or world? With whom do I interact where the principle might be germane? How can I get some additional clarification from a review of content within the EVOLVE text? And then go back and review previous sections or seek out the references, resources, and suggestions that are discussed herein.

To recap: the CNSU framework proposes that the Competitive, Co-Operative, and All-Win Modes are dependent on the "relevant conditions" that exist between the negotiators, and simultaneously that the Co-Opetitive Mode is always an underlying threat. When astute CNSUF™ negotiators are uncertain about the relationships between the parties, they do not guess. They do not revert to an emotional or historical set of assumptions or estimates. They rely on an assessment of the Relevant Conditions from the Competitive Mode.

When we do not know something, when we are uncertain about something, we rely on the Relevant Conditions of the Competitive Mode, and we follow the Seven CNSUF™ Competitive Rules as a guideline for the development of hybrid strategies to meet a challenge. Perhaps the most important CNSUF™ rule of all is this: When we do not know what mode we are in, we are, by definition, in the Competitive Mode. When we do not know what we know, we know exactly what mode we are in and what rules to follow to protect ourselves and our interests, to gain access, to build knowledge, and to use it to design and implement coherent strategy.

All CNSUF™ negotiation revolves around and must be compared with the Competitive Mode (as defined in CNSUF™), because humans tend to strive for domination of others. This is unlikely to change until the underlying perception that there is less to be gained through cooperation than from dominance changes. Not until we are on the brink of destroying the planet and all that is in it will mankind begin to put forward as much effort to build cooperation and consensus as it has invested into figuring out how the few can rule the many and possess the most.

While the condition of the Earth is currently being hotly debated on any number of fronts, all will certainly agree that we aren't yet at a place in the world where the focus of world leaders and governments can be said to be on building such cooperation, rather than exerting control and attempting to establish dominance.

Many would argue that not even the face of total destruction, clearly evident to brilliant men and women of the sciences, is enough to deter man's appetite for the competitive versus the cooperative approach. Let us all hope that wiser minds prevail before it is truly too late; but, until that day is confirmed, the astute CNSUF™ negotiator will proceed mindfully.

The Co-Operative Mode

In the CNSU framework (Exhibit XII, p. 120) the term "cooperative" has been elevated *to Co-Operative/Bi or Multilateral* to distinguish it as relative rather than the fixed term so many have come to know. As has already been mentioned, many people define *cooperative* as an action or as a feeling they have about a person or counterpart with whom they are interacting. That is not only foolish; it can be very costly in negotiation.

While this change is important for those who think of themselves as professional negotiators, it is even more important for those who do not—educators and parents, engineers, entertainment professionals, and others who just don't think they need to develop their negotiation skills and capability.

Like the Competitive Mode, the Co-Operative Mode in the CNSU framework is part of the *Conditional Mode group*. Conventional thinking has been that a negotiation has been cooperative when two or more parties involved in it reach an outcome in which each receives a part of what it had hoped to receive. This is as if to suggest that just because interactions between the parties were cordial, and each party received something he or she wanted, or reached their BATNA, that the negotiation was *cooperative*. But this definition describes the *feelings* and characteristics or *style* of the behaviors, not the underlying *intent* or *substance*.

Strictly speaking, the outcome in such instances is cooperative, because the outcome is bi- or multilateral and the parties have shared some information and have come to an agreement. The question for the astute CNSUF™ negotiator is whether all cooperative outcomes are cut from the same cloth. Virtually every negotiator will answer, "No." All cooperative negotiations are not the same, yet few can describe the difference between one cooperative negotiation and another.

The astute CNSUF™ negotiator, on the other hand, can definitively describe the difference, because the CNSU framework espouses that co-operation is relative, and the degree to which a negotiation is co-operative depends on the evolving substance and expansion of shared information underlying each side's objectives, intentions, and behavior before, during, and throughout the negotiating process. In other words, outcomes and relationships in the CNSUF™ Co-Operative Mode are conditional and relative, based on substance. They are not finite or based on style (the manner in which a negotiation is conducted—*Influence – Rapport – Results*).

As with the Competitive Mode, the astute CNSUF™ negotiator analyzes and assesses specific Relevant Conditions in order to determine where to place a negotiation on the CNSUF™ Continuum. The point at which a negotiation rests on the Continuum is where the Co-Operative Relevant Conditions are no longer expanding and substantive. As long as there is progress, as measured by the Co-Operative Relevant Conditions, a negotiation continues to move from left to right on the Continuum. When uncertain about the status of a Relevant Condition, the astute CNSUF™ negotiator will stop or slow down, reassess, recalibrate, and restructure accordingly.

Relevant Conditions: Co-Operative Mode

1. Increasing degrees of bilateral access to requested proprietary information and data.
2. Increasingly efficient/timely bilateral response to questions, including details from proprietary knowledge and data.
3. Equality of Transparency (EOT) between individuals and organizational contacts involved in the negotiation/relationship at equivalent levels on internal organizational charts.
4. Parity in Degrees of Separation (ADOS/MADS) and relative value of major and minor concessions offered and received.

Let's put things in context by taking another look at Exhibit XI (see p.112), which shows two parties engaged in the early stages of a negotiation. Remember that the responding party, assuming the two had no prior relationship, has no evidence of the underlying internal intentions, wants, or needs of the party writing the RFP until it receives and reviews it.

The party that has written the RFP will know (or believe it knows) what it is seeking. It knows its wants and needs, or it knows the solutions it hopes to achieve by awarding the business to a qualified vendor or counterpart. Thus, the two sides have unilateral positions at the beginning, with neither party fully aware of the other's wants, needs, intentions, capabilities, and so on.

Chapter 3: Mode Groups & Modes

However, once the party receiving the RFP submits a proposal, the two parties both know something about the other. Exactly what they know will depend on many factors, including what the party writing the RFP requires, what questions it has asked, what details and qualifications it prefers, and so on. But it will also depend on how the party writing the proposal interpreted the questions and requirements stated in the RFP. It will depend on the importance of the work, how badly the party writing the RFP may want or need the project, how much experience it has, what it is willing to do to win the business, and many other factors such as Geo-Socio-Poli, Org-In, and Per-Beha of the two parties.

At the point detailed in Exhibit XI (p. 112), each entity has limited information about the other and limited risk, depending on exactly what has been included in the RFP and in the submitted proposal. Each party will have already invested resources and employee hours in the development of the RFP and in the writing and submission of the proposal, but these are unilateral, with each of the parties knowing its own liability but not its counterpart's.

Another critical factor here involves the intentions of the party writing the RFP. At this point, the party submitting a proposal will have subjected itself to a level of risk commensurate to the volume and accuracy of the proprietary information included in its proposal. The party writing the RFP will have access to that information, regardless of whether it awards business to the party submitting the proposal. They have limited knowledge about one another, since the information contained in the RFP and in the proposal has not yet been fully verified.

It is important to note that, the party that submits a proposal assumes higher risk at the beginning of a relationship because it is being asked to provide insight and information about its organization with no certainty about the intended use or control of the security of that information. This risk can, however, be diminished if the party submitting a proposal recognizes its vulnerability and takes steps to neutralize or eliminate it. There is limited reward because no contract has been awarded and no commitment has been solidified. This depends both on the intentions of the party requesting and receiving information and on whether the party submitting that information has taken steps to neutralize these risks, particularly if it does not win the business. One cannot also rule out the possibility that the company submitting the proposal might do so for reasons other than the objective of winning the contract.

Given these elements, the relationship can be competitive based only on an assessment of Relevant Conditions. Once, the two entities move beyond submitting the proposal, however, the mode evolves based on the substance of the Co-Operative Relevant Conditions or on how the relationship is managed.

EXHIBIT XII

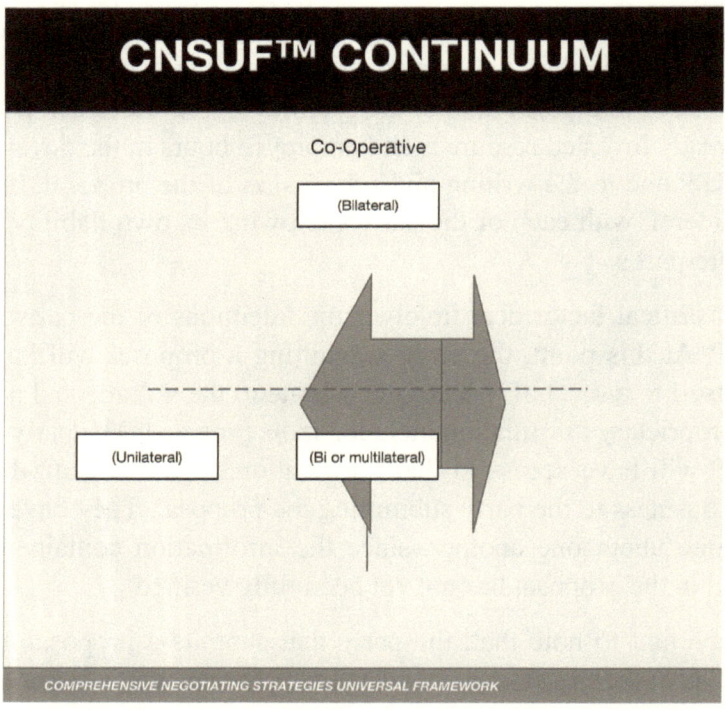

Once the RFP has been written and published and respondents have submitted their proposals, the process of evaluation begins to take shape. Depending on the protocol of the Org-In that wrote the RFP, proposals will likely be reviewed initially to ensure that all requested components have been submitted and that all preliminary qualifications (licenses, certifications, experience, and so on) have been satisfied; submissions that do not meet the criteria will likely be eliminated from consideration. Depending on any number of factors, the remaining submissions will usually undergo further review to determine which proposals will become finalists.

At this point there are several negotiations occurring. The finalists remain in a competitive relationship as each is vying to be awarded the project and because access to their competitors' proposals will be limited, if not restricted altogether. Inside the company evaluating the proposals, preferences will have begun to emerge. Many of these preferences will have already existed, and others will form as the selection process unfolds based on many elements of the Omni Modes. Those involved with the final selection will begin to formulate opinions, develop questions, and seek clarification of elements within each of the proposals.

At some point, the selection committee is going to request additional supporting data, documents, explanation, pricing, timing, and evidence of qualification and experience.

As the selection committee requests additional information, the finalists will also seek additional clarification of what and why specific data is being requested. They will have questions about terms, timing, materials, qualifications, preferences, and more. It is the substance of what is being requested and what is being provided, along with the underlying objectives of the parties, who dictate the existence, the quality, and the degree to which the process and the relationships are Co-operative.

Exhibit XII shows that as the parties provide more access to information to one another and as that information is transformed into knowledge, the relationship between the parties converges. This happens through the process of due diligence, testing, questions and answers, review of supporting materials, and identification of challenges and expectations. As interests converge because of shared information, and because there are fewer and fewer barriers between the parties, their resources, proprietary information, and Geo-Socio-Poli, Org-In, and Per-Beha, the convergence continues to move from Competitive toward Co-operative.

Exhibit XIII (p. 122) confirms that it is the expanded circle of shared information, knowledge, interests, risks, and rewards that brings the parties together. The less shared information, interests, risks, and rewards, the less co-operation. The smaller the shared access and information, the further to the left toward the competitive mode.

EXHIBIT XIII

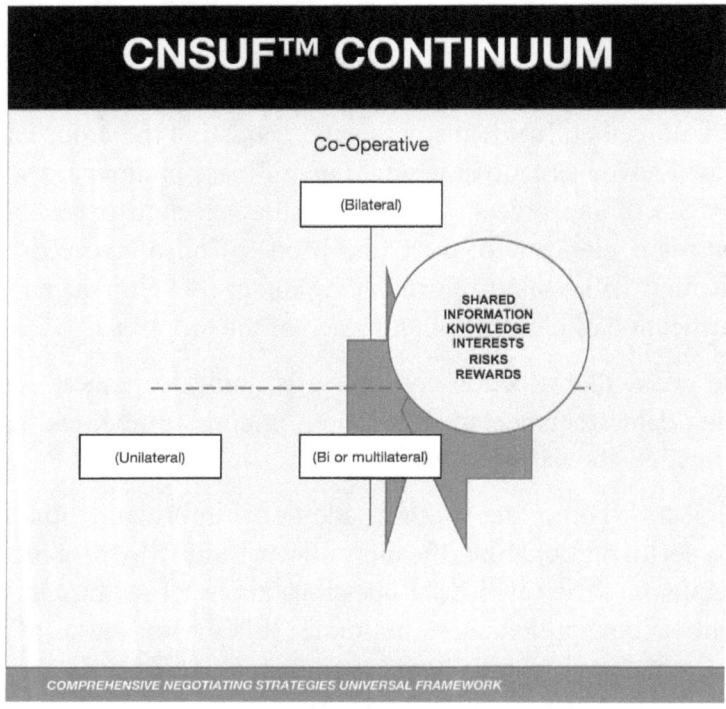

Let's switch gears for a moment from a corporate to a personal example. Let's say a woman reads George's profile on a social dating site. She and George converse by email for a week or two and then arrange to meet in person for coffee. In some ways, the profile the woman put up is her RFP. It states her hobbies, religion, food preferences, physical attributes, marital status, profession, and so on. George essentially uses the woman's profile or RFP as the point of contact. After George sends her an invitation to talk, she checks out his profile and decides whether to call or meet with him.

The first meeting is a confirmation and answers several basic questions, such as: Was his photo accurate or taken ten years prior, when he was in high school? How does he dress? What is his dating history? What is he looking for in a relationship?

Most people make their decision about whether there is even the possibility of another date in the first two minutes of meeting someone. Often, this happens much faster than that.

Back to our example. Assuming the two get through the first five minutes, they start to qualify one another more deeply. They ask probing questions; they look for hidden signs and contradictions. Depending on the attraction, they start to experience all kinds of chemical actions and reactions.

During the conversation, the woman gives more information about herself, and George provides more information about who he is. All the while they are both making decisions about what they are seeing and what they are hearing and what the possibilities will be going forward.

I do not see any difference between this and two companies engaged in the RFP process with vendors/contractors or attorneys litigating on behalf of their clients. This is also similar to a doctor getting to know a patient, two entities involved in a contract negotiation, an engineer developing designs for his company or for a client, politicians seeking to craft laws across political aisles, or executives developing policy. Every business sector, profession, or industry has its idiosyncrasies, but the essence of what is occurring as people and organizations interact inside and outside their entities holds many similarities.

At this point in the professional relationship, the initial review is an elimination round to "separate the wheat from the chaff" and identify those prospects who are worthy of additional consideration.

In fact, this is also what happens when employers are seeking prospective employees. Initially the process is competitive because there is limited access to the same information and resources. As the process moves forward beyond the first interview, the questions get more detailed; the internet search on Facebook, LinkedIn, or other sites gets more focused; and, as things move forward, there is anticipation for both parties that goes along with each new encounter.

Let's go back to that first coffee date. Imagine that instead of asking about her profile and preferences, answering questions, and sharing about himself, George asks his date for the password to her savings account. What is the likelihood that there will be a second date? Probably none at all, because people are more cautious in the early, unfamiliar, and competitive stages of any relationship. It takes time to get to know someone, to decide what you believe and what you do not, what makes sense, and what causes you to require additional information. Not everyone is going to meet this profile, but far more people are likely to act and react in this manner than not. When a second date goes well, and there is more conversation, more questions, more sharing about friends, family, past experiences, and anecdotes about your life and the other person, you either become more comfortable and move on to a third date or you do not.

Let's say things are going great between George and his date, but on the fifth date she asks George a question and finds that he contradicts himself and, even worse, she catches him in a lie regarding something of substance. What would happen then? Obviously, it depends on the specific person involved, but it's likely that if she catches someone in a lie within the first few dates, she'll back off or stop the relationship altogether. At the very least, she will probably find herself back on the internet dating site, looking with a renewed sense of purpose and new cautions for the next person.

Barring that, by that fifth date, she will likely know a great deal more about the person than she did on the first date. If instead of finding an inconsistency, let's say she finds out something wonderful. The odds are she will share something new about herself or about her life, family, and friends, and she and George will plan a sixth and a seventh date, moving further into the future with increasing expectations, decreasing suspicions, and a willingness to offer additional access to more personal information about themselves. By the sixth or seventh date, she might give George the security code to her outside gate or residential complex—which she likely would not do with someone she mistrusted.

Six months into a relationship, they've traveled pretty far from the apprehension of that first date. She knows more about George, and George knows more about her. They may have met one another's families. If one or the other has children from a previous relationship, they might start talking and thinking about whether they want to introduce the children into the picture, knowing full well that as they intertwine their lives and involve friends and family into the relationship, they move further away from the apprehension of that first date and closer toward a more cooperative relationship. They also know that the more access they provide to their private and personal idiosyncrasies, the more confidence they have in each other.

They do not have to ask if the other person likes fish, for example. Ten dates in, they probably know. They do not have to ask if the other person is a Republican, Democrat, Libertarian, Independent, Green Party, or whatever, because they have already shared that information. And as each one's knowledge about the other grows, as their confidence grows, and as their familiarity grows, the more access each one extends and expects from the other. And the more they move from a competitive toward a cooperative position in the relationship and on the CNSUF™ Continuum.

There is not that much difference between the relationships described here and the relationships between multinational corporations or small businesses, governments or countries, aerospace or manufacturing, real estate or construction entities looking to do business together. As access to information grows, as knowledge grows, as co-operation increases and perceived risk decreases, relationships move in relative degrees of separation (ADOS/MADS) from competitive to cooperative. But they rarely remain in one place for long; they may go forward or backward, but if they stall for too long at the same position, one party will begin to take the other for granted, or they will begin to look elsewhere for a better opportunity.

Again, there is little or no difference in business or professional negotiation, ranging from widgets to world peace. It's Geo-Socio-Poli, Org-In, and Per-Beha.

So, ten dates into seeing George, she knows more, he knows more, they have met one another's friends. They start to check one another's calendars for big events like New Year's Eve, birthdays, and all of that. But here is the question: where is the relationship on the CNSUF™

Continuum at this point? Where would your relationship with someone, after ten dates and six months, be on the CNSUF™ Continuum?

Are you still all the way on the left at Competitive? Or are you all the way over on the right at All-Win? Only one answer is correct of course, and it will be different for everyone. The answers will vary among the least and the most experienced negotiators, the young and the more mature, because "perception trumps reality."

For the astute CNSUF™ negotiator, the central question would be this: Is access to some information sufficient rationale to extend access to all information and to all proprietary knowledge? What do you think? How do you manage these questions in your personal and professional lives?

Ten dates in, how do you tell where you are from your own perspective? As an astute CNSUF™ negotiator, you would review the relevant conditions, evaluate, and then measure the difference between the access to previously guarded information and knowledge about the other person from the point of the first date to whatever point you are measuring to. Based on this you would make a guided judgment and determine the next steps. If your partner asked you for the password to your home network now, what would your response be? What would your partner's be?

Some people would offer to enter the password on your computer or device for you. Others would offer the password freely, not considering the issue a big one. Others would struggle silently within themselves and feel they were in a difficult position, because they would not feel comfortable giving the password, but they also would be concerned that their partner would be offended if they didn't. Where do you stand? What would you do?

What about the password to your social media account? Would you give that to someone after ten dates? How about your bank account and safe deposit box? What is and isn't on the table for you? The answers to these questions will have a direct correlation to Geo-Socio-Poli, Org-In and Per-Beha. And the answer will also have a direct correlation to how large the circle of shared information is between you and your partner. What if you gave your partner the passcode to your account and he or she would not give you theirs in return? Would that impact the position

Chapter 3: Mode Groups & Modes

of the relationship on the continuum, or would it not affect your perception, trust, and thoughts about the relationship at all?

For most people, the more they get to know someone and the more dates they have, the more interaction, the more shared knowledge, the larger the circle of shared information, the closer people move toward their limitation or resting point in the relationship, the longer and more substantive the relationship, the greater the access to personal, private, and sensitive information, and the farther the relationship moves from left to right toward co-operation on the CNSUF™ Continuum.

Looking back at the Relevant Conditions for the Co-operative Mode, we should have new insight and understanding:

1. **Increasing Shared Information.** All information is data. Data is inanimate, and thus it has to be translated into knowledge.

2. **Increasing Shared Knowledge.** Data translated through effective communication and analysis into congruent meaning and quantifiable evidence and action.

3. **Equality of Transparence.** As the parties share information, as access to resources is granted or restricted, the transparence of the information and access are relatively equal in value and significance to the respective parties. Not that parties reveal, share, and expose everything, but what they share is not intentionally misleading or encrypted.

4. **Parity in Degrees of Separation.** As major and minor concessions are withheld/granted/received, the level of cooperation recedes, remains stagnant, or increases, where perceived benefits or consequences are about the same for the respective parties. If one party consistently gives minor concessions and receives major concessions in return, there eventually will be an imbalance that will often lead to that party receding from the co-operative mode back into the competitive mode, using the cumulative benefit(s) of the imbalance as leverage.

Returning to personal relationship as a metaphor in the co-operative status at the center of the CNSUF™ Continuum, it is equivalent to the matrimonial engagement of dating parties. Getting engaged represents a new, higher level of intention, commitment, access, and shared information. But it is not the same as marriage, and it does not guarantee that a wedding will ever take place.

Engagement, in part and in theory, removes more of the barriers that exist between a couple. Conversations about children, finances, lifestyle, size, location of the wedding, employment, education, retirement, vacation, and other critical subjects are now expected, acceptable, and perhaps even encouraged by the couple and by those around them, including close friends and family.

Their focus turns to opportunities and the challenges they will face until the wedding. Anything that is left undone or unaddressed during the engagement is likely to resurface and affect the bliss and tranquility of the union once the wedding has taken place and the marriage is fully consummated.

One has only to study the history of torts, partnership, merger, and acquisition to make a connection between the metaphor of personal relationships and the complexities of Geo-Socio-Poli, human beings (Per-Beha), and corporations (Org-In) that try to combine and/or cooperate. Despite great expectation and due diligence, things do not always work out as anticipated. One can simply open the business section of any news source to see the details and stories of those who have ignored the history of competition and cooperation and trudged forward to their peril.

When I was growing up in Southern California, I remember hearing people of African American descent saying that social interaction was easier in the southern United States, especially in the "Deep South," as it was often called, than it was in Southern California and the West. People knew where the lines were drawn in the South: "Colored was Colored," White was White, and from a Geo-Socio-Poli standpoint, the two were never to meet. They were "separate but equal," or at least that was what they said.

Chapter 3: Mode Groups & Modes

Today I see that sentiment's underlying meaning as more evidence that it is easier for human beings to be at odds with one another than at peace. It is easier to be competitive than to co-operate. This is true outside of alliances of convenience that occur when bad factions threaten the greater body and divergent factions than unite to defeat a common enemy. Of course, five minutes after the common enemy is defeated, the coalition of convenient factions returns to the issues and elements that had separated them before.

I think when people said it was easier to navigate in the Deep South, they meant that there were no "Colored" or "White Only" signs in Southern California, but there were as many if not more invisible barriers. There were "sundown towns" that minorities might work in or visit during the daylight hours, but where they should not be seen after dark. There were sections of town where the races were relegated and contained. There were schools and jobs that were unattainable for minorities. There were high schools that had "Z" classes, which minorities of every grade level attended in a single classroom so they would not take time and attention away from students who were college-bound.

The deeds to many real estate properties that were sold even as late as the 1980s and beyond blatantly stated that the property could not be sold to a person who was anything other than "White." But since people of color rarely had the means to buy those properties, the issue was not transparent. An environment where there were no public signs and barriers was more difficult to navigate than one where divisions were clearly stated and highly visible.

I believe I learned the same lesson while serving in the Marine Corps and in Vietnam. I grew up learning about World War II, where the lines of good and evil were clear and the men and women who served their country were heroes. But in Vietnam, the lines of friend and enemy were so blurred during the 1960s that young Americans of that era began to question everyone and everything. Eventually, Americans of every age and Geo-Socio-Poli also began to question every aspect of the fabric of America, and the country is still emerging from the residue of that period, never to be the same.

Surely it was easier for some when the world was not struggling to clarify new definitions and new lines for race, gender, sexuality, religion, social equality, and other issues with which we continue to wrestle. Surely it was easier to hang up a sign that said who could and could not enter or use a facility. Surely it was easier when women were expected to do what they were told and have supper on the table when their husbands came home from work. Surely it was easier when superpowers did not have to acknowledge the humanity and rights of those from whom they demanded and took so much so inexpensively and with great harm to environments worldwide. Surely it was easier when superpowers could put their own growth and prosperity above and beyond the growth and prosperity of others. Surely it was easier for kings and dictators to command by decree and by force rather than by consensus. Surely it must have been easier; but for whom?

One thing is certain—it does not matter for whom it was easier, because that world will *never* exist again. The world will not return to its former self. We are intertwined in an Emerging Integrated Global Economy (EIGE) now. We are conjoined, and despite the convenience of a black-and-white world or of black-and-white competition where the boldest competitor wins or where doing a little better than you expected to do is cooperative, we go forward as astute CNSUF™ negotiators, seeking the highest and best level of cooperation possible for each negotiation. We go on for each set of circumstances as measured by relevant conditions and by how much more we know at the conclusion of a negotiation than we did at the beginning. This means how much *more* we've learned, not how "good" we feel or how "nice" our counterpart does or does not appear to be.

We do not measure competition or cooperation in terms of *style*, or the manner in which a person or entity appears or conducts themselves, but rather, we measure competition and co-operation in terms of the *substance*—of the actions, risks, and rewards we can quantify. We know the outcome of most negotiations will be determined by what we did not know at the beginning of the relationship or negotiation, and more importantly, by how we reacted to finding out what we did not know.

Ultimately, we know that competition and co-operation are relative, ebbing and flowing back and forth along the CNSUF™ Continuum, in relative degrees of separation.

The All-Win Mode

The All-Win Mode in the CNSU framework is the polar opposite of the Competitive Mode, and it is rarely achieved organically or by happenstance. It is more likely the result of a long-term, deliberate evolution from Competitive to Co-Operative that evolves over time and is measured and analyzed from a *Symbiolateral© perspective.* (A *Symbiolateral perspective* is a simultaneous multidimensional analysis and evaluation of each entity or element on every level, from every angle, including every component of the CNSUF™ Continuum). Where the iconic terms win-win and both-win have come to represent a range or perception of mutual satisfaction by the negotiating entities—often based on each entity's predetermined or preconceived desired outcome—the CNSUF™ All-Win Mode is differentiated, even from the CNSUF™ Competitive and Co-Operative Modes. These modes recognize ranges of Competition and Co-Operation based on relevant conditions. All-Win, in theory, has no range. As its name suggests, the CNSUF™ All-Win Mode is an *all-in mode*. The entities are either All-Win, fall at best on the right edge of the Co-Operative Mode, or reside where the corresponding relevant conditions warrant. (See Exhibit XIII, p. 132).

Relevant Conditions: The All-Win Mode

1. Virtually no restriction on access to information or resources.
2. All knowledge is shared knowledge.
3. Total Equality of Transparence (tangible and intangible components).
4. Total Equity of Risk(s), Consequences.
5. Equity of Reward (Interests of the parties is intertwined in such a way that the impact of any event or accomplishment inextricably binds and affects all parties equally, whether negatively or positively, and neither party gains an intended or unintended advantage.)

EXHIBIT XIII

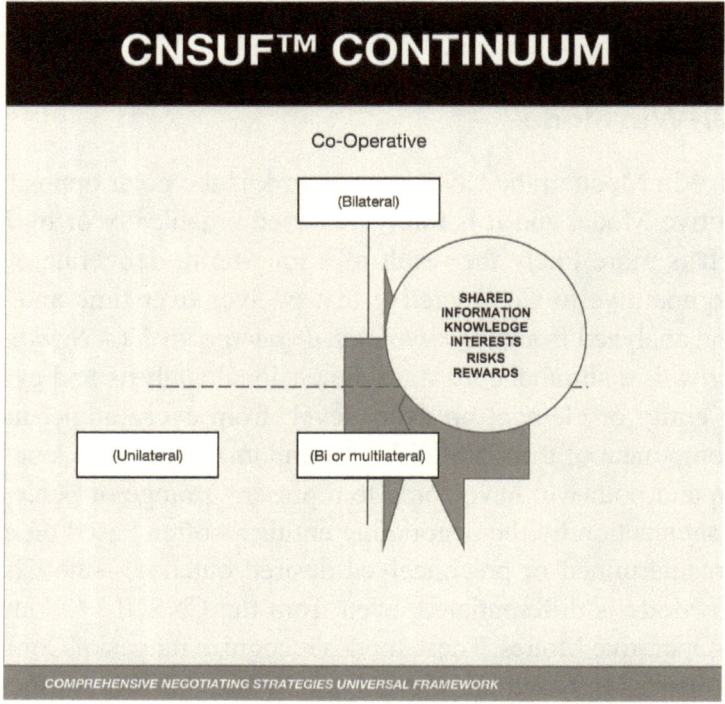

As relevant conditions are achieved and verified as shared information, interests, risks, and rewards, they bind counterparts together and move right to left or left to right along the CNSUF™ Continuum.

Exhibit XIII represents two entities whose interests and association have created what many would consider a "win-win" or "both-win" status. This means that the interests of the parties that appear are *nearly* the same, except in the few and relatively smaller areas that remain outside the circle of shared information. Having moved from left to right on the Continuum, each side will have received some portion of what it wanted. They will have fulfilled some relevant conditions, or they will have altered their wants and needs enough to encourage and achieve the expansion of their collaboration. By contrast, the astute CNSUF™ negotiator will recognize the position of the parties in Exhibit XIII as having achieved Co-Operative status on the CNSUF™ Continuum.

Chapter 3: Mode Groups & Modes

Precisely where to place the relationship within the Co-Operative area on the CNSUF™ Continuum would be different for different CNSUF™ negotiators, business sectors, and professions and for different Geo-Socio-Poli, Org-In, and Per-Beha considerations. However, no astute CNSUF™ negotiator would consider Exhibit XIII to represent the achievement of All-Win status.

Why is this true? If you cannot immediately answer this question, I recommend going back and reviewing previous content on relevant conditions until you achieve a clear understanding and can address and discuss this question with confidence.

Let's return for a moment to the dating metaphor we used in the Co-Operative Mode discussion. It was suggested that if George and the woman he met online dated continuously, they might ultimately become engaged. Now, questions and issues that might have been inappropriate or even damaging to the relationship early on have become not only part of the discussion, but part of the fabric of the relationship. As mentioned previously, one primary purpose of an engagement is to allow time to plan and finalize arrangements for marriage. Addressing questions about debts, finances, children, housing, and work usually go hand in hand. When a couple is dating and they break up, there are usually no legal ramifications. Each party is responsible for their share of expenses, rent if they are living together, and separating furniture and things that were purchased during the relationship, but unless there was an express contract of some sort, neither party has a legal claim to property that was owned or purchased outside of the relationship.

Once engaged, however, there are usually some additional cultural and/or legal responsibilities. If, for example, George bought an engagement ring for his fiancée and then she backed out of the engagement, most courts in the Western Hemisphere would likely rule that his fiancée would be obliged to return the ring. If, on the other hand, it was George who backed out, his fiancée would likely be permitted to keep it. The issue with the ring applies to both of them, aside from special circumstances and situations. The point is that with the engagement, the Equity of Risk for the parties is expanded, the circle of shared information, knowledge, risks, and rewards all expand, and, as George and his fiancée move closer to the wedding day, the circle would be expected to expand further. In essence, the engagement looks a lot like Exhibit XIII (p. 132) on the CNSUF™ Continuum. Engagement is certainly more serious and more involved than dating, but engagement is not the same as marriage.

For that reason, the Co-Operative position of the parties as shown in Exhibit XIII is not the same as an All-Win relationship in the CNSUF™ negotiating framework, although many if not most negotiators might characterize the relationship in Exhibit XIII as "win-win" or "both-win." The difference in the CNSUF™ negotiating framework is that entities that start in the Competitive Mode and evolve over time to the far right edge of the Co-Operative Mode are still in the Co-Operative Mode. All-Win status in the CNSUF™ framework means that the circle of interests, information, and risks have expanded so far that the two (or more) parties involved in the negotiation or relationship become a single entity. *All-Win*, then, is tantamount to marriage in a community property state where "two become one" (Exhibit XIV).

As such, the circle of shared interests, information, equity, and transparence encompasses all separate interests. For example, while each state in the U.S. has a great deal of autonomy; its ultimate allegiance is to the Union and interests of the United States as a whole. When the events of 9/11 occurred in New York, the entire nation was attacked. Every American (exceptions not withstanding) felt the pain and loss of those who were directly affected, because every American was directly affected. Those who were lost were not viewed as New Yorkers, but as mothers, fathers, sisters, and brothers of America. Perhaps not everyone cried, but I did. Even my children, who were quite young at the time, understood that something evil and significant had occurred.

And then, as America had done before, we banded together as a nation united against terrorism, committed to defending our nation, our principles, and our way of life. Despite the divergent Geo-Socio-Poli, Org-In, Per-Beha of the individual states, America came together as "one nation under God" seeking "liberty and justice for all." While we have never achieved every principle perfectly, the foundations of America, such as the Declaration of Independence and the Constitution, embody the principles of the All-Win Mode of negotiation in the CNSU framework. In America, and surely in this Emerging Integrated Global Economy (EIGE), the words of Laurie Beth Jones, author of the book *Jesus CEO,*

Chapter 3: Mode Groups & Modes

1995, have never been more appropriate: "Nobody wins unless we all do."

So, what does All-Win look like? (See Exhibit XIV.) All-Win in the CNSUF™ negotiation framework brings all separate risks, rewards, transparence, information, and interests together so completely that the separate risks, rewards, transparence, and information of the individual entities converge to form a single coherent Symbiolateral entity whose combined strength and capabilities subordinate those of its individual players or parts. The Hope Diamond may be rare, but All-Win status is equally rare—or rarer. Marriage consummation may bring joy and celebration, but the morning after is when the true test of intention and sustainability begins.

Thus, in the CNSUF™, entities are either *ALL-WIN*—to the extent that all overt and underlying interests, risks, benefits, and liabilities are equally shared as if the combined entities become a single unit—or they are not. There are no exceptions.

EXHIBIT XIV

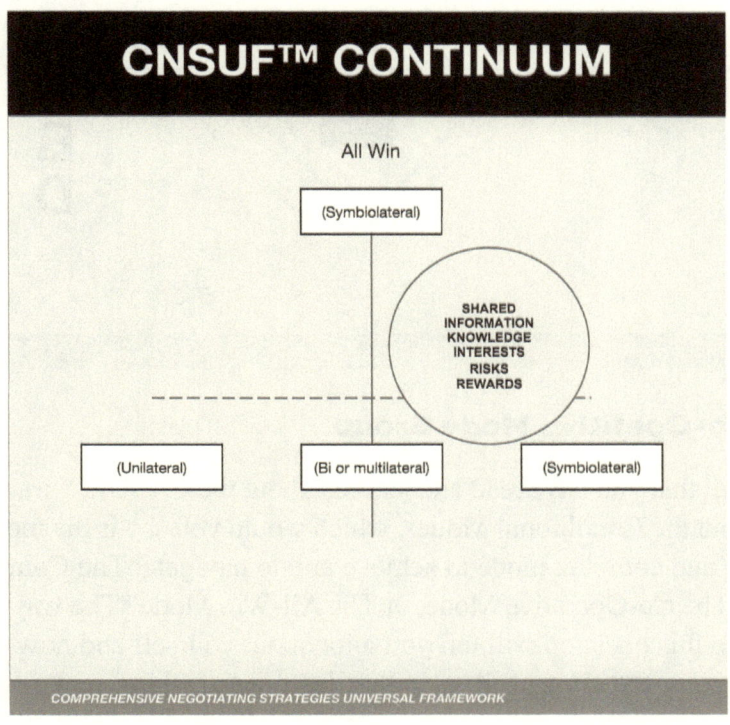

When combined, the Competitive + Co-Operative + All-Win Modes form what is called the Triangle of Conditional Dependence or Axis of Dependence (Exhibit XV). This is a visual reference that reminds the astute CNSUF™ negotiator that the status of a negotiation/relationship is best determined by a review and analysis of Relevant Conditions, and that the status of every negotiation/relationship expands and contracts continuously.

EXHIBIT XV

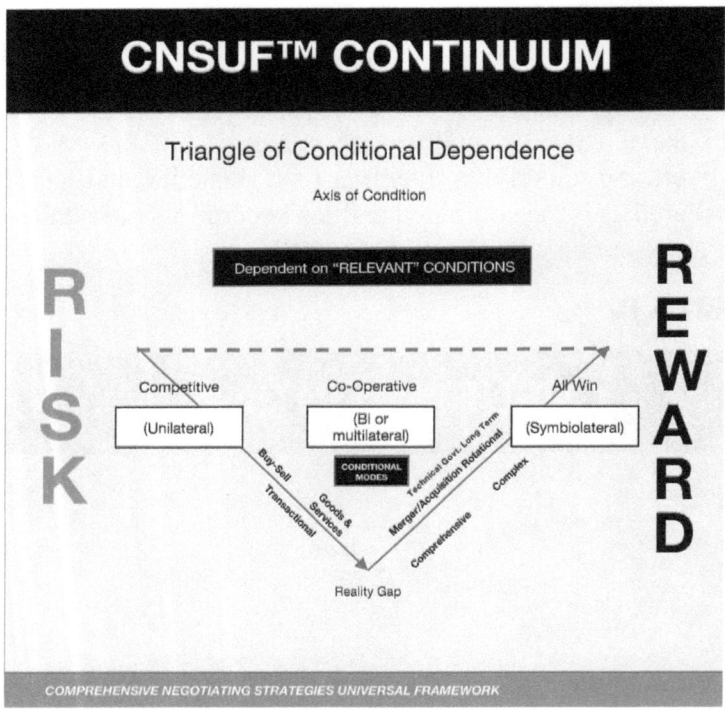

The Co-Opetitive Mode Group

Given all that you have read and learned about the CNSUF™ framework and about the Conditional Modes, which would you say is the most challenging and complex mode to achieve and to navigate: The Competitive Mode, The Co-Operative Mode, or The All-Win Mode? The way you respond to this question will tell you a lot about yourself and how you are synthesizing the content. Remember: learning anything new requires a

Chapter 3: Mode Groups & Modes

process called IKSEAR (Information to Knowledge to Skill to Expertise to Action to Results). If you have read *Influence-Rapport-Results,* you were introduced to this concept in the chapter titled: "Three Fundamental Reasons Negotiators Fail." If you haven't read that book, I strongly recommended that you do in order to have a well-rounded perspective on the CNSU framework. I hope you are able at this point to articulate key elements of CNSUF™, especially some of the key differences between CNSUF™ and your own thinking when you began reading this book.

What questions do you have? What changes have taken place in your own thinking? What makes complete sense to you, and what makes no sense at all? Where are the insights and revelations, and where do you see complete fallacy or idiocy? How does CNSUF™ stack up against other negotiating frameworks, and what are you using as the basis for your analysis?

These are all important questions, and the answers will be different for each individual reader and for every group. And that is exactly as things should be, because CNSUF™ is an evolving framework. It will grow and evolve as we continue to evaluate the principles, build and implement strategies, ask and debate approaches, and then integrate what we are doing individually and collectively.

So back to the questions at hand: What is the most challenging and complex of the Conditional Modes, and why? The All-Win Mode is hands-down the most challenging, the most complex—and the most elusive. It is one thing for the astute CNSUF™ negotiator to know that what many other negotiators call "win-win" and "both-win" are more often than not actually Co-Operative outcomes. They stretch along the CNSUF™ Continuum depending on the Relevant Conditions as defined in the CNSUF™ framework. But it is quite another thing to realize that, while the All-Win Mode is conceived at the point that all of the interests, information, risks, and rewards of all of the involved parties converge to form a single entity, the real evidence of All-Win can be determined only based upon what happens thereafter. This is among the chief reasons that All-Win is so hard to achieve and even harder to sustain.

If one party has truly committed itself wholly to the All-Win relationship, it has left nothing beyond the grasp of its new partners. Everything is on the table: all the information, all the proprietary assets and intellectual capital—all of it. If anything has been withheld, the relationship recedes from All-Win and becomes Co-Operative. Remember: in the CNSU framework, one cannot be a little bit All-Win. One is either married or committed to a single entity with one's partner, or one is not. What if there is a prenuptial agreement—that is like being a little bit married, right? Yes and no. Yes, from a legal perspective, because a marriage with a prenuptial agreement limits the division of property if things go south. But in these instances, the party that has a greater share of assets often uses the prenuptial agreement to limit his or her risks while providing some level of protection and risk limitation to the other party. If both parties have substantial assets, then both are limiting their risks to one degree or another. In the CNSU framework, a relationship (marriage) with a prenuptial agreement (where the prenuptial is a contractual limitation) is Co-Operative and not All-Win.

Another reason the All-Win mode is so difficult and so elusive is that once either party decides to submit proprietary information, resources, and access into the shared circle, that party becomes vulnerable to the surreptitious use of whatever has been shared. Once given, it is often difficult, if not impossible, to retract or erase the fact that the other party is now in possession or aware of whatever it has learned. The question then is how it will use what it has learned. What impact will that knowledge or access have on the behavior/intentions of the other side?

For example, what happens if, in the exchange of information or access, one party learns something unanticipated? What if that *something* exposes a weakness or vulnerability that had been hidden? Does the party having the realization ignore it, use it, and continue to move forward as planned? Or does that vulnerability fundamentally change the balance of power and/or the intentions of the party having the realization? These issues are relevant to significant Co-Operative negotiations/relationships too, but remember: in the Co-Operative Mode, neither party is extending unbridled access. There are limits to what is exchanged and shared. Some of these limits are known and some are not, so vulnerability is limited to one degree or another (depending on what is hidden, restricted, or retained) and to whatever contingency plans and alternatives are in place. Conversely, there are not supposed to be any separate self-serving what-ifs or buts in an All-Win scenario; it's either "one for all and all for one," or it's controlled, limited Co-Operation.

Imagine two people exchanging marriage vows that include caveats such as, "Until death do us part or until I find out you have cancer," or "Until death do us part or until you lose your hair or gain fifty pounds." Notwithstanding the fact that many marriages might be strengthened by this kind of honesty, most of us do not think these examples are appropriate evidence that people have the intention of spending the rest of their lives together. Suffice to say these limitations do not engender the total confidence or trust one might expect in an All-Win union.

There are many more reasons why the All-Win Mode is so challenging. Among them is the fact that history is replete with examples of individuals, organizations, institutions, governments, and countries that started out with the best of intentions and lost their way. There are an equal number of examples of individuals, organizations, institutions, governments, and countries that are intent on an outcome and will do whatever it takes to facilitate that outcome. This gives birth to the *Co-Opetitive* Mode of negotiation in the CNSU framework.

The Co-Opetitive Mode Group is a conundrum, because, like the Conditional Mode Group (Competitive, Co-Operative, and All-Win), it is dependent on Relevant Conditions and therefore might just as easily be included as a Conditional Mode. Because it is a hybrid (Competition + Co-Operation), and for clarity, it is separated as a mode group unto itself. Another unusual element is that the Co-Opetitive Mode Group contains only a single mode with two variations—the Mimic/Trojan variations.

"Start with the end in mind." That was the first of seven habits Dr. Steven Covey detailed in his hugely successful book, *The Seven Habits of Highly Successful People*. I have often expressed my admiration for Dr. Covey and for his book, and I highly recommend it as a great read. (I was privileged to be included with Dr. Covey and Dr. Ken Blanchard on a book project titled *ROADMAP to Success*.) I mention "Start with the end in mind" because this habit represents one of the underlying foundations for the CNSUF™ negotiation framework. To the extent that CNSUF™ seeks to achieve the "highest and best possible outcome"—the "end in mind"—it stands to reason that we aren't going to succeed by focusing on what we already know. We will get there by seeking to gain insight into the things we do not know and by protecting ourselves as we move from one point on the CNSUF™ Continuum to another. This bears repeating many times and should never be forgotten.

During a recent CNSUF™ Consulting session, a client asked, "How do you know when you've learned all there is to know about your counterpart? How do you know that you are in an All-Win position?"

These are great questions, and the answer is easy: "You don't." Negotiators are seldom in a position when they have learned all there is to know. If they are, it's called a rut—a position you want to avoid at all costs. You generally know only that you are or were in an All-Win negotiation/relationship when you are evaluating it in hindsight. (I'll revisit this later in the section.)

The moment you conclude that you know everything there is to know, or that you've learned everything there is to learn, you enter one of the most vulnerable positions that a negotiator ever can be in. Even if you are correct about what there is to know and what there is to learn, that realization will likely change in an instant. So, the astute CNSUF™ negotiator recognizes that most (if not all) of the time we negotiate in a *State of Flux (SOF)*, where things are always changing, always evolving, and always requiring reassessment and recalibration. Perhaps this is an idiosyncrasy of the EIGE, or perhaps this has always been true. What is certain is that the astute CNSUF™ negotiator recognizes the SOF and seeks to recalibrate continuously.

As I've suggested, the time for determining whether we have learned all there is to learn or whether we have truly achieved an All-Win position may be the period when we are looking backward and assessing the nature and qualities of a negotiation from a historical perspective, well after the negotiation and the relationship(s) connected to it have ceased.

But even then, there will be a great deal that will remain unknowable and/or unsubstantiated.

While a few anecdotes and stories are included in this book to illustrate a point or principle, I have purposely resisted the temptation to include a great number of specific examples about specific clients, situations, events, or companies, because I believe that while a specific example might be relevant today or to one reader, it may have no relevance tomorrow. What I want to do most in this book is share the philosophy, principles, and structure of the CNSU framework, so that a reader of any generation might apply and evaluate these elements at any given time to the specific circumstances of their interest or choosing and thereby raise questions or find solutions that are relevant to themselves. Also, I believe that many of the foundations and principles included in this book have universal characteristics, so there is a good chance that readers can research the internet, pick up a publication, or listen to virtually any reputable news outlet and find specific examples that demonstrate and confirm many of these principles and content.

Do people/institutions start out with the best of intentions and become intoxicated by access and opportunity? Or do people/institutions seek access and opportunity because they are competitive? Or is it lust for the things that access and opportunity can do or provide for them? Yes, yes, and yes again. But which people and which institutions are most susceptible, and when does one become susceptible?

Despite our best efforts to answer these questions ahead of time, we cannot do so with certainty. Therefore, the astute CNSUF™ negotiator's interests in any situation are best served and protected by seeking to understand and to know more about what is not known, and by limiting our risks as we move throughout the process.

The CNSU framework guides and supports negotiators to do this by encouraging the development of extreme competency in the principles, tenets, rules, and strategies included in this book, the other books in the *Beyond Negotiating* series, and the works of those listed herein on the Acknowledgment pages.

Relevant Conditions: The Co-Opetitive Mode

1. Negotiators use elements of the Co-Operative and/or Win-Win, both-win modes for the purpose of seeking to secure and/or achieve a strategic advantage, with the intent of using such advantage to undermine the position and/or interests of partners, friends, clients, customers, competitors, or allies.

2. Imbalance of Transparence. Rather than being transparent, the Co-Opetitive negotiator seeks to provide only what is necessary to move the negotiation/relationship forward. There are fewer, if any, limits on what is ethical or fair; rather, the focus is on exchanging minor concessions for major concessions. As the Co-Opetitive negotiator is successful, counterparts are at increasingly greater risk, while the Co-Opetitive negotiator's risks decline.

3. Imbalance of Risk(s). Tangible and/or intangible risks for one party are significantly greater than for the other party in the negotiation/relationship.

4. Imparity in Degrees of Separation. Co-Opetitive parties purposefully and successfully yield more than their counterparts in as many concession areas as possible. As the Co-opetitive negotiator gives less and gets more, the balance of power and risk shifts to favor the Co-Opetitive negotiator.

5. Fatal Flaw. Negotiators act on the belief that previous cooperative interaction is a guarantee of future co-operation and/or a basis for entering or pursuing the All-Win Mode.

The Mimic Variations

According to Dictionary.com the definition of mimic is: to imitate or copy in action, speech, and so on, often playfully or derisively.

While the research is often inconclusive and fractional, a great deal has been written about the percentage of crime and criminal behavior that is primarily the result of opportunity and/or access. One conclusion is undisputed: *some* percentage of crime occurs because the means and opportunity to initiate criminal activity are present. That said, what differ-

Chapter 3: Mode Groups & Modes

ence does it make if it is 0.5 percent or 70 percent of criminal behavior? The fact remains that if you are the victim of a crime that occurs because of access or opportunity, 100 percent of the crime that occurs in your world is the result of access or opportunity.

What is important for the astute CNSUF™ negotiator is to recognize that governments, institutions, organizations, and the human beings that run them are susceptible to opportunity and to access. Once the individual or entity has achieved that access and opportunity for more, that entity becomes a formidable potential counterpart.

The *Mimic Variation* occurs when one or more parties in a negotiation or relationship mimic Co-Operative actions or words to gain increased opportunity and/or access to proprietary information and then use it for unilateral advantage.

One *hypothetical* Geo-Socio-Poli example might be where a government, having been accused of annexing territory from another sovereign country, equips a convoy of military vehicles reportedly filled with humanitarian aid and crosses into that country without seeking permission and without allowing the contents of the convoy to be inspected, either by international humanitarian inspectors or the appropriate authorities of the country the convoy has entered.

The act of providing (or claiming to provide) humanitarian aid to people who are distressed certainly mimics positive co-operative behavior, but the unilateral decision to cross the border without permission is competitive. Ultimately, what will the determining factors be for understanding the intruder's actions? Why wouldn't the country being intruded upon take aggressive military action to stop the convoy when it crosses the border without permission? Who would appear to be the irrational party? From an international or political standpoint, the country that had been intruded upon might take considerable heat, even from its own citizens, if it engaged the convoy. This would shift the wrongdoing on itself while providing a shift in favorable sentiment toward the intruder. Should such a possibility be considered?

On the other hand, what if the intruder's convoy is actually filled with logistical equipment and supplies—not with humanitarian aid, as it claimed—to support its own personnel as they seek to establish a land connection to an area they had previously annexed but that lacks viable access, so that goods and resources can be easily transported into and out of the area? Given superior military capability once access is established, it will be increasingly difficult for the country that has been intruded upon to repel the intruder.

In this example, are the intruder's actions ultimately co-operative or competitive, humanitarian or militarily strategic?

Either way, this example illustrates the Geo-Socio-Poli power and complexity of the Mimic Mode and also serves as a potential illustration of utilizing a Mimic approach together with a Trojan approach.

While negotiators may not start with the expressed intention of taking unfair advantage of their ally or counterpart, many find it impossible not to do so when opportunity arises or is inadvertently revealed. This temptation increases further with the perceived absence of significant negative consequence to the mimicking party. Intended or not, the consequence to the party being taken advantage of remains the consequence either way.

A historical example: Early European arrivals to North America could not possibly have known the enormity of the beauty and resources that awaited them beyond the shore. It is likely that the first Europeans to arrive in North America did not intend to perpetrate the unfathomable horrors and genocide they would inflict upon the native peoples who were in North America. Yet access and opportunity decimated sixty million buffalo and millions of Native Americans to provide access and opportunity for the Europeans and others who followed. To this day, the negative consequences endured by native peoples still reverberate, leaving many of them deeply impacted and isolated while America itself is among the strongest and richest nations on Earth. Is this purposeful mimicry? The first Europeans surely did not disembark saying they had come to claim the entire country or decimate native culture that first winter, yet they did indeed claim the entire country and decimate native culture as the result of access and opportunity.

Chapter 3: Mode Groups & Modes

In 1619, when the original twenty Africans landed in North America, they were believed to have been indentured, as were many Irish and others. In fact, of those original twenty, some would go on to achieve their freedom and even own indentured servants of their own. In time, however, access and opportunity would bring forth the creation of one of the most heinous and inhuman forms of slavery imaginable. While progress has been made, the impact and negative consequences on the descendants of those original twenty remain clearly evident, even in this twenty-first century, as the wealth gap between them and the descendants of the Europeans who brought them here continues to widen.

These are by no means isolated examples. Pick a time period, pick a continent, pick a people, and history will be replete with examples of people who, driven by access and opportunity, have committed unspeakable crimes against their fellow human beings in order to create more access and more opportunity to be dominant for a given time. While one might argue that the size and severity of one inhumane act is greater than another, if it is your humanity—if it is your mother, father, sister, daughter, uncle, cousin, friend, or aunt who was adversely affected—then, for you, all inhumanity is disdainful. And yet history shows that once the dominated are dominant, they are capable of atrocities equal to if not greater than those of the ones they once suffered beneath.

The Trojan Variation

Trojan, as in Trojan Horse. Any decoy, act, or strategy that causes an individual or group to unwittingly permit access into a protected area, space, group, organization, and/or institution, especially for purposes of sabotage, compromise, or surreptitious activity.

As defined above, the Trojan Variation in the Co-Opetitive Mode occurs when one party uses a decoy of any kind to gain access to protected areas, especially when such access is achieved for surreptitious intent or purposes. Perhaps the most illustrative example of the Trojan Variation comes from the legendary conflict in Greek mythology from which the term is derived, involving a great wooden horse used to provide cover for Greek soldiers who hid inside until the horse was taken inside the gates of the city of Troy. In 2025 many will relate the term *trojan* to computer viruses used by intruders to access and take control of computers or data systems.

In the war of my generation (Vietnam) and before, they were called booby traps. In the wars of this present time, they are called Improvised Explosive Devices (IEDs).

The array of IEDs is staggering, from small charges hidden on the ground to boys, girls, women, and men wearing vests filled with powerful explosives. There are fighters of every persuasion hiding among civilian populations. There are drones hovering virtually silent in the sky; cameras mounted at stoplights, on walls, and in hidden corners; satellites peering into tiny crevices from high above us; and computer hacking by enemies who are reading the mail of our allies and the correspondence of our politicians and leaders. There has never been a time when trojan-type threats have been more prevalent. And ongoing advances in the development and use of trojan variations, along with advances in areas such as artificial intelligence, have improved and increased trojan capability, ensuring that the world "ain't seen nothing yet."

Combined, the Mimic/Trojan variations of today and those that are to come represent an increasingly significant and likely unstoppable component of business and warfare, and thus of negotiation theory and practice, from the simplest transactional exchange involving the buying and selling of goods and services to the most comprehensive multilateral, multinational, long-term negotiations, to complex global negotiations involving every element of the Geo-Socio-Poli, Org-In, Per-Beha, Emerging, and Integrated Global Economy (EIGE).

My sense is that the Co-Opetitive Mode is already the most significant and dominant negotiation mode in the world today. If it is not, there can be little doubt that it will be as we move further into the twenty-first century and beyond.

An old television commercial used to ask, "Is it real or is it Memorex?" I still use that phrase, though tape has long yielded to digital technology. Many audiophiles and stubborn folks who refuse to change still use reel-to-reel tape, but where negotiation is concerned today, and more so into the future, the astute CNSUF™ negotiator is reminded to ask, "Is it co-operative or is it co-opetitive Mimic/Trojan?"

None of this means we should stop seeking to collaborate or to Co-Operate or even to work toward All-Win relationships. It simply means that the astute CNSUF™ negotiator must be prudent and must focus on Geo-Socio-Poli, Org-In, Per-Beha, relevant conditions and the balance of risk and reward to an appropriate degree in every circumstance. That is precisely what the CNSU framework is designed to help CNSUF™ negotiators achieve.

Chapter 4:
Competitive Intelligence

From the biblical story of Samson and Delilah to the contemporary complexities of Julian Assange, Edward Snowden, drones, social media, spyware, malware, cyberwarfare, and the like, the indisputable reality is that privacy and personal security are now relics of a time long gone. In the Emerging Integrated Global Economy (EIGE), competitive intelligence (CI) is as available and as prolific as the internet. No doubt programs and applications for anonymity are being developed and marketed at this moment, but privacy ultimately will become a luxury for the few rather than a right for the many.

Since virtually every aspect of life today is digitized, captured, recorded, and stored in perpetuity, it's pretty difficult for anyone to actually get off the grid. At some point in the not-too-distant future, the concepts of paper currency and minted coin will be relics, memories artfully displayed in showcases in places such as the Louvre, the Smithsonian, and other museums and archives. In some of the most remote locations around the world, paper already is being replaced by bitcoin, and digital currency exchanges are being made at the speed of light.

A few simple clicks on a keyboard and less than fifty dollars on a credit card can render the names and addresses of relatives, friends, and enemies of virtually anyone. Even those who don't show up in an internet search can be located with just a bit more time, money, and research. And depending on whom and what we are seeking, millions have made finding out the past and present, personal, and professional lives of others possible just by sending friend requests on Facebook, LinkedIn, TikTok, or one of the dozens of similar sites that exist today, and those that will follow.

Chapter 4: Competitive Intelligence

What all of this means is that gathering insight and competitive intelligence about those with whom we negotiate, while infinitely easier today than it was just a decade ago, will likely become even easier and more expansive long before it becomes more difficult.

The astute CNSUF™ negotiator must therefore become a perpetual student of competitive intelligence, understanding that regardless of what we know and what we do, the sharp edges of CI will cut both ways. We are simultaneously the hunter and the hunted, so make no mistake about it— while you are gathering CI about your counterparts, they are likely doing the same about you. At some point in the next decade or so, the pendulum will undoubtedly shift in the other direction as millennials and their contemporaries reap the consequences of putting every facet of their lives online and inviting everyone to be included in their escapades.

History suggests that each generation drifts away from whatever they did in their youth as their perceptions and realities collide and as they reap the consequences of their decisions. Millennials are sure to develop a renewed appreciation for the value of privacy and personal decorum, and they will become intent on passing their wisdom on to their children. They will see them reject it, just as millennials rejected the wisdom of their youth, just as baby boomers and Generations X and Y did, too.

Competitive intelligence is the action of defining, gathering, analyzing, and distributing intelligence about products, customers, competitors, and any aspect of the environment needed to support executives, managers, and anyone else making strategic decisions for an organization, family, or other entity.

Such competitive intelligence will continuously evolve as a byproduct of the integral components of CNSUF™, such as the Six Foundational Tenets:

- Predict Responses
- Test Assumptions (Estimates and Presumptions)
- Influence Actions
- Minimize Risk
- Maximize Results
- Increase Knowledge and Skills

Competitive Intelligence is also the byproduct of and the rationale for the astute CNSUF™ negotiator's continuous pursuit and strengthening of his or her understanding and integration of what is derived from the Omni, Conditional, and Co-Opetitive Modes. Virtually every aspect of the CNSU framework is designed to encourage, support, inform, and/or expand our competitive intelligence. In turn, that competitive intelligence is scrutinized, vetted, compared, and contrasted to historical data and resources before being integrated as one of many components used to identify Geo-Socio-Poli, Org-In, and Per-Beha behavioral patterns and nuances. Those patterns and nuances inform our overall analysis and discussion, which culminate in the creation and implementation of strategies composed of classic negotiation tactics and techniques combined with the hybrid variations that result from the unique and proprietary elements of the CNSU framework.

Types of Competitive Intelligence (CI)

Overt competitive intelligence is just as the term implies: CI that is conducted out in the open and *observable,* not *hidden.* This might be the simple act of looking up something or someone on the internet or in social media such as Facebook or LinkedIn without the precaution of setting your search criteria to hide the fact that you were making an inquiry. The value of overt CI can be enormous with regard to the OMNI Modes. Even if we can't get a detailed picture of our counterparts, we can get glimpses and gather tidbits that point us toward greater insights and intelligence.

Covert competitive intelligence is the opposite of overt CI, because some level of effort is made to conceal its accumulation. On the most basic level, this might be placing parameters on a LinkedIn search to hide or restrict the party you are researching from seeing your identity.

On the other end of the scale, covert CI might involve using spyware, malware, worms, trojan programs, hidden cameras, microphones, or undercover private investigators and embedded plants to collect and report what they find. A simple internet search of the term "competitive intelligence" will yield hundreds of companies offering a full range of

Chapter 4: Competitive Intelligence

services from industrial research, pricing intelligence, and competitive data to degrees and certificates on how to conduct CI for you, for your company, and for hire.

But none of this is new. In her books *The Moscow Rules* and *IN TRUE FACE,* author and former CIA chief of disguise Jonna Mendez recounts many stories and experiences involving the use of simple and not so simple tactics and disguises created and used by herself and others during her twenty-seven-year career spanning 1966 to 1993.

In a presentation Jonna did in 2023 in Sun Valley, Idaho, she shared slides with photographs of herself in various disguises that were so effective, even her own family, colleagues, and friends did not detect who she was. I certainly could not recognize her, even as I observed the photos and compared them to her standing ten feet away, live and in person.

Unbeknownst to most civilians, these disguises served, and serve today, to protect American lives, as well as the lives and sovereignty of people and nations the world over, by providing covert intelligence that is then used to guide, structure, and influence global policy and many elements of geo-politics and diplomacy.

So, who is in the bed next to you, or in the adjoining office or cubical? Who is your next-door neighbor, or the negotiator sitting at the other end of a virtual meeting or negotiating table? We may have no idea.

What do you want to know? How much time and other resources are you willing to invest? What is your risk tolerance? What are your moral parameters? What do you stand to gain if you conduct covert CI, and what do you stand to lose if you do not?

Of course, the value of whatever you learn or gain will be equal only to your ability to discern fact from innuendo and presumption and, more importantly, your ability to turn what you learn into knowledge that leads to practical strategies and tangible outcomes and behaviors that would not have occurred had you not had the CI.

Short of these, CI can be nothing more than a data stream of incoherent noise. As such, one might provide CI and access to CI that is purposely misleading as a means of testing what our counterpart knows or does not know. Here again there is no one-size-fits-all where covert CI (or any other type of CI, for that matter) is concerned. The methodology and components are best determined not on the basis of some standardized formula and not even on the basis of the risks and rewards of an individual negotiation; rather, the parameters of covert CI are best determined by an analysis of a combination of these and on the basis of the determination, intent, and veracity of our counterparts. The astute CNSUF™ negotiator understands that fire is not always best met with fire; sometimes it is more quickly extinguished with water, and at other times with oil. The astute CNSUF™ negotiator may have parameters, but what they are and where they are permitted to go will be as fluid and as varied as the challenges encountered.

Ethical competitive intelligence can be overt or covert, even though many suppose that "covert" CI conducted without the knowledge or awareness of the other party means it is questionable, unfair, unethical, or wrong. For the astute CNSUF™ negotiator, the fact that something is done without the knowledge of the other party does not necessarily mean that it falls outside of ethical bounds. Ultimately, that will depend on the intent and actions that follow. But that is not to say that overt or covert CI necessarily falls within a predetermined definition of what ethical means, either.

Given the enormous range of Geo-Socio-Poli backgrounds and idiosyncrasies, the bounds of what is ethical and what is not are as wide and as complex as those who define the term. By definition, the term "ethical" is *moral approval* or *disapproval* and to whether or not an action, a thought, or an idea *is right or wrong, good or bad, sanctified* or *unholy.*

Clearly, people from different Geo-Socio-Poli backgrounds and experiences do not share the same conclusions about what those terms mean. Choose any cultural element you want to analyze, and it immediately becomes clear that what one group finds completely *moral, good, right, or wrong* is absolutely *immoral, unacceptable, or unfathomable* to another. Each group holds fast to its convictions and justifies every sort of behavior to defend what it believes. As John Mayer wrote in his song "Belief," "Is there anyone who ever remembers changing their mind from the paint on a sign? .... Oh, everyone believes."

In order to maintain dignity, astute CNSUF™ negotiators need to know what their ethical boundaries are. But in order to achieve the highest and best outcome in any negotiation, astute CNSUF™ negotiators also understand that there must be a clear comprehension of the ethical bound-

Chapter 4: Competitive Intelligence

aries of their counterpart(s). They must also admit to themselves, if to no one else, that a self-imposed decision to remain unaware in their own boundaries is also a decision to make themselves vulnerable to those who will use their limitations as the very threshold of their access and the foundation of their efforts to prevail.

Unethical competitive intelligence is another misnomer, since by definition it means *not ethical, improper,* or *inappropriate.* Again, who is making that judgment? What is unethical for one is absolutely appropriate for another, given specific Geo-Socio-Poli and given the Per-Beha attributes of each individual.

Where ethics are concerned, the astute CNSUF™ negotiator will tread carefully regarding fixed standards, platitudes, and hyperbole about what is and what is not ethical in every situation prior to his or her engagement in a particular challenge, negotiation, or battle.

Examples where CI may be relevant:

- Market Analysis
- Competitive Analysis
- Opportunity Assessment
- Technology Assessment
- Financial Modeling

Background Search

- Financial Status
- Legal Status
- Habits and Hobbies
- Community Service
- Civic Clubs/Affiliations
- Family Structure
- Religious Affiliations

- Cultural Attributes
- Location Search

Examples (Abbreviated List) of How to Use CI:

- **Identify Geo-Socio-Poli** elements that might influence the way an organization or individual thinks, functions, or negotiates. Ethical boundaries, beliefs, strategies, and so on.
- **Get specific insights** into the personal and behavioral preferences of someone with whom you negotiate.
- **Identify specific tactics and strategies** that might work better than others, based on organizational or personal background and experience, cultural elements that you may already have in common, or those that may limit your ability to be effective.
- **Determine specific strategies** to avoid, as they may be behavioral triggers that could impact the way an individual or organization reacts to specific proposals or concessions.
- **Determine the level of interest** that exists for a particular product or service, or determine the level of competition you will encounter when introducing a new product or expanding into the geographical area where another similar product or service is already established.
- **Identify time parameters** for yourself and for your counterpart. This is an integral part of implementing strategy.

Chapter 5: Overcoming Objections

Almost everyone who has had professional sales training or experience recognizes the phrase "Overcoming Objections," because they have no doubt attended workshops, studied, or received some training in this area. Oddly, though, I have rarely come across procurement professionals who have training in this area or who have any idea what *overcoming objections* means. Outside of sales and procurement, the number of professionals who have formal education or knowledge about overcoming objections is slight at best.

I find this omission flabbergasting, because not only do sales and procurement professionals deal with objections on a daily basis, but virtually every human being on the planet encounters objections of one sort or another from the moment they are born until the moment they die. Yet so few people receive formal education about how to deal with the objections they encounter or even how to recognize the role objections play in our personal and professional lives. This is especially true for those whose education, work, or professional responsibilities fall outside of sales or procurement.

Let's start with this question: What is an objection? Is it a question, a demand, a request for more information, a roadblock, an excuse, a reason, statement of fact, a strategy, an opportunity, or a gross exaggeration? The answer is *yes*! An objection can be any one or a combination of several of these elements rolled into one and used in the same instance; so, obviously, we all encounter objections every day.

Because astute CNSUF™ negotiators know that objections play an enormous role in the areas of communication, influence, negotiation, and all other human interactions, they work diligently and as quickly as possible to rectify the fact that most of us are not aware of these objections or don't know what to do when we encounter them.

To put objections into perspective, we need to understand that an objection is any form of request or resistance. It may be a person, policy, question, reason, rationale, barrier, fact, movement, thought, belief, perspective, process, an organization, an excuse, or any combination of these and other elements. But whether physical, verbal, or non-verbal, tangible or intangible, objections stand between CNSUF™ negotiators and the objective(s) they are pursuing.

Clearly everyone deals with objections; it's just that many people who work outsidem the professional sales arena or outside a courtroom don't recognize the connection, because they don't use the term or think of it in the broad way we are defining here. Certainly, we are all familiar with the idea of asking for the cost of something. For example: "How much is this cell phone without a contract?" and then saying, "Nine-hundred dollars! That is really expensive." To sales professionals, your reaction is a price objection, plain and simple. The vast majority of sales professionals would react to your objection by explaining that the price of the phone is only "Ninety-nine dollars" when purchased with a two-year contract. An attorney in a courtroom hearing his opponent repeat a question that she believes has already been asked might say, "Objection, asked and answered." Most of us have watched enough movies or television to be familiar with those two types of objections.

But how many parents have said to their six-year-old, "Okay, go to bed now," only to have the child say, "I don't need to go to bed; it's too early." Probably everyone who has a child has encountered some form of that one. But how many parents think, "Gee, my kid just raised a *needs* objection." Probably not many, even though most parents are going to overcome their kid's objection by providing a distinct reason, perhaps even more than one, as to why their child does indeed "need" to go to bed.

Chapter 5: Overcoming Objections

Teacher, lawyer, doctor, engineer, CEO, administrator, janitor, politician—regardless of your job title, business sector, or profession, the top ten objections across the board will come from the areas I will list. Where price is a factor, it will inevitably rank number one more often than not, especially in transactional negotiations. However, for those who do not deal with dollars and cents or in personal, business, or professional situations where price is the primary consideration, there is no particular significance to the number or ranking of the objection areas as listed.

The top ten all time objections are as follows:

1. Price
2. Time
3. Interest
4. Need
5. Risk
6. Quality
7. Change
8. Trust
9. Image
10. Approval

Going back to the original question: What is an objection? Let me ask another question: in your personal and/or professional life, have you ever had to deal with a demand, a request for more information, a roadblock, an excuse, a reason, a statement of fact, a strategy, an opportunity, or a gross exaggeration? The answer is probably *yes*!

At some point you have had to deal with all of these and many of the variations that come along with them. If that's the case, you have dealt with and will continue to deal with objections all the time, regardless of what you do in your personal life or what you do for a living.

When you have encountered a question, a demand, a request for more information, a roadblock, an excuse, a reason, a statement of fact, a strategy, an opportunity, or a gross exaggeration, has it occurred to you that dealing with any one of these involves negotiation? Do you always understand how to eliminate or neutralize these objections as you encounter them?

Your answer may be "somewhat," but no matter how good or how experienced you are, you probably don't always recognize and effectively neutralize or eliminate all of the objections you encounter. If you do, please put me on the list to receive a copy of your book when it is published, because if you always successfully recognize, neutralize, or eliminate every objection that comes at you, you are head and shoulders ahead of folks like me, and I am eager to know how you are so successful.

While it probably isn't possible to recognize, neutralize, or eliminate every objection that comes our way, becoming aware of the primary objections we encounter and learning how to recognize, neutralize, eliminate, or otherwise effectively deal with the majority of these objections is not only possible with a bit of awareness and lots of practice over time, it's also highly advisable and something astute CNSUF™ negotiators will seek to achieve as an important element of their negotiation arsenal.

Depending on what you do for a living and the business sector you are in, there is going to be a subset of the top ten objections that you'll encounter repeatedly throughout your career.

That subset will be a reflection of the Geo-Socio-Poli, Org-In of your personal experience, comprised of and inspired by the jargon and idiosyncrasies of your particular environment. Every personal and professional environment has peculiarities—words, phrases, jargon, and challenges that are specific and common to that environment. People are going to do things a particular way, use particular forms, nomenclature, and so on.

Essentially, objections fall into three categories:

Tactical Objections

Tactical objections are primarily determined by the intent of the individual or group using or introducing them, which is what makes tactical objections the most difficult ones to identify, neutralize, and eliminate. The objection may or may not be legitimate, accurate, or truthful. (Remember, *"perception trumps reality."*) It only matters that the party encountering the objection perceives that it is legitimate, accurate, or truthful. If an objection is primarily being used to affect a specific tactical advantage or objective, then it is a tactical objection.

Chapter 5: Overcoming Objections

For example, let us say a fashion designer is fitting a dress for a client. After making a few adjustments and turning the client toward a full-length mirror, the designer says, "I am wondering if the length is too long. What do you think?" It is unlikely that the client is going to realize that the designer's question is actually the introduction of a tactical objection to gauge the opinion of the client and ultimately elicit the client's approval.

By wondering if the length is too long, the designer has not actually said how he or she feels one way or the other. The designer's statement gives the client an opportunity to agree or disagree without feeling that her answer will offend the designer. If the client says, "Yes, I think you're right," the client exposes his or her opinion to the designer and thus feels as if the two are on the same page. The designer then completes the adjustments and *appears* to be the consummate professional. If the client says, "No, I think it's perfect!" the designer gets the approval he or she was actually seeking.

A designer who is less sophisticated or is an inexperienced negotiator might have asked, "Is the length too long?" This is an actual question, because if the client says, "Yes," she may be in conflict with the designer, who may be looking only for confirmation that the length is perfect. If the client says, "No," it may be only because she does not want to contradict or offend the designer. Either way, neither party is fully satisfied, and the inexperienced designer/negotiator may be forced to change the length when he or she does not believe it is in the best interest of the dress or the client. Once altered, the client may second-guess her decision and wish that that the designer had never commented on the length of the dress in the first place.

A word of caution: do not get hung up on the fact that any example included in this book is set in one business sector or another. I use this particular example because I have a client who sells and fits designer wedding gowns and other apparel, and I have learned a great deal about working in the fashion sector. Because it may come from a perspective, profession, or industry that differs from their own, astute CNSUF™ negotiators are most interested in the principle being discussed, as opposed to the specific circumstances of an example. Put the principle into your own Geo-Socio-Poli, Org-In, Per-Beha realm. If you find that you are unable to do that, go back and reconsider the underlying principle until you can adapt it and work it into your own circumstances and challenges.

In this instance, the underlying principle is that whether an objection is being used for tactical purposes or not depends on the intent of the individual, not on the objection itself.

For instance, if you were asked to complete a project or task within a specific period of time, someone might say, "We need you to get the project done by the end of the week." Now, you could simply respond, "No problem," get the project done, and go on with your other responsibilities. On the other hand, you could respond by saying, "The end of the week is only three days from now, and that project is going to take at least a week and a half to do properly; three days just isn't enough time!" Now, if you are responding this way because you really believe that the project is going to take a week and a half, then your objection is what? Yes, *Time*. So, in this instance, your objection is not purposefully tactical; it's actually a technical objection. By raising the objection, you may or may not receive an extension of the timeframe.

On the other hand, if you respond by saying, "The end of the week is only three days from now, and that project is going to take at least a week and a half to do properly; three days just isn't enough time!" because you purposely want to see if the person giving you the assignment will give you additional time, then you are using *Time* as a *Tactical* objection, because the underlying purpose for raising the objection is to find out whether additional time will be made available to you.

Astute CNSUF™ negotiators would likely use the tactical approach in this example for at least three reasons: 1) If there is absolutely no additional time available, they are at least aware from the beginning that they need to make the project a priority and get it done. 2) If they actually believe that the project can be done in the three-day period and they deliver the project in three days (without raising the objection), they do not get much credit, do they? All they have done is what they were expected to do, never mind that getting the project done in that timeframe might mean they get a total of three hours' sleep during the three days they're

Chapter 5: Overcoming Objections

working on it. 3) If they raise the objection tactically, get the extra time to complete the project, and then deliver the project early, they've under-promised and over-delivered. They end up increasing their perceived Added Value.

Virtually any objection can be used as a tactical objection. It is not so much the objection itself but the fact that the negotiator introducing the objection does so as a means of getting more information, obtaining a concession as described above, or, conversely, dissuading a counterpart from asking a question or seeking a concession such as a discount, a pricing increase, or change of scope or time.

On the procurement side of the equation, some objections that have been used tactically by H-C's client sales counterparts include the following:

We don't want the business.

We need more time.

The price we've extended is the lowest we've offered to any of our customers/clients.

Our internal policies and procedures don't allow us to do that without an additional fee.

It's part of the overhead.

There's no profit at all if we agree to those terms.

That would expand the scope of the project considerably.

On the opposite side of the equation, some of the objections that have been used tactically by procurement professionals from various business sectors include:

The price is too high.

The R&D is outrageous.

Your competitor doesn't do that.

The quality is inconsistent.

We need more detail in the breakdown.

The Board won't accept or allow it.

The proposal is poorly written.

While these are actual examples encountered by sales and procurement professionals and by negotiators from a wide range of business sectors, they are only a small representation of the objections that might be encountered. If you do not work directly in sales or procurement, the words of the objections you hear may be very different, but the vast majority of the objections will fall into the top ten list detailed above.

Case in point: according to an article published in the *Los Angeles Times* regarding the 2014 meeting of the Asian and European (ASEM) leaders in Milan, German Chancellor Angela Merkel "signaled at the start of the summit that she expected [Russian President Vladimir Putin] to show convincing steps toward making the cease fire [in the Ukrainian Territory] *a reality*." Let's consider the objections just from this tiny example:

"she expected" = Interest

"convincing steps" = Quality

"a reality" = Change

Given that Chancellor Merkel made these remarks at the beginning of a summit that was intended to focus on trade and not on military brinkmanship, the comments/objections raised by the statement were certainly used tactically, ostensibly in an effort to influence President Putin to take concrete action. Thus, the title of the article: *"Putin Defiant In Face of Criticism Over Ukraine at Asia-Europe Summit..."*

The point is that it does not matter what you do for a living or what business, political, non-profit, public service, educational, engineering, scientific, humanities, or other sector you operate in, objections are a part of your world every day without exception. What you have to do now is pay attention to those objections. Listen and write them down, and you will find that while there may seem to be a million new objections every

Chapter 5: Overcoming Objections

day, the reality is that every business sector or profession has a limited number of objections that are filled with vocabulary and jargon specific to that business sector or profession. You will also find that once you list what those objections are, you'll be able to categorize them by using the list of the top ten objections. Of course, there are going to be instances where an objection might fall into more than one category or be difficult to categorize altogether. In such instances, the astute CNSUF™ negotiator will treat the objection as one would treat a land mine and develop a strategy based on the Seven CNSUF™ Competitive Rules, for example, to learn more about it.

Once you have a base list of objections, you will need to be mindful of changes and evolutions as they occur over time, and you'll need to update the list continuously, remembering that in some professions and some business sectors changes will occur more quickly than in others. Astute CNSUF™ negotiators will then familiarize themselves with that list, even memorize it, and then, one by one, develop strategies for responding to those objections. This will be dependent on the circumstances and the Geo-Socio-Poli, Org-In, Per-Beha and relevant conditions that occur in each instance or during the course of every negotiation in which we are involved.

Technical Objections

Technical objections are objections that can be weighed, measured, or objectively analyzed. A technical objection is therefore an objection that can be quantified in one way or another. These would include, for example:

> I don't have the authority.
>
> The architectural drawings were not follow correctly.
>
> You signed a contract with specific terms and conditions.
>
> The tooling is too expensive.
>
> There are flaws in the house that were not included in the disclosures.

The engineering costs are 20 percent over budget.

Volumes are much lower than quoted.

We don't have the capacity.

The square footage is less than three thousand square feet.

The poling results indicate a six-point spread between the two initiatives as of Friday.

The administration is requiring everyone to sign contracts that include the same terms and conditions.

The X-rays are inconclusive.

The ad campaign generated only a 6 percent return on investment.

Each of these examples represents an actual objection used or encountered by an H-C consulting client, and each one involves a technical objection, because all of them can be counted, measured, tested, or quantified in one way or another.

Where technical objections are concerned, it is not a question of whether the objection can be quantified, it's a question of whether the negotiator or entity encountering the objection is able to get access to the people, data, and/or resources that can substantiate it.

Astute CNSUF™ negotiators will request the source data for any technical objection, and then they will take the time to fully analyze and evaluate what they receive as well as what may be excluded. And they will keep asking questions, requesting access, and evaluating what they receive until that accessed data stream is exhausted. Then they will ask for more access until every possible molecule of access and data is obtained and evaluated, given the objectives and circumstances of each negotiation. (Remember, the mode of the negotiation will then be determined by the Equity of Risk, and the Equality of Transparency between the parties at the point our access to data or competitive intelligence is exhausted.)

Typically, the greater the access and the more fluid the data stream, the further a negotiation moves from left to right on the CNSUF™ Continuum—if both parties are sharing access and data. If they aren't,

Chapter 5: Overcoming Objections

then the increased access and data received by one party are used to minimize their risk and help formulate their strategy. Remember: in the CNSU framework, negotiations move from left to right—from competitive toward the co-operative mode—by expanding shared information, interests, goals, risks, and so on between negotiating parties.

Where one party provides access and data and the other party does not, the balance of risk and transparency shift accordingly, and the party extending access and data becomes increasingly vulnerable, unless that access and data are extended as co-opetitive diversions intended to increase the perception of co-operation to "rope-a-dope."

Astute CNSUF™ negotiators are going to seek as much access and data as they can get in order to evaluate any technical objection, but they are also going to be cognizant of what is being asked for in return for what they are receiving, and they are going to be skeptical if the balance of risk seems to tip too much in or out of their favor. The higher the risk, the more comprehensive the negotiation, the more cautious, the more attentive, the more focused CNSUF™ negotiators become.

By contrast, responding to a question or request depends on the specific Geo-Socio-Poli, Org-In, and Per-Beha for each specific negotiation. As in many CNSUF™ negotiations, this is an area where there just isn't a one-size-fits-all application, because despite many negotiators' desire to have one, and many pundits' desire to provide *five easy rules*, doing so is often a recipe for disaster unless the rules are tailored to the people, objectives, and risks involved at a given place and time.

As I've already written, CNSUF™ is a negotiation framework that is adaptable to virtually any negotiation situation. Thus, the prescription that might be suitable in one instance would not be appropriate in another because of the differences in the Omni Modes, differences in relationships, and the objectives of the negotiators.

However, from a competitive perspective, a rule of thumb for the astute CNSUF™ negotiator is to raise technical objections primarily when scrutiny of the technical aspects fully supports the objectives being pursued. When that is the case, CNSUF™ negotiators focus on the technical elements as they connect to their objectives. They limit discussion outside these technical elements, they move in appropriate degrees of separation (ADOS/MADS), they maximize their use of time, they seek greater concessions or greater collaboration (if that is beneficial or desirable), and they close—repeatedly.

When the technical elements do not favor the astute CNSUF™ negotiator's objectives or position, they might ignore them, minimize the relevance of technical elements in relation to the scope of the overall negotiation, dispute the validity of the technical elements, shift the focus away from the technical elements and onto areas or elements that do support their position, or shift focus toward an extreme personality or group, making the counterpart's behavior the focus instead of the technical elements.

Should anyone doubt the effectiveness of these strategies with regard to technical objections, one has only to research the history of the tobacco industry or, more recently, review the debates on global warming and the environmental impact of fracking, or become a student of politics anywhere on the face of the Earth at virtually any time in history. It is not a question of whether these types of competitive strategies are relevant or useful to the astute CNSUF™ negotiator, it is always a matter of how and when to implement these strategies, and why these strategies rather than others? What are the short, intermediate, and long-term benefits/consequences both known and unintended? All of this will be dependent on Geo-Socio-Poli, Org-In, Per-Beha, and relevant conditions.

Remember: even technical objections can be and frequently are used tactically. For example, an engineer might specify a particular range of tolerances for a project, or a procurement professional might request that a part meet specific metrics, knowing that the metrics fall just outside the capability of the supplier's technical capacity but also knowing that the metrics themselves fall within acceptable ranges for the intended application.

When the supplier delivers the end product, the engineer will then use the difference between the metrics delivered and those specified in the Scope of Work to obtain any range of concessions using the technical objection of the differences as the rationale. Is that fair? Is it ethical?

Chapter 5: Overcoming Objections

I'll let you decide, but I can tell you that not everyone will see it the same way. For every negotiator who believes that this example is not only unfair but unethical, there will be others who believe that all is fair in love, war, and business.

By way of example, in 2014 the automaker GM was alleged to have known about a life-threatening defect in an ignition part used in some twenty-nine million vehicles for more than a decade before congressional and public scrutiny exposed the issue. This brought GM's then newly appointed CEO, Mary Barra, to a congressional hearing to admit fault and accept responsibility. One might ask why, if GM *knew* the part was faulty to the point of potentially killing human beings, it didn't address the problem and fix it. Certainly, it is not fair or ethical that people lost their lives or that people purchased automobiles that GM knew had faulty parts. Perhaps most will say they agree, but the fact remains that GM did know, and GM did not address the issue until it was essentially forced to do so.

GM's ordeal, while tragic, is hardly the only example of a company placing its bottom line above quality, fairness, and ethics. Since 2014, there have been numerous examples and inquiries raising similar issues from other automakers, including Volkswagen, Ford, BMW, Toyota, and Tesla, as well as questions, legal actions, and claims in other sectors from pharmaceuticals, construction, finance, real estate, aerospace, food safety, and the list goes on. Astute CNSUF™ negotiators understand that while they have power and command of their personal beliefs, code of ethics, and morality, they do not and likely never will be able to dictate the personal beliefs, code of ethics, and morality of everyone with whom they do business. This has always been true and will become even more evident as the EIGE continues to evolve.

Again, what is most important initially is not our personal or collective morality or ethics in dealing with objections. What is important is determining how to understand the morality, ethics, and behaviors of those with whom we are negotiating. Our strategy and the tools we select to implement it must respond to the Geo-Socio-Poli, Org-In, and Per-Beha of each negotiation. What we do when we learn about and clarify these elements regarding our counterparts will determine our professional competence, our personal and even our collective morality. Then our actions will most accurately define our moral compass and our ethical guideposts as well.

What is most important to astute CNSUF™ negotiators is what we do and how we respond when there are risks and potentially costly consequences, what we do when the rubber meets the road—not what we say or think what we'll do before the negotiation begins or before an issue arises, because we aren't going to know what we will do or how we will respond until we are faced with and evaluate the costs, benefits, and circumstances at the moment we discover the issue and are compelled to take action.

Neuro-Associative Objections

The third category of objections is neuro-associative objections. *Neuro* refers to how we are wired from the inside out. Simply put, neuro-associative objections cause an *internal reaction to an external event*. For example, imagine if someone—let us call him Joe—takes out a ball-peen hammer and, with as much force as he can generate, slams his open hand with the small end. His fingers burst open, and blood splatters on your face and into your eyes; Joe convulses in pain and screams out at the top of his lungs. How does this description make you feel? What is your reaction internally?

Just the thought makes my hands shake and my internal organs squirm. In fact, I feel a little revolted just writing it. But your reaction, whatever you are feeling from the inside out, is your neuro-associative or internal reaction to an external event. Most of us are wired to recoil, or to feel at least a little revolted just thinking about an ordeal like this, let alone how we might react if we actually saw something so disturbing.

The example is pretty extreme, but it makes the point. And even though it is only a hypothetical example, it likely brings up the same kinds of reactions we have when we read about, hear, or see tragedies in real life, or on film or on television, incidents such as the beheadings of American journalists Steven Sotloff and James Foley by Islamic militants, and more recently the 2023 attack by Hamas-led militant groups against

Chapter 5: Overcoming Objections

Israeli civilians, and the impact of Israel's response on the people of Gaza.

Depending on your political persuasion, some readers are having an internal reaction just reading the words in this section. But keep in mind, while the news was focused on the Hamas-Israeli War, there was genocide, killing, beheading, insurgence, mutilation, public flogging, hanging, and more occurring in many parts of the world that most people have no clue about, and thus, most had no internal reaction at all to these tragedies. Regardless of when you are reading this book, there are heinous crimes and revolting atrocities happening at this very moment, somewhere in the world.

Most people do not limit their internal reaction to tragic events based on race, color, religion, or nationality, unless there is a neuro-association of some sort already established inside them.

But not all neuro-associative reactions require something as extreme as these examples. An internal reaction to an external event can occur with far less stimulation, and it does not have to be repulsive; it can be pleasant, too. Have you ever looked at someone and felt "butterflies"? Have you ever walked past someone, gotten a whiff of perfume or cologne, and melted inside? Conversely, have you ever had someone tell you to shut up or sit down? Or address you with a negative gender or racial slur? All of these can evoke neuro-associative reactions, and depending on our individual Geo-Socio-Poli, Org-In, and Per-Beha attributes, the things that will cause these reactions and the reactions themselves will be different for each person.

It isn't just what someone says or does. Our reaction will be the result of a lot of factors, such as the people involved, when and where it occurs, and how it compares to experiences we have had in the past. By being aware of how certain things affect us and how they affect those with whom we interact, we can minimize the negative impact of neuro-associative events or objections when we encounter them, and we can learn to use neuro-associative actions, events, and objections when it is appropriate or advantageous to do so.

Below is a condensed list of neuro-associative objections encountered by a wide spectrum of H-C clients from a broad range of professions and business sectors. These are just some of the objections you may deal with in your personal and professional activities:

Are you nuts?

We don't want it.

We don't need it.

I want it now!

No!

Do not ask that question again!

Take it or leave it.

We're done.

Leave!

Absolutely not!

No way.

If it isn't completed by Wednesday, we're canceling.

The board is going to reject that proposal.

That's a conflict of interest.

Shut Up!

Get Out!

HELP!

The best way to see a list that reflects your specific business or profession is to build it. Starting now, make a list of the objections that you and your colleagues encounter, and then work together to categorize and refine a master list that can be updated and revised.

We have now reviewed the three types of objections in the CNSUF™ framework: Tactical, Technical, and Neuro-Associative. Each has specific characteristics, advantages, disadvantages, potential risks, and rewards, but none of these types is black or white and set in stone. They overlap, and each type varies in every dimension, depending on the specific Geo-Socio-Poli, Org-In, and Per-Beha of CNSUF™ negotiators and the negotiators' counterparts.

IARCNC

There aren't five simple rules to fit every situation, but there is an acronym in CNSUF™ that helps to focus and refine our strategy where objections are concerned. It is IARCNC:

Identify

It stands to reason that if someone raises an objection and we fail to recognize it, our response will likely be to miss it or to react to it on a visceral level, rather than to think about how to react to it as an astute CNSUF™ negotiator. Missing an objection is always bad and often deadly, but identifying one may be easier said than done. If an objection is correct from the perspective of the negotiator who raises it, it won't come across as an objection per se, or as a tactic at all. Remember: an objection is intended to get our attention and impact our thoughts and behavior. Used appropriately, it will do what it is intended to do, especially if the other party is unaware, untrained, or unskilled. If an objection isn't successful, we hope it's because an astute CNSUF™ negotiator has initiated IARCNC.

If astute CNSUF™ negotiators raise an objection that fails to get the attention of their counterpart, it may be that they are interacting with a skilled counterpart, or it may be because they selected the wrong objection for that situation. This is okay because astute CNSUF™ negotiators will learn something. As CNSUF™ negotiators, we gain insight, we reflect, and then we raise another objection or revise the one we've presented. Like all concession-making in CNSUF™ negotiations, objections are symphonies, not one-note wonders.

It may be that the objection was delivered poorly. Sometimes inexperienced negotiators deliver objections as if they are reading from a script. For example: "Oh, that is impossible!" As if to say, "I just read a book on negotiation and it says here to raise objections, did that one work?" "No, it most certainly did not." "Sorry, what do you want me to do?" From that point on it is the counterpart who dominates and the negotiator who concludes, "I tried to use your negotiation strategy, but it didn't work." Often it isn't the CNSUF™ negotiation strategy or tactic that isn't working, but rather an untrained negotiator who lacks knowledge, skill, and confidence.

When you raise an objection, do so as if you know it will not fail, as if you know it will indeed get the other party's attention and influence their focus and behavior. If that does not happen, learn something, refocus, reload, and execute with an alternative approach.

When someone else raises an objection, the first thing you want to do is *identify* it as one. *Bang!* A million synapses fire inside you, and immediately Geo-Socio-Poli, Org-In, Per-Beha, type of objection, communication style, communication type, and so on all happen simultaneously, and you know instinctively to move from identify to acknowledge.

Acknowledge

After identifying an objection, you want to acknowledge it to yourself. This will help you focus and determine how to react, depending on many factors about the relationship, prior interaction, the Omni Modes, and so on. Are you speaking to someone in person or on the phone? If it's in person, they will see your physical reaction and you will see theirs. Are you communicating in writing via email or by some classified means? Are there time constraints? If there are, who set them? What are the risk factors for both sides?

Now, if you don't have any idea about any of this or you aren't sure at any moment, what should you do? Slow down and rely on the seven CNSUF™ competitive rules. What is the first rule? "Ask IWWWWWH questions or reframes."

Examples:

What? Would you repeat that, please?

Thank you. It sounds like you're concerned about quality. How can you elaborate on that?

What do you mean?

I see, and I agree that issues involving specifications are critical. What do you suggest as first steps?

These examples demonstrate how you might clarify the objection that is being presented and at the same time acknowledge the objection to yourself and to the other party. If you misunderstand or if there are additional objections, you want to identify them as soon as possible. IWWWWWH questions lead the other party to provide further information and clarification. Once the objection has been acknowledged, you reframe it.

Reframe

Reframing is one of the most important and powerful tactics in the CNSU framework, because it can shift the balance of power from one person or entity to another and bring "congruence of meaning" to words, so that *effective communication* occurs, rather than "conversations of the deaf."

In the CNSU framework, reframe means to "repeat verbatim the words, tone, and voice inflection of the person with whom we are conversing." It is that simple and that complex. To experience the power of this simple technique, you have to use it on someone else. You will be amazed at what happens and what you will learn from this powerful device. This tool is particularly useful when you are talking with someone who holds a title or position that is higher than yours. You may not be in a position to challenge that person, but you are always in a position to influence him or her. Used skillfully, influence is often more powerful than position. (see *Influence – Rapport – Results*)

When you use a reframe, you discover that people most often will not simply answer yes or no, they'll clarify or even change what they said. For example: If John said to you, "We need to schedule an emergency board meeting for next week," you might reply, "To be clear, you're saying that we need to schedule an emergency board meeting for next week." Now, you would expect John to simply say, "Yes," wouldn't you? But often he will not just say yes, because your reframe will cause him to think about what he said. Rather than offer a simple yes in response to your reframe, he will likely respond with something like, "Oh, wait a minute, we'd better check the calendar again and make sure we don't have conflicts. Or better yet, call our vice-chair, ask her what she thinks, and get back to me."

Without the reframe, you might have simply followed John's direction and scheduled an emergency board meeting, only to discover that there were various conflicts of schedule and/or priorities among the board members. By reframing, you have clarified what John really wants you to do, and you've moved from simply conversing with John to effectively communicating with him, because there is a "congruence of meaning" between you that goes beyond his initial words. (see "Effective Communication," *Influence – Rapport – Results*)

Here is another example of the power of a reframe. Say you are an engineer, and you get a call from a colleague, Ed, who says, "Hey, I was reviewing your drawings and I think we need to make several changes in order to strengthen the integrity of the bridge on the Anderson project."

You reframe and reply, "So after a review of the drawings you think we need to make several changes in order to strengthen the integrity of the bridge on the Anderson project." Here again, you would expect Ed to say "Yes," because all you've done is repeat—reframe—exactly what he just told you. But what you will discover is that Ed won't simply say yes. Depending on their Per-Beha, different people will have any number of reactions to the reframe. Some people will be offended that you are questioning their competence. Some will immediately assume that your reframe means you disagree, and they will immediately start defending their position. Some people will assume that you agree with them and expect you to give your approval. Some people will back off completely and start to second-guess themselves. There are a dozen if not a hundred other possibilities, but one thing is certain: few of those possibilities will include the other person simply saying yes.

Depending on the response, you are likely to end up with a lot more information and insight into the person's thought process and rationale. You may find out how important your approval and support are. There is so much you can learn before you have even raised a single question or made a single comment. All you will have done is to reframe precisely what the other person has said.

Chapter 5: Overcoming Objections

A final illustration here: A supplier, Jane, visits a client, Jason, and after some small talk she says, "Look, we're going to need a 6 percent price increase beginning next year, when the current contract ends." Guaranteed, ninety-nine out of a hundred procurement professionals will hear those words and immediately disclose their negative reaction: "What? Six percent? That is outrageous!" "Why are you raising the price that much?" "No, we'll find another supplier!" "We aren't paying anything more than 2 percent, take it or leave it!" Every one of these positions may be appropriate at some time or another, but rarely should an astute CNSUF™ negotiator respond that way.

In the first place, Jane—the supplier—may only be fishing. If she is an H-C consulting client, we might have suggested that she make that statement just to find out Jason's position. One of the responses has already told Jane that, at the very least, Jason will agree to at least a 2 percent increase. If that becomes Jane's starting point, she will almost certainly get more than that 2 percent when the negotiation is finished.

Maybe Jane is just trying to identify the type of negotiator she is dealing with. Maybe she is gathering competitive intelligence about Jason's organizational structure. How does he respond? What is his time frame? These are just a few of the reasons a supplier might make a pricing demand like this. There are dozens of other reasons and dozens of nuances, depending on the particular business sector and profession. The point is that by introducing a price (or some other) objection long before a contract ends, the supplier begins the process of negotiating for a change or for better terms and conditions. They obtain competitive intelligence that will help formulate their strategy.

By contrast, let's say Jane is dealing with an astute CNSUF™ negotiator and makes the same statement, "Look, we're going to need a 6 percent price increase beginning next year, when the current contract ends."

The CNSUF™ negotiator replies, "You're saying you're going to need a 6 percent price increase beginning next year, when the current contract ends?" This is a simple reframe, and you might expect Jane to simply say "Yes." A supplier who is an astute CNSUF™ negotiator might do exactly that and then shut up and wait for the client to explode. But many suppliers are not going to simply say, "Yes." Instead, they are going to give you their pitch as to why they deserve the increase. Since you likely are not the first person they've spoken to about this—they have already been "slapped around" by every other client they've spoken to—they're going to brace for your reaction the moment they make the statement. And they are going to be shocked when your reaction is a simple reframe.

From this point forward, the astute CNSUF™ negotiator will follow the CNSUF™ competitive rules to gain as much knowledge as possible. A quick note in response to the issue of two astute CNSUF™ negotiators negotiating an issue: Since negotiation is like chess in some ways, the fact that both players know the rules is not what determines the outcome. The outcome will be determined by which negotiator is better prepared and more skilled. This is no different from two excellent lawyers meeting in a courtroom. They both know the law, but the one who prevails will be the one who can find an exception to the precedents in the case. It is no different between two excellent football or baseball teams. They know the rules of their game, but who performs better once the battle begins? Who executes better? Who is more prepared to sacrifice, and who is playing just to get paid?

At some point, the astute CNSUF™ client—let's call her Jen—might say, "Six percent has got to be tough for you. It has got to be tough." "Sensing someone who has some empathy and who is very different from other clients, the supplier—let's call her Margaret—may become more personable and begin to share things about her job and about herself and start asking questions to see if she and Jen have anything in common, such as kids and family. Many people at this point will talk enough to tell you exactly what you need to do to avoid, defray, postpone, or eliminate the increase.

Hypothetically speaking, at this point where would you place this negotiation on the CNSUF™ Continuum? From your perspective, if you were the supplier, would it be to the far left, mostly on the left (meaning still quite competitive), or more to the right toward the co-operative mode? Why would you place it in that position on the continuum?

Chapter 5: Overcoming Objections

If you are focused on the description and thinking about the demeanor of the negotiation, you put it toward the middle of the CNSUF™ Continuum toward the Co-Operative Mode. If you are focused on the negotiation itself and the relevant conditions, you probably put it more to the left, because the reframe encourages the supplier to provide more information. Clarifying the example does not address how much the client has shared, it focuses on expanding what is shared as much as possible. What mode does that behavior suggest?

This example mostly describes *unilateral* behavior, where the supplier is focused on selling the increase and the client is focused on finding out everything she can about the increase, about the supplier, and about the supplier's organization. Added up, the example would be placed well to the left side on the Continuum, though not totally to the left because there is a prior relationship and because they have a current relationship. There are Co-Operative elements, but at this point the example describes a negotiation that is primarily in the Competitive Mode. If you have questions or difficulties here, review the chapter on Modes and Mode Groups, especially the relevant conditions of the Conditional Mode Group.

It is important to think about the principle of reframe in these examples and then think about how it relates to your particular business sector. If you are in the entertainment sector where actors, agents, producers, directors, and everyone else aren't often in a position to dictate the terms of their contract or the power to make things happen independently, you almost always have the power to influence what happens and to exert more power than one might expect by using the reframe, along with many other elements of the CNSU framework. Lawyers, doctors, politicians, technical professionals, educators, engineers, contractors, real estate brokers—whatever your business or profession, the reframe is a powerful tool when you become skilled at using it.

However, this example, like many negotiations, illustrates that a great number of people who are involved in a similar situation in their own business sector would place the example well into the Co-Operative mode, because they are focused on the style rather than the substance of the negotiation. (*Influence – Rapport – Results,* first edition, pp. 65–72)

The style of the "Must be tough—" is decidedly empathetic, because rather than shutting the supplier down, it encourages him or her to open up, to let his or her guard down, and to go beyond the issue of the price by moving into Per-Beha mode.

Depending on the situation, a reframe, an objection, or a close can help encourage transition from one mode toward another. Or it can encourage the perception of a transition, which results in the same behavior, because, as we know, "perception trumps reality." If the party with whom you are negotiating believes that the negotiation is co-operative, then it is for them. What they may not realize is that their perception of co-operation affects the balance of power, the equity of risk, the equality of transparence, and many other aspects of the negotiation or relationship.

Once you've used the reframe to clarify exactly what the other person is saying, you move from the reframe to confirm. This may take some time, since a reframe can open up an entirely new conversation or lead to new directions in a conversation.

Confirm: Having reframed and refined the content of an objection, you now have a clearer idea about it. But just to be certain that you have fully explored the conversation or exposed all of the objections in question, you are going to confirm your understanding by repeating it until the other party acknowledges that your understanding of the objections is congruent with what they want to convey. Using the last example, the astute CNSUF™ negotiator might say, "Just to clarify and confirm, so I am certain that I have a clear understanding, you're saying that you need a 6 percent price increase next year when the current contract ends." If the supplier has provided a rationale as to why the increase must be imposed, you might continue to confirm each of the points that have been detailed. Depending on the situation, this could also be done in the follow-up confirmation, until the supplier agrees that your understanding of the objection (a price increase in this example) and the reasons for it are clearly and fully understood: "Well, it looks like we have a clear understanding; thanks so much for coming in. I'll call you if I have questions, and we'll talk soon."

Chapter 5: Overcoming Objections

It depends on specific circumstances, of course, but more often than not we are going to follow this verbal confirmation up with an email or written memo. Sometimes a courier or express mail service that requires a delivery receipt is warranted and most effective. The message essentially repeats exactly what was confirmed on the phone or in person. Dollars to donuts, the written confirmation will reveal new clarifications, new twists, or demands on the objection. But if it doesn't, you'll have a foundation from which to shape a strategy to neutralize or eliminate any objections or challenges. Where urgent matters are concerned, this could all happen quickly. It depends on the Geo-Socio-Poli, Org-In, Per-Beha, as well as relevant conditions, objectives, and so on.

Neutralize/Eliminate: In a perfect world, I could give you three easy steps or a one-size–fits-all formula for how to neutralize or eliminate an objection. But have no doubt: there are rules and there are formulas, and anyone who tells you they will work for every situation is going to get you slaughtered at some point. It has never been true that any single rule is all-encompassing or works all the time. I have seen no evidence that this ever has been true, but, then again, perception trumps reality. What I can affirm without equivocation is that six effortless steps, or even twelve steps, will never work for everyone in the EIGE, because the only constant in an ever-changing EIGE is an erratic state of flux. Learn to deal with this or refuse to at your own peril. Nonetheless, there are some tools to help guide the decisions we make in any given situation.

To neutralize an objection is to render that objection, event, or point of view benign. It means finding a way to defuse whatever is threatening us and render it non-lethal. To do that, we need to know a simple but powerful axiom, one of the proprietary hallmarks of CNSUF™: *"The counter to any tactic or technique [objection, strategy, point of view, position, and so on] is the tactic or the opposite of the technique itself."* On the face of it, you might think it absolutely ridiculous, but after closer consideration, astute CNSUF™ negotiators will make it part of their arsenal.

What is the underlying principle? Well, it is all around us—it is used every day, and it continues to assist in the development of astonishing remedies and solutions.

When I was in college, I became part of a small band of extraordinary people, some of whom had collections of poisonous snakes in their homes, specifically in their bedrooms, in aquariums of various dimensions topped by a piece of two-by-six scrap wood that was kept in place by a heavy stone or rock. But this was in California, and now that I look back, I do not think anyone ever thought about what might have happened if there had been an earthquake in the middle of the night that toppled the aquariums! It would have been an interesting development, if not a fatal one. It is hard now to believe that nobody ever expressed concerns about it, but this was just one of a dozen things that made the group so *extraordinary*.

I recall being in a passenger van once with a few others, along with a number of pillowcases containing several species of rattlesnakes. We were climbing a hill on a two-lane rural road, and the passenger bus in front of us was going very slowly. Our driver decided to speed up and pass the bus, and he shifted lanes, only to discover a commercial semi barreling toward us before we passed the bus completely.

I'm not sure exactly what happened after that, but I do recall the van careening down a ravine, and that when we came to, there were bags filled with rattlesnakes piled up on top of us. The saving grace may have been that it was well over a hundred degrees in the van, and the snakes may have been coming to as well, so no one was bitten. As I said, I am not *sure* who was driving but I do recall that it was my van that was wrecked. Oh, the good ol' days.

The thing was, I got to go on these trips mostly because it was my van, and the others in the group assumed that since I'd enlisted in the Marine Corps and served in Vietnam, I *obviously* would have no fear of snakes. At this point you should be saying to yourself, "Test all your assumptions." I am intensely afraid of snakes, and I went to great lengths to keep that fear "close to my vest," so to speak. I reveal this now only to dispel any notion that I had the courage of my comrades, especially Barry, who would see the tail of some serpent slithering into a hole and never hesitate to pull the thing out to determine its species and particulars.

Chapter 5: Overcoming Objections

I digress, but there is a point here. Decades after going on those trips, I was contemplating the issues around objections, closes, and conflict and wondering if there is a principle that can be useful in handling objections or tactics when they come up. I scoured the literature and found that there were some ideas and formulas, but they all had distinct limitations. For a number of years, I asked participants in workshops and programs I facilitated, "What is the counter to any objection, tactic, or technique?" They would say things like, "Shut up," "Walk away," "Tell them to take it or leave it." While each of these suggestions and many others certainly have application in some situations, they are the wrong thing to do in a number of others.

Then one day it hit me—why do people collect poisonous snakes? Why, decades earlier, were we collecting them? Well, some of the snakes ended up as exotic pets, and others wound up in zoos where they served to educate and freak out grade school kids. But some of those snakes were used to produce antivenin to neutralize the poison when a person was bitten in the wilderness. When bitten by a poisonous snake, people are given injections of antivenin that is often produced from the same type of venom. The antivenin does not remove the poison from the body, it essentially neutralizes it so that the effects subside or no longer damage the organs.

This is essentially the role objections play in negotiation, since they are often venomous and viral. As this principle works in nature, it occurred to me that it could be adapted to serve the astute CNSUF™ negotiator as well. It turns out that it does work very effectively in a great many situations. This axiom isn't designed to eliminate every objection; it is designed to render the objection/challenge benign.

In chess there is the threefold repetition rule, also known as repetition of position. According to Wikipedia: A player can claim a draw if the same position occurs three times, or will occur after their next move, with the same player to move. The repeated positions do not need to occur in succession. The idea behind the rule is that if the position is repeated three times, no progress is being made.

Focus on "no progress is being made." That is exactly what antivenin does to the venom, and sometimes it is exactly what we want to do to an objection: ensure that no progress is being made by our counterpart and that we have an opportunity to consider our options, regroup, or develop a new or revised strategy for the next round.

The counter to any objection, tactic, or technique *is* the objection, tactic, or technique. If someone says, "We need a 3 percent increase," the "anti" position would be, "We are looking for a 3 percent decrease." At this point what is the status of the objection? For the moment it is neutralized, benign. Obviously, this is the simplest example, and it is clear that identifying and implementing the principle isn't always a piece of cake. It will depend on the business sector or profession, on the Geo-Socio-Poli, Org-In, Per-Beha, and relevant conditions.

First, in order even to begin to use this axiom, you have got to know what you are working to neutralize. If you are bitten by a rattlesnake, the first thing medical professionals must do is identify the species of snake. They will examine the size, shape, location, and time of the bite. They will ask about existing health conditions or allergies and will ask if you've ever been bitten before. At the same time, someone might be taking your vital signs. All of this will help determine what course of action is needed. I'm not a physician, so I'm not making any kind of diagnosis or offering any specific medical advice. I am, however, describing the actions and activities that surround diagnosis and treatment of a poisonous bite. I am suggesting that the astute CNSUF™ negotiator can learn a great deal by paying attention to the process physicians use when it comes to overcoming objections or dealing with events and challenges. Like physicians, astute CNSUF™ negotiators have to *identify* the issue they are confronting, *acknowledge* the issue, *reframe*, and *confirm*. Only then can they establish a strategy, use their skill, experience, and knowledge to apply that strategy, and move to *neutralize* or *eliminate*. CNSUF™ negotiators, like good physicians, executives, attorneys, engineers, and others, should focus on learning what they don't know, determine how to proceed without that knowledge, or create a workaround, learn, act, and evolve.

Chapter 5: Overcoming Objections

As CNSUF™ negotiators, when we know we do not know something, we revert to CNSUF™ competitive rules. We focus on defining the objection, the strategy, and the point of view of the counterpart(s) we want to disarm, while protecting our interests and making decisions using our knowledge, skill, and expertise to *minimize risks* and *maximize results*. One tool for doing that is to employ the axiom mentioned before: "The counter to any objection, tactic, or technique *is* the objection, tactic, or technique or its opposite."

To eliminate an objection, tactic, or technique means to remove it, not simply neutralize it—satisfy the objection or issue on a permanent or semi-permanent basis. If you ask me to modify a contractual agreement so that there is a five-year "non-compete" when the agreement is fulfilled or terminated, I take a moment, refer to my calendar, and counter by saying the non-compete should be three years, three months tops. You counter by requesting a period of thirty-nine months, and the two of us agree to that compromise. At this point the objection (time) has been eliminated, at least where the issue of the length of the non-compete is concerned. If there is an area in CNSUF™ negotiation that requires a combination of knowledge, experience, art, and skill, it is the business of eliminating objections and implementing effective strategy and counterstrategy. This requires everything we have covered so far, starting with a thorough understanding of the rudiments Geo-Socio-Poli, Org-In, Per-Beha and relevant conditions, continuing through each of the other points made thus far right up to this next vital component of CNSUF™ negotiation: the close.

When all is said and done, if you do not have the knowledge, the courage, or the capacity to close, virtually everything else you do will be impotent or irrelevant, or both.

No doubt there are people who do not possess this skill, yet do fine. There are people who rise to the top of their profession who have never heard of *closing,* but that does not mean they are not closing—it just means they are closing by circumstance, accident, or by osmosis. No matter how much someone accomplishes without closing skill, it will remain a mere fraction of what is possible if the individual masters it.

Identify, Acknowledge, Reframe, Confirm, Neutralize/Eliminate. Ultimately, some people and organizations eliminate objections by any means necessary. They stand between anything and a serious person or entity that wants to take what they have away, and they devise a plan to keep it or to cause serious damage if it is taken away. They are not going to study closing techniques, they aren't going to read a book, they aren't going to ask permission, and they aren't going to care if what they do is fair, moral, legal, or even sane; they are simply going to focus on how to get what they want. If negotiators are not willing to take the appropriate counter risk, they will be slaughtered. The time to prepare for the worst is long before it arrives, so that when it shows up, astute CNSUF™ negotiators can spend their energy crafting and implementing strategies that neutralize or eliminate their counterparts' objections/issues/challenges without having to violate or compromise their own ethical standards when dealing with counterparts who are willing to prevail by any means necessary.

Whether the negotiation involves the simple transactional buying or exchange of a widget, some intermediate issue of policy or procedure, or a complex issue of international policy or one of life and death, astute CNSUF™ negotiators need the willingness, ability, and the skill to close.

Close: I am always curious about this. When you read the word "close," what images or associations come up for you? During the course of the past few weeks, how many times have you thought about this word as associated with what you do for a living or how you operate in your daily personal life?

For many people, the answer to this question is, "Not at all." Because many people assume that "close" is just negotiation jargon that makes a common ordinary word sound like something, when it actually has nothing to do with their lives or their behavior in the *real world*.

Okay, I get it. But I remind you that an assumption is merely a belief, so I am not going to argue the point. But I ask you to consider that if the statement above describes your attitude toward closing, then you are likely being closed every day without the slightest idea that it is happening. That is good for those who know better and who interact with

Chapter 5: Overcoming Objections

you, but not so good for anyone depending on you to achieve the best outcome possible in a given situation. This is because, given your assumption about closing, you are unable to do the best for them most of the time.

If you are a sales professional, a realtor, a mortgage or financial services professional, an escrow officer, a real estate attorney, or a doorperson, you understand that you close every day. For the most part, I'm talking here to everyone else, but also to a great many of the folks who should know better but don't, such as the realtors and mortgage professionals who think I'm referring to the process of closing a transaction in the presence of an attorney or escrow officer, although lots of closing goes on during that process.

Here we are talking about the classic skill of knowing and using appropriate, tailored closing techniques to *influence actions, reduce risks, and maximize results* in CNSUF™ negotiation.

If you want to see a depiction of the most iconic and gut-wrenching sales colloquium of all time, you have got to see the film, *Glengarry Glen Ross,* based on David Mamet's 1992 Pulitzer Prize-winning play of the same name.

While not a single frame of the film is to be missed, there is a scene with Alec Baldwin that personifies everything that has ever been important about sales negotiation and human interaction in business. Baldwin's character, Blake, represents the alter egos of every one of the people (in particular) who have had a significant influence on the growth and development of the world as we know it. Delivered in the uncensored vernacular of truth itself, it is the blazing, raunchy, raw reality of those who matter in the world and those who do not.

We are not bogged down by the specific period aspects. We are focused on the universal essence of what is being communicated beneath all the stylized trappings, because we know there has never been and likely never will be a time in this world when titans and kings don't see themselves as God incarnate, omnipotent, and omniscient.

In that scene Blake dispenses two lessons that give us almost everything we need to know, not only about sales but about human interaction, in three simple words: "Always Be Closing."

The first lesson is that no matter what you do for a living or who you are, either you are closing, or you are being closed. And if you do not know the difference, then, to quote a phrase: *"You are the sucker."* As it happens, "always be closing," from Blake's point of view, is what everyone should be doing in negotiation.

Blake's second lesson relates to *how* to achieve the close; and for this he offers:

Attention

Interest

Decision

Action

This is brilliant for so many reasons, but chiefly because Blake, in a simple axiom, breaks the entire process of human interaction down to a single lesson delivered with brutal candor. Every Geo-Socio-Poli, Org-In,-Per-Beha interaction involves the process of getting attention, creating interest, and invoking a decision that leads to direct action. That is exactly what happens in every political arena and business sector, and in every area of our personal interactions. In some ways it is the perfect nugget of wisdom. But that lesson is the *ying*; the *yang* is that there are three critical limitations to what we can derive from the *Glengarry Glen Ross* axiom by watching the film alone.

The first has to do with Blake's delivery. No matter how universal the axiom, most people find it impossible to comprehend the genius of the message because of the abusive and intimidating delivery of the messenger, not to mention that in the EIGE there are many cultures and many geographic locations where the curse-laden thrust of the dialogue is not only prohibited but illegal.

The second limitation is that the film presents the axiom in the context of a boilerplate, white-male-only sales environment that looks nothing like the world of the twenty-first century, much less the world of the future. So many will find the essence of the message lost in translation. The business in the film revolves around the sale of vacation properties like the one I purchased forty years ago, as well as a sit-down sales pitch that is pretty nineteenth century. It is not that the lessons are any less insightful, it is simply that in order to comprehend the full value of the axiom itself, it will need to be extracted from the film and distilled for application to circumstances outside of those described in it.

Third, while Blake demonstrates each element of the axiom with flawless clarity to the sales team, which is his intended audience, the universal application of the axiom requires that every element be tailored for the Geo-Socio-Poli, Org-In, Per-Beha of each negotiation, which was not the primary focus of the film. Thus, the *Glengarry Glen Ross* axiom does not provide the full range of applicability or substance required to have the broadest possible impact outside of the sales environment featured in the film.

Because of these limitations, and because astute CNSUF™ negotiators strive to improve, refine, and evolve beyond the limitations of every tactic, technique, or approach in their arsenal on a continuous basis, we find that a few modifications elevate the basic components included in the *ABC*, *AIDA* axioms of *Glengarry Glen Ross* to an entirely new and evolved level, so as to become applicable to any type of negotiation in virtually every environment. In fact, the evolved and elevated state of this new axiom and acronym becomes the cornerstone of all negotiations and all human interaction.

CAIIDAR (Ki-DAR)

For the astute CNSUF™ negotiator, **ABC** evolves to **C. CLOSE.**

In essence, **close** is what everyone is paid to do. No matter a person's title, position, or profession, if he or she doesn't close and achieve the intended objectives of their work, that person won't succeed. Those who don't succeed won't have the work or be able to practice their profession.

If you are a trial attorney and you lose every one of your cases, you won't be a trial attorney for very long. If you are a corporate attorney and you are not billing the 200 or more billable hours you are expected to bill each month, you won't be a corporate attorney, for any big law firm, for long. If you are a mechanical, chemical, structural, or any other type of engineer and the projects you work on during an RFP process regularly fall short of the specifications and intentions of the project sponsors or investors, you will not be an engineer for exceedingly long. If you are a procurement professional and you are not achieving the savings goals and parameters you are expected to achieve, your company will find someone who can. Teacher, stockbroker, financial analyst, professor, administrator, CEO, CFO, COO, CPA, mechanic, plumber, actor, director, producer, agent, it does not matter. If you do not achieve results, if you don't close, if you consistently fail to meet the standards and expectations you are hired to meet, you eventually will lose the opportunity to pursue those standards and expectations.

If my clients do not see results they perceive as more valuable than our fee, they will not continue to hire Harrison-Chevalier. If there is anything that every human being has to do to survive and to thrive, it is to close on some level or another. Therefore, *Close* is *what* we have to do. AIDA then becomes AIIDAR, which is the *process* for closing in the CNSUF™.

A = Attention. If we do not have the attention of our counterparts in negotiation, it does not matter what else we do—we certainly will not be closing them on anything, much less how and when we want to. The entire process of persuading or influencing to create rapport with someone involves shifting their focus to where we want it to be. We obviously cannot do that if we don't have their attention.

I = Interest. If we have our counterpart's attention but fail to stimulate their interest in what we are presenting, what is the point of having their attention in the first place? We will lose their attention very quickly if they are not interested in what we're saying or how we're saying it. The process, the tools for creating that interest, will be different for every person with whom we interact, and it will be inextricably connected to the specific Geo-Socio-Poli, Org-In, and Per-Beha of the individual

Chapter 5: Overcoming Objections

with whom we are negotiating. Creating interest will require the use of specific timing and closing strategies.

What is effective in one negotiation and with one individual will be impotent in another negotiation or with another individual. Creating interest will depend on selecting a combination of elements that are appropriate for each negotiation. There will be similarities, and we may use some of the same elements from time to time, but these most often will include some nuance that was not present in a previous instance, in part because *"the devil is in the details."*

I = Influence. It is one thing to get someone's attention, it is another to have him or her interested in what we are saying. The primary purpose for achieving the first two elements is to *influence* what that person does or thinks as the result of the *interest* we created.

The book, *Beyond Negotiating: Influence – Rapport – Results*, is devoted to an examination of the primary components of influence and rapport. A good deal of the content from that book is included here, but one would be remiss not to read it to have a broader perspective on the rudiments of influence and rapport from the CNSUF™ perspective.

Suffice to say that by definition, Influence is *the ability to be a compelling force on someone's thoughts and behavior.* This is the most important evolution of the ABC–AIDA axioms, because simply getting our counterpart's attention and creating interest falls short of the astute CNSUF™ negotiator's objective. The objective is not merely to get the attention of our counterparts or to create interest, it is to be the *compelling force* necessary to *influence* them to shift their thinking, beliefs, assumptions, presumptions, objections, thoughts, and resistance away from where they are to where we want them to be, or beyond our initial objective. Getting attention and creating interest is good. Influencing our counterpart to move in a way that narrows or eliminates the gap between their objections and toward *our* objectives is *far* better.

D = Decision. Astute CNSUF™ negotiators seek to influence and encourage decisions by our counterparts that expand the Circle of Shared Knowledge, that remove or diminish restrictions to our access to pertinent proprietary information, that improve the Equality of Transparence, and that result in achieving the very highest and best possible outcome. As previously defined, we become certain that our counterparts have made appropriate decisions when they completely and unilaterally *cut away* from any action or decision that is inconsistent with the attention and interest we created and the influence we have purposefully exerted.

A = **Action**. Because action refers to the state of acting, astute CNSUF™ negotiators observe, analyze, record, and tabulate the tangible product culminating from their and their counterparts' decisions. They do so in order to assess their congruence and the accuracy and fruitfulness of their attention, interest, and influence. If they have captured the attention of their counterparts, if they have created sufficient interest, and if they have purposefully influenced the thoughts and beliefs of their counterparts, the evidence will be congruent with their counterparts' further actions.

R = **Results**. The astute CNSUF™ negotiator's skill, competence, and expertise must be measured by the tangible and intangible outcomes of each negotiation. These will be determined in large part by how much more is known at the conclusion of a negotiation, or interaction, than was known at the beginning, and by whether the best possible outcome was achieved given the resources invested and the challenges encountered.

CNSUF= **Foundation**. CNSUF™ then encompasses the tools, tactics, and rudiments for developing, refining, and implementing tailored strategies to influence actions and close, achieving the best possible outcome in a vast array of Geo-Socio-Poli, Org-In, and Per-Beha environments.

C= CLOSE =   **What** (Must be achieved)
A= Attention
I= Interest
I= Influence =   **Process** (For achieving **What**)
D=Decision
A=Action
R=Results

Chapter 5: Overcoming Objections

CNSUF™ = Foundation/Tools (To Achieve, Process, and What/Close)

To overcome an objection:

Identify

Acknowledge

Reframe

Confirm

Neutralize/**E**liminate

Close

Chapter 6:
Dynamic Closing Techniques©
An Abbreviated Survey

Closing techniques are not new. They have been used since the inception of human interaction by every culture, everywhere on the planet, in one form or another, at one time or another, under the guise of one name or another. This will continue to be true for as long as human beings exist, because closing techniques and strategies are an innate part of humanity. So, anyone claiming to have invented closing techniques is delusional, or lying, or a little of both.

That is not to say that nobody has contributed to the refinement of closing techniques by defining, refining, or developing variations. Many people have contributed to the greater body of knowledge on closing techniques and strategies, and hopefully they will always continue to do so. Certainly, some of the techniques included here are examples of variations that I have adapted and refined out of the raw material of my own educational background and professional experience.

Like many elements of negotiation, the application of concepts and strategies has to evolve in order to remain pertinent and practical. Come to think about it, the same is true of human beings. We have to evolve and reinvent ourselves continually, or we simply slip into a coma while still drawing breath. Once again—evolve or be slaughtered.

That said, I find it puzzling that closing techniques have been almost exclusively the bailiwick of sales professionals who, through training or osmosis, become familiar with at least some aspects of the techniques and strategies. You would think that everyone who interacts with other human beings would have some insight and training, but during the past

Chapter 6: Dynamic Closing Techniques©

two decades I have found that most professionals outside of sales do not have formal training or experience in this area, and that many of them pay for that lack of knowledge in tangible and intangible ways, big and small.

As has been said, everyone uses closing techniques and strategies, and everyone has had closing techniques and strategies used on them. It's just that most people don't use closing techniques *on purpose*, because they lack knowledge and experience. Using closing techniques *on purpose* makes the difference between doing something neuro-associatively or by accident and doing something skillfully. The astute CNSUF™ negotiator is both a knowledgeable and skilled perpetual student of closing techniques and strategies.

Given specific delivery and execution, Dynamic Closing Techniques have three primary purposes:

Test: Closing techniques help negotiators "take the temperature" of their counterparts or negotiations. Some closing techniques help them find out what their counterparts are thinking, and whether their counterparts are interested and paying attention or merely daydreaming about what is for lunch.

If we, the CNSUF™ negotiators, have their attention and interest, then we need to move on to the next logistical step. Depending on the situation, the next step may be to ask them to make a decision or take a specific action. For example, Fred, the CEO of a non-profit, is talking to Sylvia, a prospective donor, about supporting his organization. Sylvia asks, "How does your organization assess the specific needs of the various populations it serves?" The first thing that ought to come to Fred's mind is Sylvia's Communication Style and Type. Next, he should assess Sylvia's other Per-Beha characteristics. Does she want to see a picture? Does she want to see an Excel spreadsheet or a detailed breakdown of the non-profit's assessment tools and strategies?

If Fred has done his homework, or if he has had a prior relationship with Sylvia, he may know exactly how to answer. If he does not know her very well, he may make a quick judgment and present an Excel spreadsheet from the most recent annual report. But what if that is the last thing

Sylvia wants to see? How long will Fred go down the spreadsheet road before he realizes he has put Sylvia to sleep?

By contrast, IARCNC provides a perfect framework for identifying exactly what Sylvia is looking for, since her question relates to Needs. Fred might choose to use an alternative close such as, "Great question. I've got a detailed breakdown of the assessment instruments we use, an Excel spreadsheet that shows a summary of results, and several photographs of our service groups involved in various program activities. Which one would you prefer to see?"

Sylvia might reply, "Let's just look at the photographs."

In a similar situation, far too many people would either ignore the prospective donor's question and respond with a predetermined *elevator pitch* on their organization, or they would not only show the photographs, but immediately go on to show and explain all the other information before testing to see if the photographs alone were sufficient.

The astute CNSUF™ negotiator, however, would show Sylvia the photographs and then test to make sure she didn't have new questions or objections, or if she was ready to inquire about something else, to see the spreadsheet, or to donate.

"What other questions do you have, based on those photographs of our programs?"

Do not say another word until the donor speaks.

"The photographs are great. That is exactly what I wanted to know. When can I visit the sites?"

I assure you there will be few people, if anyone at all, who would turn and say, "Wow, that was an effective use of the Alternative Close." Where did you learn that?

While there are some who might use an Alternative Close, the liability is that it might be the only tool in their closing skill set. That is a huge limitation. Using the same tactic in every situation will be effective sometimes, but it will blow up in your face at others; different situations,

Chapter 6: Dynamic Closing Techniques©

different people, and different negotiations require different tools and different strategies.

The point is that some closing techniques can be tailored and used to assess where you are at any given point in a negotiation. This often gives astute CNSUF™ negotiators insight into what they need to do next to manage each situation, question, or objection that arises.

Transition: Some closing techniques—for example, shifting from a firmly competitive position to a more co-operative one—can help transition from one point to another on the CNSUF™ Continuum. They can be used to transition the balance of power from one negotiator to another and back again.

Neutralize/Eliminate: This is the final step in the IARCNC process for overcoming objections prior to closing. As explained, closing techniques can be tailored to either neutralize or eliminate an objection, depending on how the closing technique is structured and delivered, and by whom.

I have consulting clients who are procurement professionals responsible for millions of dollars for various products and services. Several are relatively new to corporate procurement, as is made evident by the volume, tone, pitch, and meter of their speech patterns and physical demeanor. Many of these young buyers are women who are often dealing with male counterparts who have years of experience selling highly specialized products and services. When these men hear the women's voices or see them for the first time, they often assume they can walk all over them because of their inexperience, elocution, and demeanor. But we can use the very vocal qualities, physical attributes, and demeanor that the men believe they can take advantage of to accomplish the exact opposite.

We do this by analyzing the Geo-Socio-Poli, Org-In, and Per-Beha attributes of the person with whom they are negotiating and then designing a *"Brown Recluse"* strategy that includes specific closes that neutralize or eliminate their counterparts' objections, experience, and advantage. Below is a sample:

Great to meet you. Thanks for coming in. I appreciate your investing the time to be here today.

You're welcome. Nice to meet you, too.

So, tell me, how long have you been in the business? From talking, it seems that you've got quite a bit of experience and knowledge.

Well, fifteen years or so. How about you? How long have you been in your position?

I may have mentioned in our phone conversations, this is my first year. I'm just starting out, but I'm looking forward to learning the business.

What, at this point, is the experienced professional likely to think about his or her ability to control the negotiation and achieve the outcome he or she is looking for? Certainly, there are many possibilities, and much will depend on the individuals involved, the business sector, and prior conversations. But many of my clients (men and women) who find themselves negotiating with someone who is much more experienced feel they are in way over their heads in a situation like this. They sense that their counterpart believes they have them completely outmatched, which often is exactly what their counterpart is thinking.

At the risk of opening a Pandora's Box on gender in negotiation, let me speak in wide generalities for a moment. In the situation described above, when two men are involved, they often are sizing each other up and squaring off to see who will *win*. The result is that the entire negotiation revolves around personality, and the two spend a lot of time taking potshots at one another, until the less experienced negotiator concedes. They deadlock, or they end up splitting the difference, and both claim they *won*. But if the more experienced negotiator is a man and the less experienced is a woman, as in the case of some of the clients I am referring to, much will depend on issues such as the age of the man, whether he is married and has daughters, and other similar Per-Beha elements.

Chapter 6: Dynamic Closing Techniques©

We're going to consider all Omni elements. The astute CNSUF™ negotiator's ultimate strategy will take these and other elements into consideration. But many times, the men in cases like this see an easy target and go for the jugular, assuming they can parley their superior knowledge and experience into a dominant negotiating position.

Unfortunately, without training and support, these men are correct and often dominate the negotiation from the initial meeting until the termination of the relationship. But it does not have to turn out that way, because CNSUF™ skill and strategy can frequently overwhelm superior knowledge and experience.

A reminder: do not get bogged down by the theater of the specific roles or professional sectors in these examples. I could give you a hundred examples involving male and female CEOs, construction professionals, for-profit and nonprofit executives, doctors, engineers, technical professionals, politicians, realtors, and so on. Here we are concerned with closing techniques and their ability to help neutralize and eliminate objections and obstacles in negotiation. Rather than think about how this particular example relates to you or your profession, take a moment to consider the situations where it is important to understand how to neutralize or eliminate the kinds of objections and obstacles you encounter.

Back to the example where my female client is acknowledging that her counterpart has more knowledge and experience, and she does not know how he might want to leverage it.

She could say something like, "You really do have a lot of experience. I look forward to the day when I'll have that kind of knowledge too."

"Look," her counterpart says, "I'll be happy to help. If I can ever answer a question or whatever, just give me a call."

"Thanks," she replies.

(Pause)

"You know," she continues, "I was looking at the spreadsheet you sent over before our meeting, and there are a couple of data points I don't understand. When can you give me a little more clarification to help me get a better understanding of the price increase you are requesting?"

Here my client has used a variation of the Jerry Maguire Close: "When can you explain them or give me a little more clarification to help me get a better understanding of the increase you're requesting?"

At this point, what Conditional Mode will the more experienced negotiator likely think the negotiation is in: Competitive, Co-Operative, or All-Win? And which of the two negotiators is now controlling the flow of the negotiation?

Obviously, the answer will depend on the specific negotiators involved, but many Harrison-Chevalier consulting clients in similar situations use a variation of *The Jerry Maguire Close* to transition the balance of perceived power between themselves and those with whom they are negotiating. They neutralize the counterpart's superior knowledge and experience by encouraging them to share and substantiate their knowledge and insights, which may eliminate perceived competitive aspects of their relationship.

Remember the concept of the *"Brown Recluse"*? In the CNSUF™ negotiation framework, Brown Recluse is any type of strategy, tool, or tactic where the person encountering it does not readily recognize its underlying intent. It is adapted from the spider of the same name whose bite is often misdiagnosed. In the example above, the experienced, knowledgeable professional does not immediately perceive the shift in the negotiation with a younger, less experienced counterpart. According to *Wikipedia* and many other sources, the bite of a brown recluse is "frequently not felt initially and may not be immediately painful." However, if misdiagnosed or left untreated, the bite can result in a range of symptoms, including "nausea, vomiting, intravascular coagulation, organ damage, and even death," depending on the age and health of the victim, the location and type of bite, and other factors.

In the example above, the younger, less experienced negotiator appears to be conciliatory and co-operative, but she is using the Jerry Maguire to extract more information, gain a deeper understanding of her counterpart's objectives, and discover more about his communication style and type. As long as the older, more experienced negotiator believes he is in control, he is less cautious about withholding information, since there is no perceived threat and no overt sense of competition. As a result, the more experienced negotiator is likely to become sloppy and provide information he would not normally provide. He may assume he has the price increase (or whatever else) he is seeking or make any number of other mistakes.

Think about the CNSUF™ Six Foundational Tenets, which the astute CNSUF™ negotiator should always use to connect to the strategy, tool, or tactic he or she is considering. *Test All Assumptions, Presumptions, Estimates, and Influence Actions and Minimize Risk* can be readily applied to the Brown Recluse used in this example.

I'll talk a bit more about the Jerry Maguire Close in a few moments, but the important message here is that Dynamic Closing Techniques have three primary purposes in the CNSUF™ negotiation framework: to test, transition, and/or to neutralize/eliminate advantages, knowledge, or objections, depending on Geo-Socio-Poli, Org-In, Per-Beha of the astute CNSUF™ negotiator and his or her counterparts, as well as other factors, including the objectives of each, timing, and so on.

Key Considerations: How to Decide Which Close(s) to Use

Deciding which close to use in a given situation is not an exact science. It is a combination of science, art, skill, and experience that depends on an analysis of the Omni Modes. It should be crystal clear by now that what makes perfect sense given some Geo-Socio-Poli, Org-In, Per-Beha particulars will make no sense whatsoever given different particulars. But there are some key considerations that can help us prioritize the best close to use:

- Do the issues involve major or minor concessions?
- Is the negotiation "Transactional," "Comprehensive," or "Complex"?
- What is the timeframe? Who is controlling time?

- What Conditional Mode are you in?
- What Conditional Mode(s) are you striving to establish?
- What is your counterpart's primary communication style?
- What is your counterpart's primary communication type?
- Which (if any) of the closing techniques have been used previously?
- Are there any concessions that can be withdrawn, delayed, or changed with minimum increase in risk?

These key considerations help direct our thinking, identify and weigh the advantages and disadvantages of particular closing techniques, and provide an opportunity to think about how each technique fits into our overall strategy. When we do not have sufficient time to answer or explore all of these considerations, we rely on two key questions: Where are we on the CNSUF™ Negotiation Continuum, and what are the Relevant Conditions?

Direct Close

Direct Closes are powerful and dangerous because they are straightforward and unequivocal: "Yes." "No." "Now." While a direct close is often preferred for those with *Telling* or *Intimidating* styles of communication, it can be a death trap if used at the wrong time or with the wrong person.

Imagine a junior congressperson responding to a meeting request from the president of the United States by saying, "No!" Imagine the CFO of a major corporation responding to the CEO's request for an updated Profit and Loss or Balance Sheet by saying "Absolutely Not!" One can imagine that the lives and careers of those responding so directly will look very different after such a response.

When the balance of power or significance is not clear, a direct close will often evoke anger or defiance, even if one might have complied with a request if it had come in a more subtle package. One is now predisposed to resist or to make demands of his or her own.

Chapter 6: Dynamic Closing Techniques©

A direct close then is any close, statement, or response that is straightforward and unequivocal. The most prolific of these is simply "No." Especially when repeated, "No" represents the most powerful close of all from every Omni perspective. Go anywhere in the world, and virtually everyone understands "No."

When repeated three or more times, even the staunchest of negotiators begins to believe that "No" will never be overcome. If you want to frustrate your counterpart, simply use this direct close and keep repeating it.

Astute CNSUF™ negotiators, however, understand the power of the direct close and of "No," and they resist the temptation to yield to its power. One way to address "No" is to acknowledge it and respond by saying something like, "I understand that your response is "no," but it appears you do not understand that it doesn't apply in this case, because—" You then reiterate the benefits of your position and explain why "no" does not apply.

While "It doesn't apply..." will not always eliminate your counterpart's position, it may soften the position and open the door to minor concessions that previously seemed impossible to achieve. (When combined, minor concessions can lead to new insights and opportunities between the parties.) Sometimes, however, your unwillingness to accept "No" will surprise your counterpart, which often leads to compromise.

There are three other critical tools for dealing with No or with any direct close. First, if you say *No,* and I respond by saying *No* as well, we end up exactly where we began, because the two No's cancel each other out. The second tool has to do with the dynamics of various communication types and styles. We should always try to understand why someone employs a specific communication style or close, as well as its components. Sometimes we can gather clues that provide insight about how to respond. Third, remember the power of the reframe as discussed in the objections chapter. As powerful as a direct close may be, effective reframing can often neutralize its potency.

Concession Close

The concession close is at once the simplest and yet potentially one of the most complex of the closing techniques, depending on the circumstances and the sophistication of the negotiators. On its face, one negotiator offers to give up something in exchange for something else: "We'll accept a reduction in the stress tolerances if you will decrease the cost of the unit." Or "We'll extend the deadline if you agree to include detailed data substantiating *why* you are unable to meet the deadline." I will concede X if you concede Y (fill in the blank). These are relatively straightforward examples of a concession close.

Concessions can be tangible or intangible, substantial or minute, depending on how each negotiator perceives them. But astute CNSUF™ negotiators will temper their concessions based on where the negotiation lies on the CNSUF™ Continuum and whether they want to be short-, intermediate-, or long-range with their counterpart.

Moving from left to right on the CNSUF™ Continuum depends on Relevant Conditions such as the Equity of Risk and Equality of Transparence. So, the more Co-Operative a relationship, the more access each side has to the other's strategy and objectives (unless one party is actually in the Co-Opetitive Mode). Theoretically, the more willingness and opportunity each side has to explore and exchange concessions, the greater the Circle of Shared Information and Resources. If the negotiating parties achieve an All-Win relationship, there are no restrictions on access, data, strategy, resources, and so on, because the parties are effectively a single entity.

Concessions and other decisions are based on an analysis of all available resources with an eye toward achieving the best outcome given inherent risks and potential consequences. The importance of concession choice therefore increases in relevance as a negotiation remains competitive or moves from co-operative back toward a more competitive position on the CNSUF™ Continuum. Note that in many negotiation programs, concession rules and strategy are presented exclusively within the competitive mode, while the CNSUF™ framework stresses the importance

Chapter 6: Dynamic Closing Techniques©

of concession strategy across the CNSUF™ Continuum, depending on Relevant Conditions.

That said, where Relevant Conditions are uncertain or unsubstantiated, or when they confirm the Competitive Mode, astute CNSUF™ negotiators will seek to exchange *minor* concessions for *major* ones, knowing that doing so will minimize risks and protect or perhaps shift the balance of power from their counterpart to themselves. In the international realm, where Geo-Socio-Poli, Org-In, Per-Beha elements remain in a constant State *of Flux* and where inherent risks are so substantial, sustained limited co-operation or perpetual deadlock are surely preferable to any illusion of achieving an All-Win resolution.

Major Concessions

Let's recap major and minor concessions, as they are both closely related to closing. In the CNSUF™ framework, a major concession is a unilateral concession that has a real or perceived high value to the entity that concedes. A major concession does not require the approval or agreement of anyone other than the individual who wants it. If someone perceives that a *big* dollar figure constitutes a major concession, then astute CNSUF™ negotiators will find ways to articulate the concession by using big dollar figures relative to the perception of the individual with whom they are negotiating. That is not to say that astute CNSUF™ negotiators are going to concede *big* dollars; it is to say that they will find a way to craft their concessions so that the individual or entity with whom they are negotiating perceives them to be big.

A common example of this is when a retailer spends millions of dollars advertising the *small* dollar figure of a product or service but excludes add-on charges that substantially increase the small number they've advertised.

For example, I rented a car while on a business trip. According to the retailer, the car cost $47.80 per day for four days, and the taxable total was $191.20. However, upon returning the car, the final charge to my credit card was $254.01—$63.50 per day. I took a look at the receipt, and it revealed charges that included *GRGRECPSURG, RENTALCFC, and CONRECUR1.* Why didn't the advertisement for the rental include these charges? Because the vast majority of people focus on the *small* number, not the actual cost—and retailers know it. I know what you are thinking: why didn't I look before I rented? I did, and before leaving the garage I figured out how to reduce the cost by getting two no-cost days on my next rental.

While a car rental represents a simple transactional example, the concept of getting your counterparts to share and focus on their perception of the size or value of a concession until they see it as a major concession is a skill, a science, and an art form. This is what makes an *astute CNSUF*™ negotiator. Discovering how an individual perceives a major concession is directly connected to the Omni Modes, because what one individual considers enormously important, another will disdain. Therefore, astute CNSUF™ negotiators are not focused so much on what they view as major concession, but on finding out what the other side views as one and then determining how to give it, or the perception of it, to them without compromising their own objectives.

What has surprised me throughout the years is how often a client's perception of what constitutes a major concession for his or her counterpart is based on the client's perception, not the counterpart's. I may ask a client, "What do you think your counterpart's major concessions are?" After the client responds, I'll ask "Why?" and invariably the answer will be, "Because they told me that's what they want!" or "Who wouldn't want those concessions?" But through the course of the negotiation, my clients often come to realize that what the counterparts said they wanted at the beginning of the negotiation not only wasn't what they wanted, but it wasn't really that important to them. There are any number of reasons why a counterpart may mislead or withhold the truth about their wants and objectives, especially during the initial stages of a negotiation, and over time we may or may not discover what their actual wants and preferences are. One thing is certain: astute CNSUF™ negotiators will rarely *presume* that what their counterparts are telling them is accurate until they have thoroughly reviewed and tested what they hear from the viewpoint of the Omni Modes and, at the very least, through the lens of the Seven CNSUF™ Competitive Rules.

One way to test your counterpart's perception of a concession is to use a variation of the "what if" question. Examples:

> What if we were willing to offer X? How would that affect your position on moving forward with doing Y?
>
> If we do X, how quickly are you prepared to move forward?

In either case, you are bound to be surprised by the range of responses. In some cases, your counterparts will be unable to contain themselves as they explain that your offer is exactly what they were looking for (be cautious). In other cases, you may find that something you thought was of enormous value to your counterpart is of little or no value at all (be skeptical).

Keep in mind that major concessions in the CNSU framework are defined unilaterally. Astute CNSUF™ negotiators understand that their perception about how their counterpart views a concession's value is irrelevant. If they like sardines on their duck burger, that's the way they like it, and your opinion isn't likely to change their preference. Astute CNSUF™ negotiators are interested in identifying their counterpart's genuine underlying preferences and priorities. Once they have done that, they determine how to use that knowledge to influence the outcome of the negotiation.

Minor Concessions

What is a minor concession? It depends on whom you ask. In the CNSU framework, minor concessions are defined bilaterally as any concessions that have a low cost or low value to CNSUF™ negotiators, but a high value to their counterparts. This bilateral component is what makes the minor concession so complex and so powerful. In the competitive mode in particular, the astute CNSUF™ negotiator seeks to give minor concessions and get major concessions in exchange.

Why would someone give a major concession while receiving a minor concession in return? In the first place, our counterparts may not (should not) be aware that the concession they are receiving is a minor one to us, because it may have great value to them. They may not recognize that a concession they might be offering is a major one for us, because it does not have significant value to them. Or it may be that what they are offering is a major concession for them, and they are offering it in order to obtain a major concession from us. How do we know that what we are giving is a minor concession and that what we are getting in return is a major one? The answer is that a minor concession is one that has a low cost or low value to the person offering it. In this instance, *we* determine whether what we are offering has low value to us. And if we are receiving a concession, we—not our counterpart—determine whether it has major value to us.

The mistake many negotiators make is presuming that because something has a high or low value to them, it automatically has a high or low value to their counterpart who is receiving the concession. Often nothing could be further from the truth.

Astute CNSUF™ negotiators avoid this mistake by focusing on finding out how their counterparts view a concession, rather than assuming they know based on their own perceptions or analysis. We are asking questions such as:

> How do our counterparts view a concession?
>
> Why do our counterparts view the concession as they do?
>
> What is the best way to leverage a specific concession to alter the balance of power or to influence a shift one way or the other on the CNSUF™ Continuum?

These and related questions will likely yield new ones, but they will also produce steps that help us clarify the answers. This in turn provides insight for choosing the most effective tools and strategies. From a broad perspective, it may be helpful to understand how people determine value. Obviously, much of the way people come to value something is directly connected to their Geo-Socio-Poli, Org-In, Per-Beha. These elements will heavily influence what is important, but some things still are

Chapter 6: Dynamic Closing Techniques©

universal—and one of them is that access to information plays a major role, no matter what Omni-related elements are involved.

Minor concessions are almost universally things that are readily available. In the United States, tens of millions of buffalo once roamed the plains. Herds sometimes spanned the horizon for miles. But those herds were slaughtered, killed for sport and for their fur, until fewer than 1,000 remained near the end of the nineteenth century, at which point they were nearly extinct and became protected by federal mandate. This and similar examples can be found around the world, from the oceans to the jungles to the deserts to the lakes to the rivers and everywhere in between. Repeatedly, we see that what is abundant is taken for granted until it is rare or impossible to get, and only then is it valued.

As a negotiator, I have learned this universal truth: people rarely value tangible or intangible things when they are abundant or easy to obtain; these things are taken for granted, ignored, and abused with little thought or consideration.

By contrast, when something is rare and difficult to obtain, its value can be enhanced to a point of absurdity. Imagine that a synthetic polymer paint used on canvas to depict a can of soup could bring riches and accolades to its creator, Andy Warhol, in his lifetime, whereas Vincent Van Gogh, who painted the extraordinary Starry Night, had to concede his work to pay his bar tab and rent. Only after his death did his work receive the attention and admiration it deserved.

Have you ever had someone love you or want you so much that he or she was available all the time, willing to do anything and everything you wanted him or her to do? How did you treat that person? How did you treat that relationship? One day that individual stopped being available, stopped caring what you wanted or thought, and started to walk away. What were you feeling when that happened? Even if you weren't very interested in the relationship, you may have felt sick that something that once was so available was no longer available. Perhaps, in fact, that was when you realized that you did care, only now it was too late. It proves again the CNSUF™ axiom: *"The value of what we give or do is greatest before we give or do it!"*

Why do human beings so frequently want the love they cannot have, rather than the one they do? Why do people pine for the love that was cruel, unfaithful, damaging, or abusive, rather than the love that lifted them up and offered itself true and pure of heart?" Surely there are many reasons, but part of the answer revolves around universal *human needs*. One love was available (certainty), and the other was not (uncertainty). One brought complacency (significance), and the other brought uncertainty and intrigue.

What does any of this have to do with minor and major concessions? It turns out that if one recognizes that *perception trumps reality,* and if one comprehends that people often equate accessibility with value, then perhaps it is possible to increase the perceived value of a minor concession by restricting or eliminating access to it. If you are not sure whether a concession you are providing your counterpart is perceived as a major or minor concession, take the concession away and restrict access to it, or demand a greater concession in return.

If you remove a concession and your counterparts fail to react, you make a discovery and reduce your liability. If a concession has no value to your counterparts, why provide it to them? If you restrict access to a concession by, for example, raising the demand or narrowing its availability, and your counterparts meet your increased demand, you raise your profitability and/or significance and discover that something you were willing to include as part of your service, something you were willing to give away freely, has a greater value to your counterpart than you realized.

A variation here could be to detail the costs of a concession by explaining that it is available only to a select few, or to no one at all. When the counterpart asks for the concession, cite its excessive cost, many benefits, or limited availability, and deny it. Or require that your counterpart meets specific targets in order to qualify to receive it. Focus on learning how to enhance the counterpart's perception of the concession's value or desirability, rather than on the concession itself. As the perception of value increases, you can extend the concession to your counterpart, who may then perceive it as a major concession, rather than a minor one, leaving you to demand a major concession in return.

The most astute CNSUF™ negotiators focus on developing their ability to exchange minor concessions for major ones by influencing their counterparts' perception of the value of the concessions offered. To do that, one must consider the Omni Modes, fully understand the power of influence and rapport, and learn to use variations of the concession close combined with other tailored closing techniques.

The Jerry Maguire Close

Inspired by a line from the 1996 film of similar name, The Jerry Maguire Close is a brown recluse type of close that is virtually impossible to detect. It can be a sincere request for assistance, a tool for transitioning from a competitive position toward a more co-operative one, and/or a masterful means of influencing our counterpart to provide the rationale needed to delay or avoid an action that is not in our best interest.

In the film, the line is an impassioned "Help me help you"—simple and powerful. In fact, it turns out to be as powerful in real life as it was in the film, because it can be adapted and used in a host of personal and professional negotiating situations. There are literally countless variations:

> Given your experience how easily could you help me with…
>
> I really need your help!
>
> As difficult as it is to ask, how much better would it be if you would take off the gloves and help me out here?
>
> Obviously you have a lot more experience than I do, so you can either use it to keep beating me up or help me out so we can get through this. What do you say?
>
> I hear you saying that you're looking for a 5 percent increase for next year. To make that happen, I am going to need help from you in the form of some additional data so that we can justify the change and give you what you're asking for. When can you get me that information?

These are just a few of the variations. The options are endless and can be tailored to any personal or professional situation. One of the reasons this is such a powerful close is that it is neuro-associative—it tugs at an internal set of experiences and emotions that are already built into most people. There are exceptions, of course, but no one succeeds or fails during the course of a lifetime because of them—not if one is engaged throughout the entire negotiation. When we meet an exception, we recognize it as one, and then we adapt.

Beyond the exception, how many people react differently when a credible person says, "I need your help," or when someone we are even marginally acquainted with says, "Help me."? Most people are sensitive to a request for help unless they think the request is disingenuous or calculated (that is why the way you communicate the request is so critically important). The fact is, the vast majority will respond to the request by lowering their competitive instincts and behavior and looking for ways to help, especially when it appears they are being asked to help someone get them something they want, as in the last example.

Take another look at that example: "I hear you saying that you're looking for a 5 percent increase for next year. To make that happen, I'm going to need help from you in the form of some additional data so that we can justify the change and give you what you're asking for. When can you give me that information?

Where does this example belong on the CNSUF™ Continuum? Is it leaning more toward the competitive mode or toward the co-opetitive mode? Where would you place it, and why would you place it there? What's your thinking?

In some ways it's a tough call, but upon further consideration you will likely conclude that, based on the example alone, there is no real way to place the negotiation on the continuum. The determination will depend on the *intent* of the negotiator using the close. If the negotiator is truly asking for help in order to support the request of the person asking for the increase, or if the negotiator making the request has no preconception about how to use the information he or she is requesting, then the request would move toward the co-operative mode. But if the request for additional data is an intentional effort to obtain insight that will be used to determine how best to resist or deny the request, then the close is being used as a competitive tool. And that is why the Jerry Maguire Close is a brown recluse. You do not know you've been bitten until after the fact, and even then it may be difficult to determine that it was the close that was responsible for what occurred after it was used. In all fairness, you also do not know how effective the close has been until you evaluate how your counterpart has responded. Either way, you learn something valuable about your counterpart, something about your access to the counterpart's information or resources, and about how to proceed.

As with all closes, tactics, and techniques, the most effective Jerry Maguire Close will be combined with other closes and with variations of itself, which include but certainly are not limited to:

> I need a favor.
>
> I'm wondering if you could do something for me so that I can move forward on your project.
>
> If you could get X done by end of business today, I should be able to give you Y by close of business tomorrow.
>
> This isn't getting done without your help; I can't do it alone.
>
> I'm stuck. Why won't you help so we can move forward?
>
> Work with me so we can get this done. It's the only way we'll get where you said you wanted to go. When will you help me?
>
> Look, the more insight I have about your objective, the easier it's going to be to help you get where you want to go.

I find that some variations of this close are so effective, they can become crutches. Weak, lazy, or inexperienced negotiators will rely on them too much and use the same variation repeatedly. For a dozen reasons, continuously using the same close or variation of any strategy is ill-advised at best. This is why astute CNSUF™ negotiators constantly find new ways to vary the use of every close, tactic, or strategy, regardless of whom they are negotiating with, but especially when they are negotiating with the same counterpart repeatedly.

The Urgency Close

"10, 9, 8, 7, 6, 5, 4, 3, 2, 1" Where is the greatest urgency in this sequence? The urgency is at 1, because while you may not know what is going to happen next, you are no doubt expecting it to happen at the end of the countdown. Urgency, by definition, interrupts patterns and business as usual. It encourages immediate attention that often forces people to do things they normally wouldn't. It can cause people to make mistakes or act erratically, which is why urgency can be such an effective close, if not also a dangerous one.

Deadlines often create urgency, especially when they are connected to negative consequences. Some people dissolve in the face of deadlines, and in doing so they become victims of their own assumptions. No one is completely immune from the cunning of an urgent ordeal, yet while some people run away in the face of certain business or life-threatening events, others run toward the same situation to face the urgency in front of them.

In my experience, none of us knows how we will react when things become urgent. But the more prepared we are, the more knowledgeable and skilled we are, the greater the chance that we will make the best choices when an urgent matter materializes.

The Urgency Close is another neuro-associative close, because it isn't so much what is conveyed but how it is conveyed that makes it urgent. And while the Urgency Close can be direct—"Get it done today!" "The deadline is 3:00 p.m. Tuesday!" "Take it or leave it!"—its real power is in its timing and delivery.

If you are a parent and you receive a call from your adult child at 4:00 a.m. on a weekday, what is the first thing that comes into your mind? What is the first thing you say when you pick up the phone? You say, "What's wrong?" because of the timing. If you do not have children and one of your parents calls you at 4:00 a.m. on a weekday, what's the first thing that comes into your mind? It might depend on which parent made

Chapter 6: Dynamic Closing Techniques©

the call. If it is your mom, your first words will likely be, "Is Dad okay? Are you okay? "What's wrong?"

Depending on the kind of parent he is, if your dad is calling at 4:00 a.m., then you really know it's urgent. The urgency is inherent in the timing of the call. It is an interruption in the pattern. It is unusual and it can be frightening.

While not quite the same, receiving a call from someone you work with or work for on the weekend can be disconcerting, unless you are expecting a pay raise or a promotion. So, what does this suggest about using the Urgency Close? It suggests that the Urgency Close should be conveyed with a combination of timing—when you call, email, or text your counterpart—and physiology, which involves the tone, pitch, and volume of your voice and the quickness of your breathing. All of these elements should be significantly different than they are normally. For example:

> Sorrytocallontheweekendbutweneedyourdecisionbynoontoday. Gottago!
>
> What?
>
> Sorry I have to go.

What do you think your counterpart is going to glean from that phone call? Take a wild guess. Possibly your counterpart might think you are out of your mind, or that something is *urgent*. Either way, you grabbed his or her attention, that is for sure. Then when the person calls you back—and they will almost always call you back—you can repeat what you've said. Better yet, be unavailable for the rest of the day. Few things create a sense of urgency as much as finding that someone who is normally available is suddenly unavailable.

As noted, the greater the potential consequences or perceived consequences, the greater the urgency or perceived urgency. Where can urgency be used to interrupt your counterpart's expectations or response? Where do you want to test your counterpart's reactions or find out whether the issue or issues involved are of minor or major importance to them? Where previous extensions and requests have failed to elicit a response, consider the Urgency Close.

Conversely, when you are presented with an Urgency Close, take a deep breath, separate facts from emotions, ask IWWWWWH questions, evaluate your options, review Geo-Socio-Poli, Org In and Per-Beha for insights and clues, meet with family, friends, and colleagues (depending on the issue you are negotiating), schedule a consultation with an experienced negotiation consultant, and then determine your best course of action. Start preparing for an urgent event before it occurs by honing your skills and running test scenarios. Most of all, find a way to act on purpose rather than react by accident.

The Assumptive Close

Have you ever heard the expression, "It's easier to ask for forgiveness than to ask for permission"? It is a quote generally attributed to Rear Admiral Grace Hopper, a pioneer in the field of computer science who encouraged the idea of machine-independent computer languages, which led to COBOL and much more. She is also credited with being the first to use the term "debugging," and she was often referred to as "Amazing Grace."

As far as anyone can tell, Admiral Hopper was never known to have argued that her quote about forgiveness came before or was associated with the Assumptive Close, and that is good. The Assumptive Close and its variations have been around for as long as human beings have interacted. There have always been people who ask and people who just do, people who give and people who simply take what they want as though it were their birthright.

In the CNSUF™ negotiation framework, the Assumptive Close can be distilled to a single statement: Take an action instead of asking a question. In other words, *act as if* the result of whatever you say or do is a foregone reality. Rather than asking, "Would you do X by Friday?" the Assumptive Close is, "I'll be there at 2 o'clock to pick up X." Rather than "So you'll vote for candidate Y on Tuesday?" the Assumptive Close is, "Thanks so much for voting for candidate Y on Tuesday!" Rather than

Chapter 6: Dynamic Closing Techniques©

"Is that the best you can do?" the Assumptive Close might be "We both know you can do at least 17 percent better." Rather than "Can we count on your donation of $100?" the Assumptive Close might be "Given your support last year and given your dedication to X, a gift of $150 will be great. How do you want to take care of it? That has to make you feel good, knowing it's your generosity that is making the difference. Do you prefer using MasterCard, Visa, or Amex? What works best for you?"

Granted, these are just examples, and you will want to tailor your message and your Assumptive Close to your specific Org-In, Per-Beha. But you get the idea. We are going to make a statement, ask a question, or take an action that assumes the outcome, and because the Assumptive Close is neuro-associative, we'll tailor the timing and physiology of our delivery to the style, type, and so on of the individual with whom we are negotiating.

Will the Assumptive Close always be effective? No close will be effective 100 percent of the time. However, an Assumptive Close will increase your success rate and provide insights into the other party's limitations, objections, thoughts, and rationale that you might never have been aware of.

Let's say you're in a meeting and you ask Steve, your counterpart, for a folder he had in his hand and referred to throughout your meeting. Is it likely he will give you the folder if you give him an opportunity to refuse to do it? Not likely.

Think about the last meeting you were in and what might have happened had you said, "Hey, why not let me take a look at the folder you have there?" If there was proprietary information in the folder, chances are that Steve would have politely said, "No." But if you had reached out for the folder as if you expected him to give it to you, he might have handed it to you before he thought about it. This is another example of neuro-association. Steve sees you reaching out and he naturally accommodates you before his brain registers the action and he thinks about refusing. Is it possible that he will recoil and jerk the folder out of your hands? Doing that or refusing to give you the folder would be unthinkable in some Geo-Socio-Poli environments. Is it possible that he will refuse to give you the folder? Yes, but what can you learn from his reluctance to provide access to that information? Clearly you are not too far into the Co-operative Mode and definitely nowhere near All-Win. At the very least you will discover that you do not have full access to some of your counterpart's or colleagues' information, and that is always an important part of assessing Relevant Conditions.

One obstacle that seems to get in the way of using the Assumptive Close is the fear that a question, statement, or action will appear rude or inappropriate. From a Geo-Socio-Poli, Org-In, Per-Beha perspective, that may well be worthy of consideration. But do not make the Omni Modes an excuse for not taking risks that could lead to important insights. Sometimes the Assumptive Close is an effective way to interrupt a pattern, gain insight, change a dynamic, transition, and test limits. It is an edgy and often unexpected tactical approach. And do not forget Rear Admiral Hopper's axiom, "It's easier to ask for forgiveness than to ask for permission." That is a powerful insight.

Where fear for fear's sake is determined to be the underlying rationale for not using an Assumptive Close, challenging the fear and taking steps to examine and curtail its impact on how and when The Assumptive Close is used is the right action to take. (See: *Beyond Negotiating: From Fear to Fearless*.).

The Puppy Dog Close

The Puppy Dog Close is one of the oldest, simplest, and most effective closes ever developed. This is precisely why it remains one of the most prolific closes, not only in retail sales but in every business sector and profession in every corner of the world today, and no doubt into the future. We have all been *"puppy dogged"* at one time or another, and I'll bet it's never occurred to most people that the technique has a name, much less that it goes back further than anyone can pinpoint.

Like most closing techniques, the Puppy Dog Close was developed for selling. But given the countless variations one can identify and use in situations that range from widgets to nanorobotics, its usefulness is infi-

Chapter 6: Dynamic Closing Techniques©

nite. Never forget that, at our core, we sell all the time. I am either selling you on what I want you to buy or think or do, or you are selling me.

Here is the way I originally heard the story: A father takes his son into a pet shop to buy a puppy. The only puppy the shop owner has left is the runt of the litter, and it has an injured paw. As the boy plays with the puppy, the father asks when the shop owner will get a new batch of puppies.

The father says to his son, "You don't want that puppy. We'll come back in a couple of weeks when the new puppies arrive."

"Look, son," the shop owner says, "Why not do what your dad is telling you and come back in a couple of weeks when I get some new puppies, and you can have the pick of the litter?"

Seeing the kid's disappointment, the shop owner says, "I'll tell you what. You can take this puppy home and bring it back in a couple of weeks when the new puppies come in. How would that be?"

How likely do you think it is it that the puppy will be returned to the store? Once the boy and his family get the puppy home, name it, play with it, feed it, and sleep with it, they'll have to take the boy back with the puppy and leave them both at the shop before he'll let them return it.

Variations of this close have been around for decades. Remember the instant rebate? Think about the Jewelry Channel, HSN, QVC, and the other retailers that rely on the Puppy Dog Close to put products into the hands of their customers. It amounts to billions of dollars annually. Six easy payments, free shipping, a sixty-, ninety-, or one-hundred-and-twenty-day return policy, and mail-in rebates are all variations of the Puppy Dog Close. The only thing more prolific is the "Oh, but wait, we're not done yet. Order today and we'll include X and Y! Just pay separate shipping and handling," which is usually half the cost of the item.

Many people who hear about the Puppy Dog Close realize they have been "puppy dogged" at one time or another, but then they quickly ask, "What does this have to do with being an engineer (or financial services professional, CEO, physician, and so on)?" A lot—a *whole* lot!

Remember, we are not sitting down and negotiating directly with people most of the time in these situations. We are negotiating with them indirectly, because we don't have the authority to tell them or make them do what we want them to do. A great deal of the time we negotiate by influencing others to take an action or have a thought that is consistent with the action we want them to take or the thought we want them to have.

The Puppy Dog Close is a valuable tool for doing just that— influencing people to think or act as we want.

Have you ever had a difference of opinion about an approach or about a specification, program, or idea? Depending on the size and significance of the issue, such disagreements may lead to deadlock or inertia, but often the Puppy Dog Close can help. If I am confident that your idea isn't the best, I can talk until I'm blue in the face trying to convince you that my idea is better. Or I may not be in a position to debate with you. Perhaps you are the owner of the company I work for. Your position is higher than mine. I could suggest that either we go with your idea and then make an adjustment if certain results are not achieved—the Puppy Dog Close—or I could suggest that since you feel confident that my idea is sure to fail, we go with my idea and then implement your approach if it doesn't work. If you really believe my idea is going to fail, there may be a "silver lining" to allowing me to fail and then implementing your idea, which you believe will save the day. Of course, if my idea is spectacularly successful, well...who knew?

There is no question that the Puppy Dog Close is powerful and that it has been wildly successful, albeit not always ethical and not always called puppy dog.

Consider that in some ways the Puppy Dog Close is a variation of a Ponzi scheme. In 1920 the swindler Charles Ponzi used an apparatus called *arbitrage* to pay off early investors with the deposits of later investors. Since the beginning of the twentieth century, variations of the Ponzi scheme, including the Puppy Dog Close (which I believe is even older than the Ponzi scheme), have been used to bilk billions from

Chapter 6: Dynamic Closing Techniques©

unsuspecting participants who could not resist the allure of exorbitant returns and promises of no risk.

I am not suggesting that offering flexible payments and free shipping to get people to spend money they do not have is the same as promising enormous returns to unsuspecting investors. But on a smaller scale, who has not made a purchase only to receive a product or service that was inferior to what they saw advertised on television or in print?

The thought that the product can be returned or the service can be cancelled is powerful, yet how many people wait months to return a product or to cancel a subscription or a service that should have been stopped within days? People think of Puppy Dog Close and the story behind it as *cute*. A little boy gets a puppy, and the puppy that might not have found a home gets one. But is it ethical? Is it honest? Is it manipulative? Is it merely the power of suggestion and influence? Each individual will be the judge of that, and people will come down on every side of these questions. Nonetheless, the Puppy Dog Close will continue to be an effective tool for influencing the actions and thoughts of others. Even if you do not use it, you should be aware of its potential for good and not so good.

It isn't that the tactic or strategy is inherently devious; it is the *intent* of the person or counterparts using the tactic or strategy and how people respond that make it what it is.

I am also *not* suggesting that any negotiator should perpetrate fraud by employing a Ponzi scheme or by using the Puppy Dog Close. I am simply pointing out that at their core, both are powerful. I am also suggesting that while the Ponzi Scheme is designed to take advantage of people in extremely negative ways, the Puppy Dog Close is designed to influence the actions of others in a manner consistent with the desire of the negotiator using it.

Close Three to Six Times

You will recall that, depending on the close, the situation, the characteristics of our counterparts, and other factors that we've discussed, closing techniques can be used to test, to transition, and to neutralize or eliminate objections.

The astute CNSUF™ negotiator also must have the wisdom and courage to close *three to six times* before even starting to become discouraged or think about giving up the fight. In order to do that, you must have the tools available as well as the knowledge (a well-developed reservoir of closes and variations), the skill (the ability to discern which combinations to use), and, most importantly, the discipline to close three to six times, even though your counterparts have repeatedly refused to alter their position. When closing know-how and discipline are combined, they become a formidable force, yet very few negotiators are willing to use the power of closing three to six times.

For those who are willing, some powerful closes are specifically designed to enhance your options in this area and provide additional opportunities to close as much as possible. They include the Doorknob Close and a variation of it called the Columbo Close.

The Doorknob Close

You have used two or three closes, and your counterparts still refuse to alter their position. One way to test their resolve is to use the Doorknob Close. Depending on where the negotiation is taking place, gather your notes and pack up any reference materials, spreadsheets, and so on that you brought in with you. Stand up, say you hope for a better result next time, walk toward the door, and place your hand on the doorknob. Then open the door and begin to walk out. The more important the negotiation, the less time you perceive you have, and the more pressure you feel, the more difficult it is going to be to walk toward that door—but do it.

While all you can think about is the importance of the negotiation, the lack of time to complete it, and the consequences of not reaching an acceptable outcome, it will not occur to you that your counterparts feel the same way. It will not occur to you that all they are thinking about is *their* limited time, their consequences, and the importance of the negotiation to them, their company, or those to whom they are responsible.

Chapter 6: Dynamic Closing Techniques©

In those few seconds, as you walk toward and reach for the doorknob, you will not remember that *feelings are not facts* or that *perception trumps reality*—unless you came prepared when you enter the room.

If you are prepared, your hand will wrap around the doorknob, and you will resist the temptation to speak until the last second, just before the door slaps you on the backside. That is when you will often find that your counterparts will not let you leave that room. You will discover that when you test the position and resolve of your counterparts repeatedly, they often will move from their position, invite you back to the table, and reopen the negotiation. And if they do not call you back, you will turn and go back into the room with a seemingly sudden idea to offer a new concession—a minor one that you will have decided upon prior to the negotiation. And then you will close again and again and again.

The Columbo Close

The Columbo Close is a variation of the Doorknob Close, with the primary difference being that as you leave the room or end a phone call or video conference, you turn back to your counterpart with the phrase, "Oh, by the way…" words that were famously used by the frequently mumbling, purposely fumbling, disheveled yet brilliant detective of the long running 1970s television series *Columbo*.

With "Oh by the way," you will introduce new information, a new perspective, new facts, and/or new potential consequences that were previously missing from the negotiation. Here again, there are lots of variations:

> Hold on a moment.
>
> Oh my gosh, something completely slipped my mind that may be important.
>
> Did you see the results from the [testing, validation, performance review]?
>
> Have we considered the XYZ option?
>
> We didn't realize that we could _____. Let's take another look to see if it helps us to get where we need to be.

As you read these variations, many of you will dismiss them as antiquated gimmicks and patently reject their potential to succeed. But let me say that as an astute CNSUF™ negotiator, you will come to love counterparts who reject these closes, because they will be the most susceptible to them, all while proclaiming they could "see them coming a mile away." No, they won't.

In the first place, who has not experienced being stuck and at the end of their rope, only to then find a solution or successfully navigate a challenge? Just when it appears that there is no way to solve a problem, someone in the negotiation moves, alters a demand, and becomes willing to do what they were not willing to do five minutes before. Or, seemingly out of the blue, you or someone else sees an outcome that no one saw previously, only to realize that it was staring everyone right in the face the entire time. Virtually everyone has been in this position.

The primary difference between the Doorknob and the Columbo closes is that astute CNSUF™ negotiators create an environment where the same kinds of outcomes that occur spontaneously, as in the examples above, occur strategically, rather than by chance, as the result of their skill.

The Doorknob and the Columbo closes do two things effectively. Each provides an opportunity to test the resolve of our counterpart's position and a means by which to close multiple times by making slight variations.

There are other benefits as well that make these classic closes worth their weight in gold. They often get our counterpart's attention and shift the focus of the negotiation from potential deadlock to potential resolution. They provide pattern interruption, and, depending on the benefits and risks involved, they encourage our counterpart to reevaluate the timeframe and consequences.

Rope-a-Dope Close

Sometimes our greatest weapon is not exposing or using all of the weapons we have at our disposal until we have encouraged, tested, and influenced our counterparts to expose or exhaust every weapon (tactic,

Chapter 6: Dynamic Closing Techniques©

technique, intention, threat, and strategy) available to them. Since so much of the CNSU framework is designed to test, expose, and teach us about our counterparts, this knowledge is built over the course of a negotiation or relationship, or by controlling time and other elements as suggested throughout the framework. In other words, it pays, at least sometimes, to hold back and protect ourselves by understanding that our smartest move against a stronger opponent is to play dumb or appear to be vulnerable when we are not.

In 1974, Muhammad Ali, arguably the greatest fighter ever to don a pair of boxing gloves, found himself in Kinshasa, Zaire (now the Democratic Republic of Congo), in the opposite corner of the ring from the undisputed and undefeated heavyweight champion of the world, George Foreman. Younger readers and those who have no knowledge of boxing may remember Foreman for being the spokesperson for the *Foreman Grill* and other products, but in his prime he was a formidable boxer capable of shattering bones with his crushing blows.

Many of Ali's staunchest supporters feared not only that he would lose, but that he might be permanently injured or even killed, and they begged him not to take the fight. Ali had no such fears, and he taunted and provoked Foreman before the fight so that the champion's sole focus would be on using every fiber of his body to take Ali out.

Early in the first round, Ali displayed a glimpse of the *float like a butterfly, sting like a bee* form that made him famous in his prime. He did a bit of the *Ali Shuffle,* traded a few punches, and then gradually drifted back to the ropes. He leaned back against them, put his arms and fists in front of him to protect his face and body, and Foreman pounded him relentlessly. As Ali absorbed blow after punishing blow, his cornermen yelled for him to get off the ropes. Many in the crowd squirmed in their seats, awaiting his seemingly certain demise with trepidation.

Over seven rounds, Ali absorbed the blows. He clinched, he taunted, and he waited for Foreman to punch his way into exhaustion. That point came in the eighth round; Foreman, now a saggy lump of sweat and fatigue, could hardly lift his arms to throw another punch. Sensing his moment, Ali pushed Foreman to the center of the ring, released a furious and relentless bombardment of rapid punches, and laid Foreman down for the count. Ali won by a knockout. He had, by every measure, "roped the dope."

This is a great story, but how does it apply today, and how will it apply in the future, for the astute CNSUF™ negotiator? How does the "rope-a-dope" apply in situations where we are outmatched and at great disadvantage? Some examples: A junior executive overwhelmed by a superior who is hellbent on exercising his or her authority and position; it's a great time to rope a dope. An inexperienced procurement or sales professional, physician, entertainment executive, engineer, or financial services associate saddled with the responsibility of battling someone far more experienced and far more knowledgeable. It's another great time to rope a dope by appearing to yield control and authority to the counterpart. Since only the smallest and most pathetic narcissists can restrain their appetites for significance, the astute CNSUF™ negotiator who is willing to sacrifice will eventually watch them wither as they gorge on feasts of self-importance and the need for physical, organizational, or professional dominance. Astute CNSUF™ negotiators must be willing to absorb some punishment and be humble, or appear to be humble. But as our counterparts become exhausted by their own self-importance, they will eventually expose their weaknesses and vulnerabilities, and we use these to shift the balance of power in our favor.

Silence

Indulge me if you will and participate in a simple experiment. Pick up a phone and call someone you know very well. When he or she answers, say, "Hello," and then don't say another word until you've counted: *One-thousand one, one-thousand two, one-thousand three, one-thousand four, one-thousand five, one-thousand six, one-thousand seven, one-thousand eight, one-thousand nine, one-thousand ten.*

Odds are whoever you called hung up somewhere around one-thousand three. If not, you are now connected to someone who is either frightened that something is gravely the matter with you, or believes they are the victim of a prank call, or thinks you are in danger, or believes you have completely lost your mind. One way or another, they would love to get their hands around your neck when they find out they were a lab rat in your experiment. And what is the moral of this? It is that silence is an underrated and powerful tool that astute CNSUF™ negotiators nearly always have at their disposal, yet many don't use as often as they should.

Silence in response to a direct question or a direct close will often cause your counterparts to alter their position. Acting on their assumptions about what your silence means, they may provide unsolicited information or facts, or offer new concessions, or remove an objection they had on the table. It is also effective at exposing the underlying or previously unidentified communication style and type of a normally cool counterpart who, frustrated by your silence, turns into a raging bull. Once that happens, you have essentially nullified their personal and professional legitimacy, and you may have recalibrated the balance of power between you.

It is important to think about communication types and styles here. For some reason, when people who do not talk very much suddenly start talking, others tend to think they must be saying something important. I recommend taking this on a case-by-case basis, because I've found throughout the years that it doesn't actually prove they have superior levels of intelligence or insight, but the perception is so widely held that we may be able to influence a negotiation by having someone who is perceived as the "silent type" speak up when the timing is right.

Conversely, as someone who is perceived as a "talker," I learned long ago that the best way to draw attention to myself or my point of view is not to start talking. It is when I shut up that people pay attention. If I am quiet, they immediately assume something is wrong. Others who are perceived as talkers have told me the same thing, but here again, take this on a case-by-case basis; don't leap based on a single fact or factor. That said, however, you will more often than not find that silence is more effective when it comes from someone who is perceived as a talker.

Are there risks to using silence? Of course there are, because we won't always anticipate our counterpart's reaction accurately. The real question is whether opening our mouths is riskier, especially when we do not have anything substantive to say or when we've stated our point of view more than once. Silence, when used strategically, can be the loudest noise in the room.

Silence also offers a host of opportunities to mitigate many risks with little substantive damage to our position. For instance, if we are on the phone and our counterparts blow up or become overly agitated by our silence, we can say, "Hello? Hello? Can you hear me now? That was strange. I was talking away and suddenly realized you could not hear me. Are you on a cell phone? Sorry, that was very strange, wasn't it?"

Now, was the connection broken? Were you talking? Was there a technical issue with the phone lines? Was the issue with your phone or with your counterpart's? It all depends on the negotiation and on your counterpart. It depends on where the negotiation falls on the CNSUF™ Continuum. It depends on your communication style and type, and on your counterpart's. It depends on where you want the negotiation to go and where your counterpart perceives it to be. It depends on risks, time, and many other factors that astute CNSUF™ negotiators will take into consideration. There is definitely an art to the strategic use of silence, but its foundation is skill, not creativity. Remember: silence is a friend often ignored and misunderstood; once you get to know her, she will be a powerful ally.

No doubt there are a great number of other powerful closing techniques that can and should be integrated into our arsenals. But start with those included here. Practice them, tailor them, and become adept at creating variations on each with relative ease. Keep in mind that all closes need to be modified for the medium in which we are communicating. Delivering a close in person is totally different from delivering a close via text, cell phone, email, or the internet.

So, consider the PER-BEHA and ORG-IN influences of your counterpart, their *Type* and *Style* of communication, the location of the relationship or negotiation on the CNSUF™ Continuum, the Tenets, and especially the Seven CNSUF™ Competitive Rules, as you craft your strategy. And tailor the selection and execution of every close you use.

As you do that, your confidence will grow, your capabilities will grow, and you will eventually become an astute CNSUF™ closer.

Chapter 7:
The Calculus of Deadlock

One of the surprising aspects about deadlock in negotiation is that few people truly understand what the word means to an astute CNSUF™ negotiator. So, it stands to reason that many negotiators find themselves invoking their BATNA too soon and settling for outcomes that are far less than what might have been possible had there been a deeper awareness of CEATNA to BATNA.

First things first: Quickly, off the top of your head: What, from your perspective, is a deadlock?

Don't sit there pondering what the *right* answer is, because at this point you're looking only to identify your personal perspective—the one you carry in your subconscious. Whatever is on the tip of your tongue at this moment is what's important, because it's been driving your behavior around deadlock for years. Your perspective drives what you do and how you react when you find yourself feeling that the *conditions* of your definition are present.

If you're thinking that deadlock means a negotiation is stuck or stalled, or that it occurs when either side isn't willing to give up something it wants, then that is pretty close to what thousands of professionals have told me throughout the years. And frankly, that's not bad. It is a reasonable answer that works for most people. But astute CNSUF™ negotiators are not *most* people.

Deadlock, contrary to what many professionals believe, does not fundamentally mean that progress is simply stalled, since virtually any negotiation of substance will have points at which progress stalls. In my experience, when everything goes smoothly and agreement is reached quickly, it often means that one party has been taken advantage of, and they realize it as soon as the ink is dry on the agreement they have signed. According to *Merriam-Webster*, the word "deadlock" is defined as: *A situation in which an agreement cannot be made: a situation in which ending a disagreement is impossible because neither side will give up something that it wants.*

In the CNSUF™ negotiation framework, we focus on two words from that definition—"cannot" and "impossible." If deadlock is defined as a situation in which agreement "cannot" be made or is "impossible," everything changes about the fundamental structure of deadlock.

Let's look at those two words again. According to Merriam-Webster: "Cannot": *to be unable to do otherwise than.* And "impossible": *incapable of being or of occurring.*

Using these definitions as a foundation, the question becomes: when can a negotiator conclude that a situation *cannot* be overcome or that a situation is *impossible*? For many negotiators, it is not so much that their negotiations *cannot* be successfully navigated or that they are *impossible* to navigate. Rather, it is often the case that a negotiation has simply not concluded in the way the negotiator had hoped or assumed it would conclude. Thus, situations that might otherwise have been resolved are inappropriately determined to be deadlocked.

In speaking to clients and others who have been involved in negotiations that they determined were deadlocked, I have asked two simple questions: 1) Why did you conclude that it was deadlocked? 2) What specific actions did you take before concluding that it was deadlocked?

To the first question, the answers have overwhelmingly been something to the effect of, "We offered them everything we could, and they wouldn't move." Or "We did everything we could, and they wouldn't move." Or "They were unreasonable and wouldn't budge, no matter what we did."

Okay, then what about my second question: What specific actions did you take before concluding that the negotiation was deadlocked?

Chapter 7: The Calculus of Deadlock

Inevitably, the answers to the second question have been something to the effect of, "As I said, we did everything we could, and they wouldn't move." Or "We just ran out of time and could not wait any longer. There was just too much risk for us." Or "In the end, I feel certain we secured the best deal possible under the circumstances." Or "They told us to take it or leave it. The deal on the table was the only deal they had to offer; it would not have mattered what we did."

Every one of these statements was made by professional negotiators, many of whom were experienced, successful, senior negotiation professionals. The odd thing is that I have also heard these same statements or variations of them from novices who had little professional success or experience in negotiation.

In probing further, I have learned that the negotiators invariably found themselves falling back to the BATNA they had determined even before the negotiations had begun. This is exactly why a BATNA, set and resorted to incorrectly, becomes a study in negotiating with ourselves. Furthermore, what exactly does "we did everything we could" actually mean? If we have done "everything," wouldn't you think we'd be able at least to detail the specific steps and actions included in "everything"? Yet far too often, "everything" comes down to a lack of clear comprehension of what deadlock means, and a lack of skill as to what specific steps can be taken to make certain that negotiators "cannot"—are *unable to*—do *otherwise,* and that progress is impossible—*incapable of being or of occurring*—for these are the standards for the astute CNSUF™ negotiator. Before they conclude that a negotiation is in fact deadlocked, astute CNSUF™ negotiators will make sustained, rigorous, and repeated efforts to use every tool at their disposal and to explore many avenues and many variations of those tools and avenues to ensure they are certain that they are *unable* to do otherwise, and that progress is unequivocally *impossible.* And even then, they will not fully accept that there is *nothing* more that can be done, because the words *unable* and *impossible* are too significant to permit us to do otherwise.

At the very least, astute CNSUF™ negotiators will pursue the following, along with some variations, to reveal new self-discovered suggestions, steps, tools, and approaches.

A. Test every element of the Omni Modes. Test, challenge, review, discuss, and refine every assumption upon which your own position is based and those that have been presented to you.

B. Offer/Restructure Minor Concessions that you have previously framed as major ones. Your early strategy should incorporate minor concessions that are presented to your counterpart as major concessions, so that you have an opportunity to restructure them if necessary. Also, *testing every element* includes considering whether you have accurately understood how your counterparts view the concessions you have offered. Have you accurately interpreted what they consider a minor concession? Are your major concessions also major for them? If so, compromise may rest in both sides getting a lot of what they need, rather than everything they wanted. At other times, compromise may mean both sides accepting a little of what they can get and returning to negotiate another day. That is sometimes preferable to deadlock. This is especially true in complex and comprehensive negotiations, political matters, and diplomatic negotiations.

C. Use Present Gain Against Future Pain. Sometimes your counterparts will flat-out be able to dominate a negotiation because their options are greater or their risks are fewer than yours, and they know it (or presume they do). But just because your counterparts can prevail today does not mean they are unconcerned about your ability to hurt them in the future. Remember: "perception trumps reality." It does not matter whether you can hurt your counterparts in the future. What matters is that you can create the perception that you can.

Not only is this strategy effective and useful on a corporate level, but it can also be used with individuals or divisions within your counterpart's organization. It can create reluctant allies who may not be on your team or even want to be on your team, but who see their interests will be at risk should the corporate will of their organization succeed. Perhaps total domination or victory today will cost them or those they support in the future. How can you capitalize? How can you shape individual and corporate perceptions?

Chapter 7: The Calculus of Deadlock

D. Change the Location of the Negotiation. You know before you read it that this is a neuro-associative, neuro-physiological phenomenon. (Location, like food and music, impacts every fiber of our being, every one of our senses.) Why do you think people refer to certain foods as "comfort food"? It is because comfort food evokes memories of safety and warmth and belonging and abundance and loving family members and friends, and action and choice.

The location of every negotiation should be considered an important player or member of your negotiating team. And, as with every other player, the strengths and capabilities of each location should be weighed and used to their maximum potential and benefit.

Do not just consider physical location. Ambiance is just as important. What pictures are on the walls? What is the view outside the windows? What does the room sound like? What is its color and shape? What amenities are included? All of these are assets or liabilities, depending on how they are acknowledged, utilized, or taken for granted.

And what about configuration? Does that matter? Of course it does. Configuration dictates power, prominence, and credibility, and thus it evokes feelings, emotions, and memories. It fulfills universal human needs, like the need for significance and connection, just as effectively as comfort food or an unforgettable memory. Often, conference rooms are arranged so that counterparts sit on opposite sides of a table, which immediately creates an atmosphere of confrontation. Even when tables are round, negotiators go out of their way to make sure that a clearly established line divides the sides.

While those are natural divisions at the beginning, both location and configuration should evolve during the course of the negotiation. Every change and every nuance should be used to test, to evoke different sentiments, to suggest different possibilities, and to provide different environments for pattern interruption, for risk-taking, for movement, and often for resolution. Change the room, change the configuration, go outside. Change the focus of the conversation; steer away from combat to points of agreement, such as the sun, the moon, and the stars. Consider what you have in common. Seek to clearly understand your counterpart's position and point of view. Sometimes that will mean putting a stop to talking and letting silence and location do the negotiating for you.

E. Change the Negotiators: Reconfigure the Negotiation Team or Team Structure. Sometimes deadlock occurs because the negotiators themselves are the issue. In many ways this is another neuro-associative, neuro-physiological component.

Have you ever met someone and found that, for no apparent reason, you just don't like him or her, and you get the feeling that they don't like you too? While the obvious culprits can be race, sex, sexual orientation, age, or other Geo-Socio-Poli, Org-In, Per-Beha elements, sometimes it is plain and simple—people do not always like one another.

We do not always get to choose our teammates. Just because we work for the same company does not mean we play by the same rules, have the same objectives, or even see ourselves as colleagues. Often the internal underlying divisions between people who work for the same organization can provide fertile ground for exploitation if we recognize how to react strategically. Surely it can be said that many of the most difficult elements of negotiation involve internal, rather than external, elements or people. Keep in mind that our counterparts didn't get to choose their teammates either. There will be internal differences between them, just as there will be within our own ranks.

Astute CNSUF™ negotiators, however, will acknowledge and then diminish or neutralize the negative impact of these differences by strategically changing the negotiators whenever necessary. The most successful negotiating teams are the ones whose leaders recognize that it is often necessary to place people over and above their titles, their purpose over and above the people, and the outcome over and above expectations in order to achieve the best outcome.

People Over Title. Purpose Over People. Outcome Over Challenges and Obstacles.

$$\frac{Pe = Pu = Dot}{Ti = Pe = Ch}$$

Chapter 7: The Calculus of Deadlock

While this might appear to be a simple axiom, it is among the most difficult things senior leaders do, especially when it means they need to get into the trenches or out of the process entirely. It might mean pulling out people they respect, or with whom they have a relationship, and replacing them with people with whom they do not have a strong history or affinity, but who possess the skills or attributes needed to move a negotiation toward the best resolution. Perhaps the person they know doesn't have the skill, isn't able to do a particular job or fulfill a needed role, or just isn't the right ingredient at that time, for whatever reasons.

Many deadlocks occur because negotiators do not have the courage to admit that they are the problem. And to be fair, that is the result of what they learned while working within their organizations. Who gets credit for stepping down, stepping out, or asking for help in a critical negotiation? It happens, but let's face it—it's rare.

As a result, many professionals would rather see a negotiation fail or go to deadlock than recuse themselves or admit that the task was greater than their ability to rise to it.

Not long ago, I observed a negotiation that was badly handled by a talented manager and gifted negotiator who, on that occasion, was simply outmatched and unprepared. I later heard her tell her superior that the outcome was the result of a junior colleague who refused to "shut up" during the negotiation. The truth was that the outcome was due to her lack of preparation and skill, and a counterpart who was a stellar, well-trained, and well-prepared negotiator who "took her to school."

This is one example. I could write dozens more, but they all come to the same end. Sometimes a particular negotiator is not the right person to achieve the best outcome at a given time. If the leadership and the team are focused on the task rather than any individual's ego, they will identify the negotiator who is best suited to execute a particular tactic or assume a particular role that leads to the highest and best possible outcome, rather than accept deadlock as the result of not doing so.

From an Org-In standpoint, organizations that reward people—especially senior and C-level leaders and executives who know when to allow those with lesser titles but with the ability to provide insight—will be stronger and more successful at finding solutions than Org-Ins who don't and deadlock, rather than change protocol. Organizations that involve folks who are outside of a particular issue as part of their negotiating team/strategy will often benefit greatly from doing so.

Work cross-departmentally and cross-divisionally to increase everyone's exposure to new information and insights. People who are not directly involved in your negotiation will see things you don't see, and they may have insights that surprise you. Their questions and ideas may be exactly what you need to complete a strategy or pursue a solution for compromise.

The question isn't whether this is of value. The question is, how do you begin to encourage this sort of activity in your own organization?

The advantages of changing negotiators also include the opportunity to assign roles to people, such as *good cop* and *bad cop*. One negotiator can be used to establish the parameters of minor and major concessions, only to be replaced by someone who will recalibrate those definitions and move the "lines in the sand" once they have served their purpose. One negotiator can be the *third-party restrictive force* who is immersed and immovable, only to be replaced by someone who is more flexible or who will fight to gain internal concessions from your organization in exchange for some movement from your counterpart.

Part of the preparation for any negotiation is to consider every aspect of the people who will be involved on both sides of the table. Chess is an excellent (though imperfect) metaphor for war and negotiation, but in chess only the pawn can transform into a rook or a queen by crossing the board and arriving on the other side. In the CNSUF™ framework, on the other hand, every negotiator can transform into virtually any role on the board at any time. And because our counterparts frequently overlook that capability, the transformation, regardless of its significance, often isn't perceived even after it has occurred. And even when it is, the transformation, when executed correctly, is rarely associated with a strategic negotiation framework. Allow location to do its bidding, and use its power. It will prove a reliable resource for avoiding a deadlock when deadlock is not the best possible outcome.

F. Agree to Concessions Previously Refused or Rejected. Clearly this goes hand-in-hand with changing negotiators and with an advantageous location, because averting an unwanted deadlock involves an orchestra, not a single instrument.

The elements listed here work independently and together to complement one another, rather than to step on the heels of our objectives.

As we change negotiators and locations, we also change our behavior and demeanor. Why bother to do one of these things if you are not prepared to do the others, especially given that the full force of possibility is hidden in the collective benefit of many small, discrete steps added together over time? The primary reason for rejecting a concession early on may be to accept it down the road as a means of showing good faith and progress.

Navigating deadlock in negotiation is historically grounded in theatrics and protocol; the astute CNSUF™ negotiator is a student of both.

G. Reopen Issues Previously Closed. Any student of politics, whether domestic, international, corporate, or military, understands that saying yes has extraordinarily little association with meaning yes, and saying no has little association with meaning no. While individuals and corporate entities alike decry the lack of integrity inherent in making a promise or commitment that is not kept, every individual, every corporation, and every government has done exactly that on innumerable occasions. The reality is that some organizations and people intentionally mislead their counterparts and their own constituents because they see benefits in doing so, or because negative consequences can be averted.

The other reality is that some individuals say yes or no at one point, only to reverse their course in light of new facts or revelations. If saying yes or no is going to stall progress or cause an unwanted deadlock, many people will do it to find out what is on the other side of their response. It is a way to test or discover what will happen if they agree to or reject a proposal or concession or position.

Some will rail against me for suggesting that any negotiator should say yes or no without regard for integrity. But that is not at all what I am suggesting.

What I am saying is that you see things the way you do, but there is no guarantee that your counterpart will see things the same way. The fact that they do not is often the very reason for trying to avert deadlock. Not even those within your own organization or on your team will see things exactly the way you do, so it's highly unlikely that the other side will make the same moral judgments that you make. Remember, negotiators from different backgrounds or different socioeconomic strata are going to make different judgments about what is or is not ethical or fair (Geo-Socio-Poli, Org-In-Per-Beha).

Sometimes finding out that your counterpart is willing to make an adjustment allows you to make one that might otherwise be too risky. The key is to realize that even a small thing can change negotiations. What was impossible a moment ago becomes the natural and obvious thing to do.

A variation here is to add a "what if?" element to a close. Rather than simply reopening an issue, you add a possibility. You might say, "What if we reopen our discussion on X, since we're unable to move forward on Y?"

"What if" puts the question of reopening an issue on the table without actually doing so, and thus your counterpart's reaction can be evaluated. Keep in mind, though, that asking "what if" in some instances may lessen the impact of simply reopening an issue. Nonetheless, the "what if" approach may be preferable to deciding not to broach a topic or issue at all. In CNSUF™ negotiation, as in sports and in business, "The opera ain't over till the fat lady sings."

Stick to your own moral compass, of course, but make sure that you put "purpose" above your own judgments, limitations, and prejudices when seeking solutions to critical or potentially deadlocked negotiations. Sometimes reopening previously closed issues is an effective way of driving toward the best possible outcome.

Don't forget to prepare for the fact that your counterparts, no matter how you feel about it, may not hesitate to reopen or change their position on previously closed issues. A bit of research on the Omni Modes for any number of countries and cultures will reveal that this is the norm, and it is more likely to occur than not for many with whom you might

Chapter 7: The Calculus of Deadlock

be involved. In fact, this tactic is a matter of cultural protocol for many Geo-Socio-Poli entities around the world.

Therefore, make your response part of your planning, your discussions, and your strategy. Most importantly, do not simply go running home to the BATNA you developed before your negotiation began just because things aren't going your way, or because your counterparts are doing something that is outside your frame of reference.

H. Identify/Use Personal Risk(s) to Individual Counterparts and Enlist Them to Support Your Position Within Their Own Organization. We are not necessarily talking about getting someone to spy for you, but CNSUF™ negotiators will take note of the fact that any significant negotiation is going to involve issues and decisions that are better for some folks on the other side than for others. Those who could be adversely impacted by their organization's willingness to agree to one compromise versus another may support their own organization, but when it asks them to do things or makes decisions that will affect them personally, their focus—and the focus of the vast majority of people—will be on their loss and on how an outcome or decision will change things for them personally and/or professionally. Sure, that individual may be willing to *take one for the team,* but if they are in a significant position, chances are good that they have taken more than one for the team during their career and received little or nothing in return for doing it. That individual is a potential ally, because in a *pinch,* people are more likely to put their own interests above the interests of their organization if they see a way to do so where the benefits are perceived to outweigh the liabilities. So, the question is, how do we influence their perception so that it complements our objectives?

Depending on someone's financial situation, their Per-Beha attributes, or their opportunities inside and outside of their current situation, a counterpart may not be willing to outright *betray* their own company directly. But when you strip away all the platitudes and get to the heart of it, the prominent questions on most folks' minds during a critical negotiation are: "What's in it for me? How do I benefit? How do I get hurt? And what can I do to avoid negative consequences?"

Look around and consider leaders who have gone to unthinkable lengths to convince their citizens to focus on the good of the whole at their own expense. Consider the rank and file in manufacturing, in the automotive sector, agriculture, entertainment, finance, and a dozen other sectors worldwide. Measure the cumulative gain of the few who have focused on the whole against that of those who have lined their pockets or put the interests of shareholders above the interests of their workforce. Examples are abundant and make for fertile ground. How many mergers and acquisitions have hung resolute, lifelong employees out to dry?

What about retirement, healthcare, pensions—how are they working for you today? What about the incredible array of customer loyalty benefits you are receiving from the airlines; don't they make you absolutely unwilling to go anywhere else, switch, or look for a better deal? Per-Beha attributes are going to drive that conversation in the head and heart of anyone who might be adversely affected by their partner's or employer's decision to compromise in order to avoid a deadlock, which makes for a potentially valuable resource or ally.

The point is that if we focus on the cost/risk of decisions on individuals at the table (or those folks who might be impacted but are not at the table), we may find that we can influence their thoughts and behavior by prompting them to focus on the cost and risk to themselves personally. It may be with a question such as, "If your company decides to withdraw its relationship with our company, how will that affect your role as senior vice president of the XYX Division?" We may have no idea that it will, but they do—or they hadn't even thought about it until we put it in their mind, and now it's all they think about.

If they are not certain about how a decision will affect them, that question may influence their fear of the unknown. They may never do an overt thing to hurt their own company, but they may never do a single thing to vigorously hurt us or to support a decision that may be detrimental to their own interests, either.

Sometimes the doubt created by exposing a personal cost or risk to an individual can create an unwitting ally who becomes your most significant weapon for breaking or avoiding a deadlock. Astute CNSUF™ negotia-

Chapter 7: The Calculus of Deadlock

tors must consider how, when, or even if this is a viable avenue in order to determine what the pitfalls may be, and which CNSUF™ components should be included in our strategy to explore or exploit the opportunities that arise. Then our strategy must be tailored and the selected elements refined for each situation. Like many of the tools and strategies included in the CNSU framework, the identification of personal cost/risk to individual counterparts must be used in coordination with other elements, such as Omni Modes, Conditional Modes, the location of the negotiation on the CNSUF™ Continuum, and the potential for where it might be possible to drive it, over time, with a coordinated and sustained pursuit of the best possible outcome.

I. Employ the Trojan or Mimic Variations to Set Up the *Fatal Flaw*. On the heels of the previous two sections, this may be the next step. Many won't consciously consider it, but that is what makes it a powerful strategy. The *Fatal Flaw* in CNSUF™ negotiation is a proprietary concept that refers to the point at which a negotiator begins *acting on the belief that previous co-operative interaction is a guarantee of future co-operation and/or a basis for entering into the All-Win Mode.* Actually, the fatal flaw can mean entering deeper into the Co-Operative Mode as well.

Once your counterpart concludes that you are acting in good faith and no longer pose a threat to their interests, based on whatever empirical or historical data you influence them to focus on, many barriers come down. There is no longer a perceived division between you and them as defined by the All-Win Mode in the CNSUF™.

The definition of All-Win eliminates the obstacles between you and your counterpart, but if there is a potential deadlock, you obviously aren't in the All-Win Mode.

What if you agree to drop the key demands that separate you and your counterpart? If you are willing to give them virtually everything they want, what will they give you in return? What resources will they be willing to share in order to substantiate the relationship when those barriers come down? What if you were true allies? What about the potential merger of interests and resources? What are your counterparts willing to do? What aren't they willing to do? What can't they do that you thought they could?

Employing the Trojan and Mimic variations can help ascertain the answers to these questions and more. For more than a decade and a half I had a relationship with my primary contact at a major client. When she moved from the automotive sector into the utilities sector, she called me to determine how Harrison-Chevalier could provide customized negotiation training and consulting to employees in her division at her new company.

After a good deal of work and laying foundations over a couple of years, H-C facilitated several workshops and did one-on-one consulting that resulted in an ROI many times over the fees received for the work. This included the company's investment of time and productivity for everyone while they attended the customized workshops away from their other duties and responsibilities.

As a result, my primary contact informed me that Harrison-Chevalier had been selected to provide negotiation workshops and consulting throughout the entire organization.

As part of the initiative, her company hired a third-party consulting company to assist with the rollout of the overall effort, and I was asked to work with both an internal person assigned to coordinate the overall project and with a member of the consulting team they had brought in. Given my relationship with my longtime primary contact and with many of those within her company who had participated in the consulting and attended our workshops, we gladly collaborated with the internal contact, who did not work with my contact. I also collaborated with other members of the third-party consulting company who had been brought in to help tweak the design of the overall project for folks in various other divisions of the company. The work they did was not primarily negotiation, but they could benefit from greater skills and knowledge in that area.

The fatal flaw for H-C, Inc. was believing that there was no risk in following the consultants' *normal* protocol, given my relationships with my longtime primary contact and those who had attended the workshops

Chapter 7: The Calculus of Deadlock

and participated in the consulting we had already provided. The consultants' *normal* protocol included access to our approach, curriculum, and resources by the internal contact who had been assigned to work with us, and by others from the third-party consulting company. We provided that access and worked diligently to get our overall training tweaked and prepared for rollout. Once all of the preliminary work had been done, we identified an entire slate of dates for the rollout of our programs to the overall organization.

A year later nothing had happened. Dates were missed, phone calls were never returned, misleading emails were received, excuses were made, and on and on.

Given that our company was growing and that this was certainly not the only project we had in the pipeline, I continued to believe that this client was viable and trustworthy. Occasionally I would speak with my primary contact. She had many things on her plate, but she assured me that to her knowledge there had just been issues with the overall rollout.

Every now and then I spoke to the internal contact with whom we had worked, but, again, our fatal flaw was *presuming* that, based on my relationship with my longtime primary contact, I could trust the word and commitment of the individual who had been appointed to manage the overall rollout. There are a dozen remedies I might have used in another case, but my relationship with my longtime client blinded me to the betrayal for two years.

One day I received a call telling me that my longtime client, whom I regarded as a friend, had been dealing with cancer and had passed away. I knew she had been ill previously, but her death was a shock. It was the result of a relapse that she did not want to advertise—especially to me, a cancer survivor myself. So, I understood why my client had not shared everything as she battled her illness.

Following her passing, it became clear that the internal resource and the third party with whom we had worked so diligently and with whom we had shared information, insight, and proprietary access, had used my relationship with my longtime client and with those who had participated in our customized workshops to realize enormous ROI. They used what they had gained to provide further workshops and educational forums themselves, knowing that my friend's passing made any negative consequences unlikely.

There were two significant fatal flaws in this scenario, but there were many smaller ones as well. Combined, they are a pristine example of using Trojan and Mimic variations to set up those fatal flaws.

I use this personal story, but I have many others involving a full range of clients and circumstances in various sectors. I don't want to reveal too much or too many of the identities of our clients, and I don't want to provide a lot of examples that will be relevant to one reader but not to many others, but I want to dispel any sense that just because I do what I do, I always see something coming or have a precise answer for every occasion. And I don't want to present the illusion that I don't make mistakes. Beyond the examples that I might provide, history and today's news outlets are filled with examples of the Co-Opetitive Mimic and Trojan variations being used to facilitate the fatal flaw, and of how powerful these elements can be in breaking or neutralizing a deadlock.

Given the increasing use and development of artificial intelligence, spyware, and espionage along with the loss of personal and corporate privacy, and the diminishing commitment to workers along with the expansion of the EIGE, there is little doubt that the Co-Opetitive mode, Mimic and Trojan variations of negotiation are more likely than not to continue to expand, impact, and blur the lines between individual loyalties to corporations, the greater good, and self-preservation. People are going to become increasingly likely to place their interest ahead of the interests of anything and anyone. And that means that the Fatal Flaw has only just begun to play it full part in the outcomes of negotiations large and small.

J. Caucus Inside and Outside Your Own Internal/External Resources.

One of our long-term clients of more than ten years, the director of a significant division at a top-tier global supplier, has become an expert in the caucus. Here's an example from a significant negotiation in which he and his team were involved. (I was present via cell phone using a *stealth* protocol.)

Chapter 7: The Calculus of Deadlock

First, he and his team listened to their counterparts as they presented their position and responded to questions and items asked prior to the meeting. On the basis of communications before the meeting, there were low expectations and even some expectations that the negotiation might deadlock (for which we had prepared during preliminary consultations). Then he and the manager who manages that client (also an excellent CNSUF™ negotiator) asked several IWWWWWH questions, and then they asked follow-up IWWWWWH questions. They listened and jotted down notes. Then our client, the national director, asked the counterpart if they could take a break so his team could look at options and consider what had been shared.

The counterparts remained in the room, and the director moved his team into another one close by, which was brilliant. During the caucus he asked each member of his team to provide impressions and thoughts about what had occurred. The team included the national director, the manager responsible for the relationship with the client with whom they were meeting, an intern who was not yet a full-time employee, one other person who had been brought in to observe, and me via cell phone.

After a cursory discussion, a review of the objectives, and an agreement to request clarification from the counterpart on a few of the items and comments it had made, they returned to the negotiating table.

They asked more IWWWWWH questions, and then more IWWWWWH follow-up questions. And as they did, it became clear that the counterpart's responses prior to the meeting had been presented only as "trial balloons," to see how they might fly. They did not.

Then the counterpart made a comment about his review of a possible solution from my client, a proposal he had previously called "interesting" but now admitted was something he'd "never seen before." Then the national director requested another caucus with his team.

They discussed potential tactics, closes, risks, and timing, and they reviewed their impressions of what was happening. When they returned to the room, the national director provided a recap of the meeting and put forward a proposal for resolution of the issues dividing the parties.

Despite what the counterparts were saying, there was a sense that what had seemed impossible when the negotiation began might actually have become possible. The national director and the client manager sensed that if they made a slight modification to the proposal they had just presented, they might be able to close the gap and conclude the negotiation right there.

But instead, my client stopped talking and ended the meeting— another brilliant move.

A few days later, to the amazement of the national director and the client manager, they were informed that the negotiation that included a proposal that had "never been heard before" was concluded—and even expanded in scope, with benefits to both sides, but a considerable advantage for my client.

There is no question that the masterful use of the caucus contributed to that outcome, as did the knowledge and skill of the national director and his client manager, who are both accomplished and knowledgeable proponents of CNSUF™. What also contributed to their success was the presence of the intern, the outside observer, and me, who had been involved in the planning and strategy for months.

What is most important and unique about this example is the skillful use of the caucus, because many negotiators, even experienced ones, might not have used it at all.

When I've asked negotiators why they don't use the caucus more often, their most frequent responses are: "We didn't have time to caucus." "We didn't think that this [or that] person could contribute." "Everyone was so overwhelmed that we had to get that negotiation closed."

Really? You did not have time to do it correctly, but you have time to deal with the consequences of not using the caucus for years to come? Or you did not have time to caucus, but you had plenty of time to deal with the deadlock that occurred because you kept talking when you should have stepped back? You did not think an outside resource could be of value, so you simply did not bother to ask an IWWWWWH question or review their suggestions or potential contributions to ensure that your presumptions were worthwhile? You did not have time to do your homework or use any of the educational elements and resources provided because you were so incredibly important? You had time to spin your wheels and then lament that the education, tools, and resources wouldn't have made a difference anyway?

We have heard these responses for years. Hopefully, you will find time to caucus and leave the excuses and lack of discipline to your counterparts. As for how much time you have, you have exactly the same twenty-four hours that everyone has. You might consider H-C's Dynamic Time Management Workshop. It will dispel your time myth, as well as other misconceptions you have about time.

The bottom line is this: caucus, caucus, caucus.

In your preliminary meetings, develop and decide on vocal, and/or physical cues that any member of the team can employ to signal a break to caucus. A member of the team might pick up their phone, look at it, and proclaim that they have just received a critical text or email with pertinent information that needs to be reviewed or considered immediately. A nudge under the table to a colleague, a cough, a grunt, an audible outburst—all of these and more can be used to signal the need for a caucus at any time. Virtually every significant issue should include opportunities to caucus, if for no other reason than to introduce a pattern interrupt, or raise the fear or uncertainty of your counterpart.

K. CEATNA to BATNA. The predilection for establishing a BATNA early, even before a negotiation begins, and for reverting to it as soon as things do not go as hoped is a pitfall for all negotiators, from expert to novice.

These are ingrained habits, and knowing it is an advantage for astute CNSUF™ negotiators only if we recognize the pattern as it occurs and counter it by taking a CEATNA to BATNA approach. Outcomes will evolve during a negotiation and the course of a relationship. Rarely will a significant negotiation's outcome be *exactly* what we anticipated at the start (and we should be skeptical if it is). We are going to ask IWWWWWH questions, test, close, revise, refine, research, review, and evolve throughout the process and throughout the relationship.

Our focus is not so much on winning but on achieving the highest and best possible outcome given each situation's circumstances and limitations. This is not a chess match or sporting event where one can simply look up at a scoreboard to see who is winning. Astute CNSUF™ negotiators more often than not know that the real outcome of a negotiation, the real impact of the decisions made and not made, the real value of the concessions given and gained, and the real substance of risks perceived and substantiated can't be perceived until well after the negotiation has concluded.

L. Deadlock. *"Know when to hold 'em, know when to fold 'em, know when to walk away, and know when to run."* The wisdom of this lyric from a simple but insightful country tune is powerful and precautionary. Not all situations can be successfully negotiated in a single meeting, and sometimes not even after decades. When the roots of the issues separating the parties simultaneously involve geography, cultural differences, blood, politics, significance, and history, there can be no permanent resolution for a single entity until there is permanent resolution for every entity involved and/or impacted by the outcome.

How do people forget their loss? How do they rebuild without the resources to do so? How does one rectify a wrong that occurred decades ago when memories are blurred by self-interest and self-preservation? How does one restore priceless monuments and artifacts after they have been destroyed? How does one achieve retribution and peace in the same way at the same moment?

The fact is that perpetual deadlock is the viable outcome sometimes, but far be it from me to say definitively which situations meet these criteria and which do not.

Beyond these situations there are a substantial number of instances when the best and highest outcome is derived from deadlock itself. If we are willing to deadlock, if we are willing to make the tactical choice to walk away, we are using deadlock as a close. Sometimes our greatest strength is our willingness to risk anything, to do anything, to lose everything, to suffer any consequence, any hardship, and any indignity to advance our position, or neutralize the position of our counterpart. Such convictions

Chapter 7: The Calculus of Deadlock

can be a formidable force that can topple much larger counterparts who possess many times our resources.

Beyond this, we, as astute CNSUF™ negotiators, know that creating the perception that we are willing to make such sacrifices is an equally formidable force. And doing so is undeniably easier today and will become even easier in the EIGE than it has ever been.

Advancements in and access to knowledge and technology are leveling the playing field as never before. Here again, there is no one-size-fits-all for any significant negotiation. Every situation is unique and requires analysis, finesse, reflection, skill, and its own prescription.

When these elements (A through L) are crafted, combined, refined, and modified, they create hundreds of possibilities for dealing with deadlock. Yet these elements are far from all-encompassing. Look at each element as a raw ingredient, rather than a stagnant do or do not. Think of the calculus of deadlock and the elements provided here in the way a chef thinks of how to modify a classic recipe. Regardless of your cooking ability, you are surely aware that the same roast beef, filet of fish, or chicken can be prepared hundreds of ways by altering spices, cooking time, cooking location, and so on. The cut of meat may be the same, but the preparation and treatment can create vastly different meals.

Astute CNSUF™ negotiators do the exact same thing. While we approach negotiation challenges that are very much alike within the scope of our work and personal lives, our prescriptions and behavior, decisions and outcomes will vary widely, depending on the Geo-Socio-Poli, Org-In, and Per-Beha of ourselves, our counterparts, and of the specific scope and nature of each negotiation.

Before astute CNSUF™ negotiators proclaim a negotiation is in deadlock, they will at the very least have utilized a great number if not every one of the elements included in this section. Beyond that, they will have employed a sizable number of unique variations that utilize these elements as the raw ingredients of their strategy. Following all of this, they will review their actions and scour their strategy for any hint of further opportunity to modify or introduce new elements to encourage forward movement.

Only then will astute CNSUF™ negotiators concede that progress is *impossible*, and when asked how we came to this conclusion, we will be able to provide a detailed recount of the primary actions taken and of the variations employed. This exercise will provide many benefits, including the possibility that someone will review our narrative with fresh perspective and see something we didn't, thus invigorating new life and new possibilities. Beyond this, the experience of review and reflection will provide a platform from which to improve our own CNSUF™ skills and capabilities, deepen our knowledge and understanding of the Geo-Socio-Poli, Org-In, and Per-Beha attributes, and strengthen our resolve to EVOLVE.

Conclusion

To become an astute CNSUF™ negotiator, one must do considerably more than attend a two-day EVOLVE LIVE workshop or simply read this book (or attend any other program or read any other book). At a minimum, since many principles and concepts included here were initially introduced in *Beyond Negotiating: From Fear to Fearless, Beyond Negotiating: Influence – Rapport – Results,* and *ROADMAP to Success,* these resources should be read as well.

EVOLVE or Be Slaughtered: Negotiation for the 21st Century represents the foundational framework of the Comprehensive Negotiating Strategies Universal Framework that has been built on the CNSUF™ Continuum. To see the larger picture, one must spend time studying the ideas and rationale for the concepts before deciding that any one concept or element is good or bad, right or wrong. No one will agree with everything in these resources, but the concepts are valid, and a good deal of it is based on quantitative elements that must be considered on their own merit. If the underpinning is valid and strong, the ideas are unaffected by doubt or opinion—fact does not bend to suit opinion. Thus, CNSUF™ deserves more than a cursory perusal before its acceptance or rejection. No one can absorb any negotiation framework simply by reading a book and deciding to agree or disagree with it.

The CNSUF™ framework has taken years to develop and represents thousands of hours spent studying, researching, consulting, facilitating, asking IWWWWWH questions, challenging masters and gurus, and talking with thousands of people, along with experimenting and using multiple variations of each of the elements and tools here and in the related resources.

CNSUF™ remains in its infancy, because it has been designed to evolve and grow well into the twenty-first century as many more people attend the workshops, seek out consulting services, and practice, use, question, and improve every element. The process of negotiation will become even more formidable as technology provides tools to make it so.

My hope is that I will continue to grow and evolve along with others who seek to become astute CNSUF™ negotiators. There are many other aspects of CNSUF™ that remain to be explored. Most importantly, there is much to write and discuss about the application of CNSUF™ principles, tactics, and tools in a wide range of specific situations in various business sectors, professions, and personal areas, and I look forward to being a part of those discussions and activities. In closing, repeat: IKSEAR (Information to Knowledge to Skill to Expertise to Action to Results).

In order to develop a skill or a body of knowledge, one has to undertake a process introduced in the article *Three Fundamental Reasons Negotiators Fail.*

INFORMATION—The words, ideas, and concepts included in the CNSU framework must rise up from mere words on a page to the level of knowledge.

KNOWLEDGE—This is what happens to information when it is processed, elevated, and understood beyond the simple ability to regurgitate. We must transform data into cognitive meaning to possess knowledge of its essence.

SKILL—This is the ability to execute a specific action or use a specific tool at a specific time for a specific reason, at will, and on demand. It happens when astute CNSUF™ negotiators can recall the Seven Competitive CNSUF™ Rules as easily as they can recite the multiplication tables and use that knowledge to make appropriate decisions and implement strategy.

EXPERTISE—This is gained when astute CNSUF™ negotiators can effectively apply their skill and knowledge on behalf of others. When they can effectively teach what they know, and when they can compare

Conclusion

and contrast the principles and rudiments of one framework or body of knowledge to another, they have developed expertise.

ACTION—If all we do is *know,* but we never *act*, skill and expertise are useless.

RESULTS—The value of any negotiation framework must be measured by the tangible and intangible results achieved over time. Not a one-time, big win, occasional outcome, but achievement and results measured from a Symbiolateral perspective (a proprietary term that refers to seeing or being aware of a crisis or negotiation environment from virtually every angle simultaneously) in many situations, by many people over time. What is the true ROI? What are the benefits, as compared to the liabilities?

Believe it, acknowledge it, and accept it or not, the world continues to change even as you read these final words. The underlying purpose of this book is to encourage readers to challenge themselves, to grow, and to EVOLVE or Be Slaughtered.

Harrison-Chevalier Programs & Services

Consulting – Workshops – Services

CNSUF™

EVOLVE LIVE

Strategic Sales/Procurement Mastery

Influence – Rapport – Results

Superior Customer Service

Cross Cultural Collaboration

Dynamic Time Management

Closing & Conversion Mastery

Consulting Services

545 Coaching Program

5 hours of Coaching

545 Consulting Program

Consulting On Demand

Platinum – Silver – Bronze

Customized Consulting Agreements

Negotiation Preparation

Sales/Procurement/Other Clients
Small, Medium, Large Cap Companies

Government

U.S. Military

Nonprofits

Small Business

Administrators

Entrepreneurs

Individuals

Engineers

Attorneys

Doctors

BootCamp

Mock Negotiations

Modified War Games

In-Person and Virtual Options

Acknowledgments

Over the course of the past three decades as a negotiation consultant and educator, there have been many people who have contributed to my personal growth and thinking in the area of negotiation theory and practice, and for them I am ever grateful.

But beyond those generous and insightful collaborators there are a few particularly exceptional thinkers and innovators whose individual and collective works and accomplishments have contributed so substantially to the greater body of knowledge in negotiation and related areas that they have not only guided me but shaped and changed the fabric of humanity.

To this illustrious group I want to acknowledge a debt that cannot be re-paid and offer my deepest gratitude and humble appreciation.

Socrates	Martin Luther King Jr.
Geronimo	John Nash
Plato	Chester Karrass
Alexander the Great	Roger Fisher
Attila the Hun	William Ury
Sun Tzu	All Mothers
Niccolo Machiavelli	Bruce Lee
Mahatma Gandhi	Adam M. Brandenburger
Emiliano Zapata	Peter Drucker
Tony Mendez	Barry Nalebuff
Jonna Mendez	Robert Haugh
Nelson Mandela	Zig Ziglar

www.ingramcontent.com/pod-product-compliance
Lightning Source LLC
Chambersburg PA
CBHW020242010526
44107CB00038B/1451/J